11-11-97
Memphis

For Betsy —

Thanks for organizing the
Ford for Thought meetings.

Enjoy coping with shades
of gray —

— cause that's all there is!

Webster

The You
You Don't Know

COVERT
INFLUENCES ON
YOUR BEHAVIOR

The You
You Don't Know

Webster Riggs, Jr., M.D.

Prometheus Books

59 John Glenn Drive
Amherst, New York 14228-2197

Published 1997 by Prometheus Books

01 00 99 98 97   5 4 3 2 1

Library of Congress Cataloging-in-Publication Data

Riggs, Webster.
    The you you don't know : covert influences on your behavior / Webster Riggs, Jr.
        p.   cm.
    Includes bibliographical references and index.
    ISBN 1–57392–116–5 (cloth : alk. paper)
    1. Psychology. 2. Human behavior. I. Title.
BF121.R48   1997
150—dc21
                                                                96–48012
                                                                CIP

Printed in the United States of America on acid-free paper

Contents

tion. Deception is the rule in the world of nature and in interpersonal relations.

behavior. An example is expecting the world to be "fair."

These aspects of our behavior exist on the border of our ability to control them. Workaholics exemplify this. Many of our self-deceiving actions serve as devices to disguise and lubricate the rough edges of reality.

We unconsciously choose our actions by weighing time expenditure against benefit. Our modern world's obsession with time has produced many urgency addicts.

So tightly bound are we in the wrappings of our culture, we can barely give an authentic wiggle. Our ambiguous, postmodern culture shifts rapidly and overwhelms us with high-technology influences and superabundant role models.

A social construct that does not exist as we think of it. Our changing culture confuses and contradicts our self-image. We cannot escape being like a chameleon tumbling around in a rotating kaleidoscope.

weighing options and making statistical cost/benefit analyses. Our behavior is often adversely affected by erroneous understandings of mathematics and logic.

Your posture toward life depends on the answer to the question "What's it all for?" Plato, Spinoza, and Sartre all influence our thoughts today, as do general discussions of free will and existentialism.

Acknowledgments

Many valuable suggestions were offered by members of the Riggs family: Sandy, Rollin, Russell, Ryan, Warren, Sandra, Christy, and Melissa. Others providing support included Drs. Louis Parvey, Sarah Fitch, Sidney Wilroy, and Aram Hanissian. Roy Smith, Jennifer Smith, and Keith Bell were very helpful. Geneva Reid provided beneficial editorial assistance and Ginger Hoskins and Cindy Owings were patient in their valuable stenographic contributions.

Preface

We think we are in charge. Strolling through our daily lives, we blissfully assume we consciously control our behavior by using our reason and common sense. Only occasional events—such as forgetting a name or erupting in anger—remind us that we lack total command. Though we know that life is complicated and that we are the products of both environment and heredity, we underestimate the infinite number of influences on our actions and tend to lurch from one simplistic conclusion to another to explain our own behavior and that of others. We tend to overemphasize certain limited causes, such as being weak at math or being the youngest child. Seemingly enlightened people argue that genetics is *the* cause of criminal behavior, while others are convinced that *all* differences between male and female behavior are cultural. Criminal defense lawyers often argue that their clients' violent acts are caused by episodes of abuse early in life, or even by premenstrual syndrome. We indulge in easy absolutes, unwilling to admit that we have more covert masters than we realize.

Actually, we are oblivious to our own ignorance, misinformation, and illusions. We are unaware of the overwhelming influence and deception of popular culture in the form of media distortion, advertising, political rhetoric, and superstition. We don't appreciate the effects of many physiological and medical factors on our brain function. We don't acknowledge our unconscious and genetic behavioral determinants. We don't understand the broad trends in physics and philosophy that question our very concept of self.

The purpose of this book is to make readers more aware of the unbounded number of hidden and unreliable influences on their lives. Socrates admonishes us: "Know thyself," and I believe any contribution to self-knowledge is worth the effort. Our freedom of action is dependent upon an awareness of the unseen forces that influence our thoughts. Surrounded by a hyped-up, existentialist society, we should recognize and accept the infinite complexity of the causes of our behavior.

Much of this book represents a compilation of my reflections and interests. As a practicing physician, I struggle for objectivity and truth. I hope that being aware of the overwhelming nature of the influences on human conduct will help readers face life with more equanimity. I am not trying to change the direction of your life or convince you of any particular way to live. Rather, I want to convey certain ideas as objectively as I can, using an open-ended, scientific approach and eschewing teleological thinking directed to some purpose in nature. For a millennium, from the fall of

Rome to the Renaissance, such purposeful thinking (for the glory of God) impeded progress in the physical and social sciences, and likewise for most of this century in the Communist world (for the good of the state). Following rational thought down certain paths inevitably leads to opinions that give discomfiture, if not offense, to many people with firmly established belief systems of religion, politics, or philosophy. Numerous books now offer one simplified psychological gimmick for "empowering" yourself immediately, usually to make money or to gain love. Some of us yield to the short-term comfort of a constricting ideology in a particular philosophical or scientific discipline. I support the more long-term benefit of confronting the vast intricacy of our behavior, an approach that has helped me face myself and others with more tolerance.

In this book I hope to integrate the psychological, physical, medical, and basic scientific aspects of our behavior. We need to stress the relationships of the different fields of knowledge to make sense out of recent discoveries and topics; unfortunately, there is not enough communication among today's disciplines of psychology, medicine, genetics, philosophy, and theology. Frequently, these ideas are presented to professional groups in scholarly journals using technical language, but I have tried to make these subjects more accessible and concise. Current books on the self tend to limit discussions to its psychological aspects and ignore its more basic scientific components, like genetics and physiology; likewise, many scientists, such as those in physics and chemistry, are unaware of the broader psychological aspects of the individual.

Since physicians are basic scientists often cast into the most poignant interpersonal relations, I believe my profession well qualifies me to function as a synthesizer of the disparate disciplines in our chaotic world.

The chapters of this book progress in subject matter from the influence of the most obvious and superficial elements of our culture to that of the broadest philosophical aspects of our minds. The concluding chapter ties the many components of our behavior together and relates them to current chaos-complexity theory.

You will notice that my writing style is forthright and unadorned. This stems from my many years of dictating X-ray interpretations. It is crucial for these reports to be honest, concise, precise, and without effort to impress anyone with flowery language.

You are even more complex than you think. I hope this book amply demonstrates this one salient fact.

1

As a Radiologist

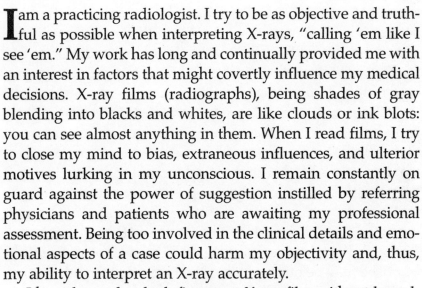

Iam a practicing radiologist. I try to be as objective and truthful as possible when interpreting X-rays, "calling 'em like I see 'em." My work has long and continually provided me with an interest in factors that might covertly influence my medical decisions. X-ray films (radiographs), being shades of gray blending into blacks and whites, are like clouds or ink blots: you can see almost anything in them. When I read films, I try to close my mind to bias, extraneous influences, and ulterior motives lurking in my unconscious. I remain constantly on guard against the power of suggestion instilled by referring physicians and patients who are awaiting my professional assessment. Being too involved in the clinical details and emotional aspects of a case could harm my objectivity and, thus, my ability to interpret an X-ray accurately.

I have learned to look first at an X-ray film without knowledge of the patient's clinical background so that I can decide what I think the film shows in a truly unbiased way. Then, after obtaining clinical information from the referring physician, the patient, and/or the hospital record, I look at the film again. I often see something I didn't see in my first inspection because of the specific clinical information I now have, such as the exact location of pain. I might notice a subtle rib fracture, or, if I learn that a patient had a malignancy, I might then see a tiny lung metastatic deposit because I am specifically looking for this possibility. If, however, I know the clinical information first, I am apt to look too hard for something that would fit the clinical picture. I would never know what my unbiased opinion would have been.

A pediatrician once brought a child's skull radiographs to me and told me the films were evidence in a malpractice suit in which another radiologist might have missed evidence of a brain tumor. He asked if I thought the sutures (the lines between the skull bones) were widened from increased pressure. I could only tell him to consult another radiologist and for him not to tell that doctor this information because my objectivity had been destroyed.

Referring doctors often tell the radiologist that their patients have fever and pain in a particular area of their chest and that with the stethoscope they hear evidence of pneumonia in that location. With this clinical background, it is amazing how the normal lung markings in this particular area of the lung X-ray seem to coalesce and simulate pneumonia. It is easy to over-read pneumonia when it has been so strongly suggested. But if a radiologist does go along with the suggested diagnosis, he or she may be hurting rather than helping the patient.

There is a compelling tendency for physicians to "over-call" X-ray films. Above all, they are trained to search for disease and destroy it. Therefore, the expectations prevail that the conscientious doctor *finds* something, and *does* something. The patient wants the radiologist to find something (in part to justify the expense of the diagnostic procedure), and the referring physician also wants the radiologist to find something to justify the request for an X-ray procedure. If the radiologist obliges them, everybody is happy (for the short term). Sometimes in such situations the truth has no advocate.

When dealing with the pediatric patient, there is the extra distorting influence of sympathy; after all, a small, helpless child deserves the benefit of the doubt. Because we feel that we absolutely can't miss anything in such a case, we often try too hard to find an abnormality.

In interpreting X-rays, physicians sometimes forget normal anatomic variations and technical artifacts. The range of normal (a bell-shaped curve) should be constantly considered in interpreting X-ray films. In school, we took this variety for granted: there were always tall and short kids, fat and skinny kids, and black and white kids, and all these individual variations were the norm. However, when some physicians look at radiographs, many tend to forget about normal variation; they have an idea fixed in their mind of an absolutely perfect radiograph. If the film at hand deviates one speck from this image of perfection, they often call it abnormal.

Doctors sometimes have a tendency to make things more complex and interesting than they are. In looking *too* hard for pneumonia, they, including radiologists, may tend to seek out clinical information that confirms their belief in pneumonia rather than refutes it. For instance, a doctor may learn that a child has fever and therefore feel justified in diagnosing pneumonia. The doctor may forget, however, that the child has no cough or chest pain. To say a film is normal is too blah, but uncovering a subtle finding shows he or she is "sharp."

In debate, when someone makes a positive statement or changes the status quo, it is this debater's job to prove the point, not his opponent's job to disprove it. Those who cannot see subtle findings on the X-rays are not required to disprove them. We hold others to such a standard: for example, viewers of UFOs should be responsible for proving the existence of UFOs. Disbelievers should not have the burden of disproof.

A failure to appreciate mathematical probabilities may influence the interpretation of radiographs. Uncommon presentations of common things are more likely than classic presentations of rare things. A common anatomic variation (a mole on the skin) or a technical artifact (the X-ray film is too light), uninteresting though they may be, are statistically more likely to be the cause of a possible abnormality than the typical manifestation of some exotic disease the doctor may have read about the night before. For instance, there is a finding in the breast bone of a child that is present in 80 percent of children with the Down syndrome (trisomy 21), but is also present in 20 percent of normal children. When we see this finding in a case where no clinical information is available, the chances are overwhelming that we are dealing with a normal child rather than one with Down syndrome. Only if there are other signs of Down syndrome, such as an enlarged heart or prominent lung vessels, should we seriously entertain the diagnosis of Down syndrome.

Sometimes radiologists tend to see order in a random chance situation. If we happen to encounter films from a large number of vehicular wrecks in the emergency room one night, we might conclude that there must be something going on that is causing these accidents to happen throughout the city. But purely from statistical probability, on some nights there will be a cluster of wrecks.

Problems in reading X-rays arise from inexperience and from lack of knowledge; that is why we have specialties and subspecialties in medicine. We all make honest mistakes. Mostly, we don't know that we don't know. We realize that we have strengths and weaknesses of knowledge, but we are not aware of the specifics of these. An elderly teacher of radiology once told my group of residents, "Half of what I tell you is wrong. The only problem is, I don't know just exactly where that half is." His words reflect the inexact nature of medical science.

We all indulge in wishful thinking and self-serving distortions. Those of us who have been radiologists for many years tend to blame our mistakes on external circumstances rather than on our intrinsic lack of skill. We always believe we are correct. We often don't get the negative corrective feedback we need that results from genuine disagreements among our fellow physicians.

Often the clinical information that radiologists are provided is given to us in an overly concise manner. The patient's background is often distorted when busy referring doctors are compelled to inform us of the patient's symptoms in one sentence. Since radiologists are likewise encouraged to be concise and to give a specific opinion following the report, there is a tendency to squeeze a diagnosis into a cubby hole that it doesn't quite fit.

Other factors that may sway a radiologist's judgment are various ego needs and peer pressures. Am I trying to be a star radiologist by "hot dogging" and always finding a positive diagnosis described in ostentatious language? I might get away with this if the referring physician is relatively inexperienced and not skeptical.

All radiologists are limited by the inherent vagaries of language in conveying their findings precisely. Trying to express ourselves, we will use a word that doesn't quite fit, creating a slight distortion of thought. We all face this constantly in everyday life.

Radiologists are also influenced by physical circumstances. I might be apt to shorten my dictated X-ray reports if I have a cold and laryngitis. Do I interpret radiographs differently when I stay late and am tired and hungry? Could I be swayed by having a latent overactive thyroid or an incipient brain tumor? What about the heat and humidity in the room in which I am working? What effect on my mood does the wall color in the room have? Am I wearing a shirt with the tag scratching the back of my neck? All of these factors may be affecting me unconsciously.

What other psychological factors are influencing my diagnostic ability? Will I tend to overassess a case (make a false positive) if I recently missed something on another case and feel guilty? What are the effects on me of some long-forgotten, traumatic childhood experience? What hereditary factors are influencing my decision? The same problems that I have as a radiologist when I try to be objective and honest beset people in all walks of life.

Finally, in trying to establish the truth of any conclusion, we have to ask, "What is truth?" We have to acknowledge philosophy and physics, even to the high levels of Heisenberg's uncertainty principle, which creates doubt about whether there is any objective truth. My final radiology report remains only my interpretation of the X-ray films based on my professional training, my personal perspective, and my limited perceptions.

These are some of the ideas that led to my interest in self-knowledge and in the hidden persuaders of our actions. Self-control and free will are not operative in the simple and straightforward manner we often presume.

2

Ignorance, Half-Truths, Buncombe, and Fibs

It's a formidable task for most people to face the fact that much of their behavior is based on false, incomplete, or obsolete information. An old adage in medicine advises, "It isn't what you don't know that will hurt people, it's what you don't know you don't know." When the oracle at Delphi called Socrates the wisest man in Athens, Socrates said that the oracle couldn't be right because he (Socrates) didn't know anything. But the oracle said that because Socrates knew that he didn't know anything, he was ahead of everybody else. Socrates being the ultimate skeptic, I suspect that he was even skeptical that he knew that he didn't know anything.

Ignorance

Each day I confront my lack of knowledge. I had always thought that Eskimos lived in igloos until I learned that igloos were used only by hunters as temporary shelters when they were out far from their homes, and that Eskimos should actually be called Inuits since this is their tribal name. Often we are ignorant of local culture. Thumbing a ride in certain countries, such as Nigeria or Iran, may not be well received, since in these countries the gesture is considered obscene. Clearly, what you don't know *can* hurt you.

As the amount of knowledge increases, much of what we know becomes obsolete. For snake-bite therapy, most people are surprised to learn that tourniquet application, incision, and suction are now strictly discouraged. The mainstay of current treatment is the administration of the appropriate antivenin. You can also forget the old unquestioned truth that emotional stress causes peptic ulcer. The new cause is often a bacterium, *Helicobacter pylori*.

Sometimes incomplete information is all too willingly accepted. Based on a single view X-ray of an extremity, I have at times thought that there was no fracture, but another view from a different angle revealed an obvious fracture. Also, another test such as a radionuclide bone scan* might demonstrate the fracture that was not visible on the X-ray film.

---

*A radioactive isotope is injected into the blood and is taken up locally at the site of the healing fracture.

Half-Truths and Exaggerations

Examples abound of truths stretched by advertisers and the media. Disclosures such as satanic cults leading to child abuse have been proven to be highly exaggerated. Child abuse in satanic cults has no doubt occurred, but most of the reports about it have been shown to be fallacious and based on hysteria and media hype for secondary gain. Although child pornography does exist, government agents using various solicitation traps to search for child pornographers usually run only into other such government workers. The "satanic influence" on rock music has been overstated as has the efficacy of subliminal records in learning and influencing behavior.

Sexual abuse of women, from childhood incest to workplace harassment to date rape, is real, and it is proper that it has finally been elucidated. Its overall incidence, however, has been hyped to ridiculous extremes. The media has captured a cause *du jour* for profit, and some women have found an explanation—the evil inherent in sex and men—for all of life's problems. Certain books now mention that if you have headaches, feel unmotivated and have interpersonal problems, you probably were a victim of abuse or incest, and if you can't remember the events, you are obviously *in denial* of them. Campus feminists exaggerate episodes of sexually offensive behavior and have defined a proper, idealized sex role for men that is bound to lead to disappointment.

The ability of financial gurus to foretell stock prices has been shown under close analysis to be overrated. John Kenneth Galbraith said, "There are only two types of economists; those that don't know what will happen in the future and those that know that they don't know." Certain rare examples of skill do provoke comment, but these almost always prove to be temporary chance happenings. The hero one year is the goat the next.

The health industry is certainly subject to promoting half-truths. Patent medicines are mostly worthless but do provide some benefit on occasion. Claims for the benefit of health foods likewise are pushed beyond reason. "Natural" foods sold at health food stores are generally no more healthful than many other foods: e.g., nuts have a high fat content, and honey is pure sugar (simple carbohydrate consisting of fructose and glucose). The effects of biorhythms on our physiology, although having some basis, is often overstated. Many medical treatments using diathermy, vitamins, steam baths, and massage, although of minor benefit, are usually given more credit than they deserve. Diets and diet pills usually cannot deliver on their promised results. There is a great placebo effect in medical therapy, because patients usually get well quite naturally after the treatment, not because of it, but in spite of it.

Scandal sheets such as the *National Enquirer* are skilled at twisting the truth, usually including just enough fact to barely scrape by the legal requirements.

Buncombe

We are all conditioned to believe in superstitions and myths. Early in childhood, we learn about Santa Claus, the tooth fairy, and the Easter bunny. Most of us playfully accept superstitions such as the dangers of Friday the 13th, walking under ladders, and black cats crossing our path. We enjoy reading the fortune cookie predictions and tend to incorporate athletic superstitions, such as wearing the same clothes in which we have previously won contests. Having a vague general belief in luck, we accept such things because they make life lighter. Further down the line is the tendency to believe in UFOs and the ability of such seers as Nostradamus and Jeane Dixon to predict the future. Acceptance of invalid concepts such as Von Däniken's story of ancient astronauts on earth is widespread. Belief in unproven parapsychology, such as ESP, is much with us, as is the false dietary benefit of bee pollen, ginseng, and wheat germ. Many believe in the poppycock of the New Age concept of crystals and channeling.

New Age ideas such as numerology are pushed by people wanting to make money from the gullible. The popular near-death experience (NDE) is nothing but the effects of an ischemic (oxygen-deprived) brain that was lucky to have the ischemia resolved. Mineral water spas and mud packs to the face are of no value. The Bermuda Triangle does not exist, and there is only mud at the bottom of Loch Ness. The Shroud of Turin is considered nice to believe in, but the scientists who declared this image of Christ a fake produced in the Middle Ages were considered not so nice.

The amount of Dark Ages thinking in our modern world is incredible. We read about the local police hiring psychics to find clues to unsolved crimes. During the administration of President Reagan we were told that the White House schedule was established after astrologic consultation. And there are many who still believe in the alleged extraordinary feat of mental spoon-bender Uri Geller. Gallup polls have consistently shown that half of Americans believe in the existence of UFOs and that the government is covering up what information it possesses about them. James Randi, noted magician and skeptic, warns, "To mix our data input with childish notions of magic and fantasy is to cripple our perceptions of the world around us."

In a world nearing the twenty-first century, where education is compulsory and prolonged, it boggles the mind to think that there are vast numbers of people who believe in astrology and join religious cults.

Fibs and Fraud

Groucho Marx quipped, "The secret of life is honesty and fair dealing. If you can fake that, you've got it made." We live in a dishonest world, from padded resumes to padded bras. Have we become a nation of liars? In order to be a successful salesperson or to win an election, or even to be popular, many people believe they have to fudge the truth and tell white lies. And many of us accept this. A common pretense on many campuses is to wear the shirts of other colleges, those of Harvard and Yale now being in vogue. Fake IDs and diplomas are ubiquitous. The overlap between frank dishonesty and cosmetics is exemplified with hairpieces, breast implants, plastic surgery, and hair coloring.

As we shall mention in chapter 16, philosophers have given up trying to define truth. Therefore, they also cannot define lying. Situation ethics is criticized in theory yet universally used de facto. Most people say they value honesty in another person, but they wouldn't be able to live around that person very long if he or she were completely honest. A completely honest person would be considered blunt, cruel and cynical. Dishonesty is our social lubricant. Columnist Mike Royko states, "If truth-mongering ever becomes the norm in all our everyday dealings with one another, civility would collapse and our society would suffer from a national nervous twitch." We say to a speaker who looks terrible and has put everybody to sleep, "My, you're looking good. You gave a great talk." Proper social intelligence demands that we let many lies go unnoticed. Only the uncouth reply with candor to "How are you doing?" We withhold the facts about our ingrown toenail or the recent spat with our spouse. We don't tell our young child that there is no tooth fairy. When invited to a party, instead of blurting out that we don't want to come, we make an acceptable excuse (fib) that we have other plans. A more finely tuned social nuance is to make the excuse obviously flimsy, thereby telling the inviting person that one does not wish to be invited again to such an event.

Lying comes about quite naturally. At the Robert Wood Johnson Medical School in New Jersey, researchers have shown that 70 percent of guilty three-year-olds lied about peeking at a toy when an adult left the room and told them not to peek. At age seven, 95 percent lied. The brighter the child, the more likely he or she is to do so.

Nature abounds with examples of deception. A mother bird leads predators away from her babies by pretending to have a broken wing. Is she a liar?

Mendacity has been easily observed in primates. Evolution has designed our human brain to be capable of deceit. Those who are most adept at this live on to procreate and continue this genetic endowment.

Most people lie regularly—to themselves as well as others. All social interactions involve degrees of polite deception. We *act* pleasant to others, using tact and discretion. We laugh at our bosses' jokes and *act* authoritatively to our subordinates. We continuously alter our personality depending on whom we are with. The truly smart person is smart enough not to *act* smart. Everyone enjoys the entertaining raconteur who embellishes stories for interest and whose

metaphors and similes display hyperbole in expressing reality. The engaging conversationalist has to go pretty far out
before he or she is considered a purveyor of "bull." Doctors
commonly shade the truth toward gentleness and optimism
when discussing a terminal illness with a patient. They
sometimes give placebo therapy which, when combined
with a patient's own self-delusion, is often helpful. Patients
expect their doctors to *act* the role of a proper doctor; if he or
she doesn't perform the part well, the patient may not trust
the physician.

We hide the truth at the lowest levels when we scratch an
itch in a delicate place only when others are not looking our
way. At the highest levels, lawyers argue a Supreme Court
case, always shading the truth in favor of their clients. We
deceive the enemy in espionage and war just as the police do
when trapping and interrogating criminals. We practice deception regularly in all games and sports, such as bluffing in
poker or faking a punt and throwing a pass. We temporarily
forsake honesty when we indulge in fantasy, pretense, or fiction. Forms of guile are fully expected to be employed in
advertising, diplomacy, and negotiation. It is not questioned
that politicians twist the truth in favor of their reelection
potential and that business people twist it to put their product (even tobacco) in the best light.

Minor deception is so common that we accept it with only
a wince. Envelopes come in the mail stating, "Urgent, open
immediately." We've all learned that these are always come-
ons. Some now pose as important government documents. A
letter labeled "From Bureau of Control" was only an ad from
a credit card company. Another ploy is "Second Notice,"
which is merely a second mailing of an ad.

We treat dishonesty lightly, as evidenced by secretaries

who now tell callers that the person they wish to speak with is "in conference" rather than playing or napping.

One consequence of this liberal fibbing is that we become skeptical of everything. We don't believe an ambulance is really in an emergency situation just because the siren is blaring.

In 1958, I enjoyed the television program "The $64,000 Question" and was disappointed to find out it was a hoax and that the brilliant people who could answer impossible questions such as the batting average of the third baseman for the Boston Red Sox in 1938 were frauds. We still hear of séances by people who are willing to take the ignorant and gullible to the cleaners. Nobody really believes that magicians do magic, but current spectacular shows tend to condition us to accept such concepts. Professional wrestling is almost an art form with a great deal of symbolism, but it is amazing how many people actually believe that it is something other than a show. Faith healers have been shown to indulge in fraud, although I am sure there is some placebo effect and benefit for true believers.

Dishonest people are abundant in all walks of life. They can be stockbrokers, insurance salesmen, doctors, and clergy. Scams abound, most depending on the greed, vanity, and wishful thinking of the victim. Job placement bureaus, recording studios, and agents for inventors—all offer to make their naive clients famous and wealthy for only a down payment to get the work started.

We must constantly be aware of the ignorance and dishonesty that both surround and lurk within us. We'll discuss our constant, low-grade forms of self deception in the chapter concerning psychological defense mechanisms.

David Nyberg, author of *The Varnished Truth*, writes, "Deception is an essential component of our ability to organize and shape the world, to resolve problems of coordination among individuals, to be civil and achieve privacy as needed, and to flourish as a person. . . . But we deceive carelessly, thoughtlessly, inhumanely, and selfishly at our peril."

References

Capaldi, Nicholas. *The Art of Deception*. Amherst, N.Y.: Prometheus Books, 1987.

Frazier, Kendrick, ed. *Paranormal Borderlands of Science*. Amherst, N.Y.: Prometheus Books, 1981.

Gilovich, Thomas. *How We Know What Isn't So*. Free Press/Macmillan, Inc., 1991.

Gold, Barry S., and Willis A. Wingert. "Snake Venom Poisoning in the United States: A Review of Therapeutic Practice." *Southern Medical Journal* (June 1994): 597–99.

Goldberg, Steven. *When Wish Replaces Thought*. Amherst, N.Y.: Prometheus Books, 1991.

Lear, Martha Weinman. "Should Doctors Tell the Truth?" *New York Times Magazine* (January 24, 1993): 17.

MacDougall, Curtis D. *Superstition and the Press*. Amherst, N.Y.: Prometheus Books, 1983.

McLoughlin, Merrill, Jeffery L. Sheler, and Gordon Witkin. "A Nation of Liars?" *U.S. News and World Report* (February 23, 1987).

Miller, David, and Michael Hersen, eds. *Research Fraud in the Behavioral and Biomedical Sciences*. New York: John Wiley and Sons, 1992.

Nyberg, David. *The Varnished Truth*. Chicago and London: University of Chicago Press, 1993.

Randi, James. *Flim-Flam! Psychics, ESP, Unicorns and Other Delusions*. Amherst, N.Y.: Prometheus Books, 1986.

Randi, James. "Help Stamp Out Absurd Beliefs." *Time* (April 13, 1992): 80.

Roiphe, Katie. "Date Rape's Other Victim." *New York Times Magazine* (June 1993).

Rothman, Milton. *The Science Gap*. Amherst, N.Y.: Prometheus Books, 1992.

Tavris, Carol. "Beware the Incest-Survivor Machine." *New York Times Book Review* (January 3, 1993): 1.

3

Media Distortions and Hype

We *are* what we read, watch, and believe. Our understanding of the world around us, and consequently of ourselves within this world, is profoundly influenced by the media. The best way to gain insight into people and predict their potential for success is to find out what they read, what they listen to on the radio, and what they watch on television. Those who read newspapers, professional journals, and magazines such as *Time*, *Forbes*, and *National Geographic* are blessed with a different view of the world than those who read only romance novels and *People* magazine. People who watch "60 Minutes," "Washington Week," and "Nova" see things from a higher level than those who watch only sitcoms and sports. Television, movies, magazines, and newspapers all establish our concept of reality, which, in turn, establishes our self-image.

Limited by their imperfect technology and the requirements to earn a profit and entertain, the media are fallible.
Though we know that much of the media output is false, our
natural skepticism recognizes only part of the overblown
statements and distortions, while the remainder sinks deeply
into our unconscious.

Sometimes we overlook the most important way that the
media control our thinking: the media decide what is news
and what to present to us, thereby telling us what to think
about. We forget that many events, such as small protest dem-
onstrations, would not have existed to us (we would not
have known about them) if the media had ignored them.

Politicians are skilled at manipulating the media; con-
versely, media responses can also influence the kind of political action that is shown to please the populace. Leaders such
as Hitler, Stalin, and Saddam Hussein realized early that propaganda is more effective than honest thought. We should
never underestimate political authority and media propaganda in distorting reality. Stalin killed millions of his coun-
trymen, but Russians wept when he died, even those in Siber-
ian labor camps. I can remember the World War II American
propaganda image of our beloved ally "Uncle Joe" Stalin. The
marriage of politics and media is becoming stronger; the
chances of getting elected now are in direct proportion to a
candidate's skill at image management and the ability to buy
air time. All politicians now know that it is important to make
everyone happy and to present an optimistic image. Jimmy
Carter unwittingly depressed his chances in the political
arena by speaking of the American "malaise."

Politicians have always used the media in manipulative
ways, employing different ads to target specific groups, with
selected emphasis to black voters or other racial minorities.

Pictures of a white political candidate surrounded by black friends are never given to those in the white communities. Politicians use zip codes to differentiate neighborhoods, sending blue collar workers different mailings from the ones they send to professionals. Politicians can obtain lists of voters with strong religious backgrounds, and tailor the brochures to this group accordingly.

Media leaders sometimes withhold information from the public, justifying this by claiming a higher morality that they have defined themselves. Such items as tax revolt, the recidivism rate after drug treatment, and the small percentage of murderers apprehended are all topics that media moguls feel would be bad for the typical American to know.

Media attention can be capricious and vicious. A comment made by a presidential cabinet official can be seized upon and emphasized so much that it can provoke calls for the person's dismissal. The media can select individuals for a feeding frenzy, as they did with evangelist Jimmy Swaggart, Vice President Dan Quayle, and convicted hotel mogul Leona Helmsley. Who decided that Leona Helmsley is the most evil female who has ever lived on earth and that Marilyn Monroe should be revered? Who decided that one-time presidential candidate Gary Hart is a satyr and John F. Kennedy a saint? Jimmy the Greek was fired because of a media uproar about his comments concerning black athletes. Shortly thereafter, when black athletes were studied in a PBS television special in much greater detail, the same things were said, and no one objected.

It's illogical to assume that media selectivity is always or even ever valid. The media present musicians, movie stars, and athletes as deities, with certain types in vogue at particular times. After thirty years of being out of the limelight, old rock stars Chuck Berry and Little Richard are now sought-after. The adoration of such figures as Michael Jackson and Madonna is ridiculous, but unconsciously we go along with it. Worship of such celebrities is an indirect put-down to all other productive, creative people in more mundane walks of life and reflects how our priorities and values can easily become distorted by a lifetime of exposure to the popular media.

Media attention often gets disproportionately centered on certain topics at the expense of those of equal or greater importance. For twenty years a simplistic good guy–bad guy drama was stressed about South Africa, but the far greater genocide in neighboring African countries such as Zimbabwe, Uganda, and Nigeria went almost unnoticed. Corrupt tyrants in these countries murdered and enslaved millions, making South Africa look relatively peaceful by comparison. The silence of the Western press has protected these other African despots from public scrutiny.

The major media are corporations that sell exposure to privileged audiences to other businesses. The concentration of ownership of the media is high and increasing, with the number of corporations sponsoring the bulk of print and visual media activity shrinking by half in the last twenty years. Those who hold the purse strings are in a position to determine what is socially constructive and to convey this through the media using the mechanisms of the political system. Pressures for corporate profits prevail over desires for artistic quality and creativity.

Manipulation of the media and outright propaganda have been justified in the past because there are always those who believe that the "common people" are not the best judges of their own interests; the elites are. Thinking that disaster would follow if the masses were allowed to influence the decisions of the leaders of industry and government, the media moguls believe the people must be fooled for their own good and necessary illusions must be created. If the propaganda is not effective and the population becomes uncontrollable, the state is then forced into covert operations, such as occurred with the Iran-Contra scandal.

During the Vietnam War, news reporting reached its nadir because of the mutual distrust between incumbent politicians, military leaders, and reporters. Toward the end of the war, the Tet Offensive was actually a profound defeat for the North Vietnamese, but the press, justifiably suspicious of any optimism on the part of the military, reported it as a continuation of the military stalemate. The media tended to think that the U.S. forces in Vietnam, the military-industrial complex, the CIA, and the U.S. government were the real villains of the world. Perhaps at times the media were too enthusiastic in the adversarial role against these functions of government. Yet, in the Persian Gulf War, instead of an adversarial relationship between the military and the press, there was almost too much cooperation, with the press acting as a cheerleader.

The media have created certain classic images that we take for granted as valid, but the stereotypes remain in our minds. The old American West was basically fiction, since historical analysis has shown that there were few quick-draw fights, that the saloon constituted only a tiny part of the total activity in a Western town, and that the classic shoot-outs in front of a saloon were extremely rare. With the stereotypical images of Chicago in the 1920s, you would think that anybody who lived there in those days had only to look out the window to see Al Capone's black cars speeding through the city with machine guns blasting away. I well remember the surfing fad in the 1950s. Songs by the Beach Boys were always on the radio, and movies were saturated with the antics of tanned surfers, boys and girls. Living in Memphis, I thought that I was missing out on all the surfing that everyone else in the country was enjoying. Only years later did I realize that only a tiny percentage of Californians surfed and that in no other place on either coast was there significant surfing activity.

In the past few years, the pressure to make news entertaining has intensified. TV ratings are more important than depth of research and integrity of reporting. Publications such as the *National Enquirer* or the *Star*, which were previously ignored by serious publications and reputable newspapers, now enjoy some rank in the reading material of many Americans. Their ubiquitous presence at supermarket checkout lines attests to this. Those who fill their minds with this current fluff condemn themselves to a disadvantaged sense of reality.

The media produce a concept of reality that we eventually buy after looking at it for many years. *Black Rain* (1989), a movie about the Japanese underworld, showed more violent murders in Tokyo in thirty minutes than there actually have been in thirty years. We know such movies are fiction, but they eventually exert an effect, particularly on the young and poorly educated. With the media seemingly becoming less honest, our threshold for feeling disgust has heightened. We really don't mind being entertained rather than informed.

Newspapers

Most people have an erroneous idea of how news is gathered, thinking that almost all is acquired by reporters going out and conducting investigations as portrayed in the movies, à la Lois Lane. A significant part of the news is phoned into the newspaper offices, somewhat distorted by people who have personal motives.

The freedom of press selectivity has First Amendment protection. There is no law that says the press has to be fair or objective. Objective news reporting doesn't exist, and never has. Reporters and editors are mere errant humans who first must decide, with their inescapable bias, what constitutes news. They vary in their background, education, and experience. They subjectively choose which of many competing events to cover for the news and whom to interview, and then select words from their own personal vocabularies to tell their story. Readers, with their own unique backgrounds and unconscious motives, choose how to interpret these stories.

Good news is no news but all things aberrant and bizarre are considered newsworthy. Joggers in Central Park who don't get mugged aren't considered newsworthy and banks that aren't robbed go unmentioned. These constitute the unrepresented silent majority. Readers have an exaggerated sense of the true incidence of crime and catastrophe due to media overrepresentation and distortion.

Newspapers don't give us a balanced view of the world. For example, they tend to report medical studies that show positive correlations rather than those that show no correlation. Of two articles in the *Journal of the American Medical Association* on the effects of radiation exposure, one article showed a significantly higher incidence of disease in an area of radiation exposure while another concluded that there was no such correlation. Newspapers reported predominantly on the article that showed the positive correlation between radiation exposure and disease. Considered not newsworthy, the article that showed no correlation with radiation exposure was hardly mentioned. It became a casualty of "publication bias."

This bias can also originate primarily with investigators, who tend not to submit articles that have negative conclusions, and with the editors of the scientific journals, who tend not to accept them. Studies that conclude there are no significant effects on behavior by food additives, such as an artificial sweetener, tend to be dull and are overlooked by newspapers. Public readers (which also includes doctors) are therefore likely to encounter a distorted view of controversial health issues.

Researchers often are stimulated by a new idea and suffuse their work with a spirit of optimism. Research that doesn't pan out is met with disillusionment, although the negative findings may be of significance. I am reminded of the cartoon showing two dejected scientists in their lab amid a large number of disheveled test tubes and trash. One says to the other, "What is the opposite of eureka?"

Newspapers want to gain a "scoop" on medical information and are looking for breakthroughs and flashy events. Some years ago, I published an article on X-ray findings of sickle cell anemia in children. When I presented a talk on this subject at a national meeting, the local newspaper sent a reporter to interview me. While I was flattered by the attention, I became worried when the reporter stood at my office door, writing on a tiny spiral notebook, and asked, "What is sickle cell anemia, anyway?" I cooperated, in spite of my better judgment. My worst fears were realized several days later when the article declared that I had discovered ways to diagnose sickle cell disease that would lead to saving many lives. This was a gross exaggeration of the true situation, and I was embarrassed because I was sure my colleagues thought I had made some overblown statements in the interview.

A physician friend presented a paper at a meeting concerning the occasional complications to the eye from sinus surgery. The article appeared in the newspaper with the headline, "Physician Says Sinus Surgery Causes Eye Damage." The true facts were buried in the article.

The content of newspaper news is sometimes determined by the powers of the established domestic authority. Although we should take a defensive posture and seek protection from this control, often any questioning or infringement on the media power by the populace is considered an evil. The freedom of the press is considered sacred, but we must realize that industrial and political powers have already tainted its purity. After the Vietnam War and the Watergate hearings, there was some thought that the general public had too much power in the area of political debate and that this power should be curtailed. Some leaders thought that democracy had to be squelched in order to save democracy itself. The general public was considered an enemy to be reduced to a passive and apathetic body. There was great fear that the media had become too liberal and was in opposition to the views of the larger society and the government.

Newspapers share the blame in propagating blatant superstition. Articles on haunted houses, the Loch Ness monster, visiting space aliens, the Bermuda Triangle, or the search for Noah's ark on Mount Ararat are frequently featured. Yet we never see the follow-up stories stating that ghosts in the haunted house were never photographed, Nessie was never seen, and Noah's ark was never found.

Horoscopes are a staple among newspapers. Derived from the ancient theory that movements of stars and planets influence human affairs, astrology presents a vision of a world ruled by forces that operate in a precise manner. Astrology has been increasing in popularity for the past twenty years, with many more newspapers than ever before now carrying astrological material. Studies show that believers tend to be female, strongly religious, and feel that they are controlled by external rather than internal forces. Astrology, along with other fortune-telling schemes, is a multimillion-dollar business.

It is difficult to argue with believers in astrology. They look at you in all seriousness and state, "I have been studying astrology for many years and know astrology and its powers, just like you went to medical school and studied medicine. I don't attempt to give medical opinions and you should likewise not give an opinion about the validity of astrology because you haven't studied it for many years like I have." Bunk, studied for many years, remains bunk.

The final result is no different for so-called end-of-world prophecies which always make good press because people like the excitement of preparing for the end of time. After the prophesied fatal date has passed uneventfully, newspapers drop the subject, but they never retract their initial fascination with such unsupported claims of gloom and doom.

Newspapers always report such amusing bits of Americana as the weather prophecy of Groundhog Day. The humor blends with blatant superstition to make it seem like acceptable press. Only real curmudgeons would scoff at Groundhog Day.

The economic realities of newspaper operations are quite meaningful today, since newspapers are closing all over the country because of decreasing readership. This economic difficulty further distorts news content of daily papers because in tough times the long-term benefit appreciated by the readers of responsible journalism is sacrificed to yellow journalism, which provides a fiscal quick fix. With profit being the bottom line, newspapers now run surveys to see just what people want. Not surprisingly, a survey in my community showed that readers wanted more coverage of sports and food. The newspaper promptly obliged.

Because of the public's short attention span, some popular newspapers now give little tidbits of trivialized news. Newspapers are considered the first draft of history, and future historians looking back at our newspapers will obtain no meaningful depth or detail, only half-true factoids.

Newspaper content panders to the tendency of people to want to vicariously experience the exciting rather than the mundane or neutral. Our desire for the exotic makes us want to believe that captive prisoners of war still remain in Vietnam and that some sinister, complicated plot was successful in assassinating President Kennedy.

News Photography

We need to be skeptical of news photography. In *selecting* news, the photographer picks out for human interest and excitement particular subjects to photograph, which are not necessarily the most *representative*. A photograph, like a word, distills a complex thought down to one simple point, a process that is inescapably distorting. My son, a publisher as well as news photographer, told me that he was once assigned to cover a memorial service for John Lennon at a public square in New Haven, Connecticut. Most of the people attending this service were casual and laughing, but one young lady with a candle lit in front of her face was crying. The picture of this unusual individual was portrayed throughout the country as exemplary of the attitude of the people at this service.

A single photograph can produce an overly strong emotional reaction on the part of the national leaders as well as the populace. Seeing Somalis jeering over the dead body of an American soldier overwhelmed rational, long-term military policy by its immediacy. However, a photograph can create far-reaching positive effects; such as the napalm-burned Vietnamese girl jolting us to the horrors of that war.

We don't realize that a photographer's opportunities are often limited by government or public relations officials who grant access only to well-selected material, thereby altering the accuracy of the visual account of an event.

Sometimes news photographers who try to be excessively artistic skew objectivity and create a false sense of reality. We must be aware of deceptive and staged photos. With digital technology, the photographer can now more easily manipulate images, such as putting one individual's head on the shoulders of another. The claim that "the camera doesn't lie" may still be true, but the photo processor can lie. A photo of President Reagan in the hospital after he was shot had the intravenous tube cropped out to hide the severity of his situation from the public.

Movies

Movies influence us in many ways. Certain fictional events, when seen repeatedly, tend to be accepted as reality. In the movies, Lassie could obviously understand any human conversation. I had a collie when I was a child and was always disappointed in him after seeing Lassie movies.

Like television, movies contribute to the acceptance of casual, sometimes even humorous violence. In *Home Alone* and *Home Alone II,* the burglar "bad guys" are the recipients of repeated bashing. Director Chris Columbus says, "The higher the pain factor, the higher the audience reaction level. As long as they know the guy is not going to get killed, they laugh harder when it hurts more." On another level, the casual violence of *Pulp Fiction* and *Natural Born Killers* provides a numbing elevation of the threshold for experiencing a normal emotional response.

I have seen skull fractures caused by people striking others in the head with a pipe, thinking that they would only "knock them out." In reality, such injured people don't wake up after an appropriate few moments, rub their heads, and say, "Where am I?" I have also interpreted hundreds of films of hand fractures, so-called boxer's fractures, that usually occur in teenage boys. Clark Gable and John Wayne can hit each other in the face repeatedly in a movie barroom fight without sustaining fractures to their facial or hand bones, but real people can't get away with it. Hollywood continues to fatally distort reality for some suggestible people. Children have been known to die by putting on Superman capes and jumping from high buildings. Another movie myth suggests that anybody who gets fatally shot dies immediately rather than languishing in pain for a long period, and almost all nonfatal wounds are ones involving the shoulders, allowing for treatment with only an arm sling.

The movie and television doctor in the past has been a paragon of virtue who has the time to become truly involved with his patients and sometimes their entire families. The physician could go to the patients' homes and solve social and criminal problems while curing their illnesses. This unrealistic view created disappointment when patients went to their own doctor's office and realized that he or she sees many other patients before and after them in one day. More recent medical depictions, such as television's "ER," provide more realism.

Several movies have stereotyped blacks living in south Los Angeles as gang members. The movies *Colors*, *Boys 'n the Hood*, and *Grand Canyon* all portray this distorted image of violent blacks. People may not realize that the vast majority of blacks in Los Angeles are peaceful individuals holding down stable jobs and watching these movies with possible concern.

Movies have increasingly become obsessed with the supernatural. *The Exorcist*, *Ghostbusters*, and movies about haunted houses have become so prevalent that it is little wonder that our young people believe in all sorts of fantasy and superstition.

Movies have propagated the idea that there are many American prisoners of war still alive in Vietnam. *Uncommon Valor* with Gene Hackman, *Missing in Action* with Chuck Norris, and *Rambo: First Blood Part II* with Sylvester Stallone all served to promote this view.

Television

You are what you watch from your sofa. Television is undoubtedly our most powerful means of mass communication, although the extent of its influence on our personalities is hotly debated. The influence of any sort of fiction on the human mind has concerned thinkers since Plato, who warned against fiction. We're so inundated by media sources, the sheer number of competing effects tends to moderate any one. Compare the influence on us of the hundreds of movies and the thousands of hours of television that we watch with that of the influence on a child from a tiny African settlement seeing one movie during a trip to Nairobi. Typical Americans will spend about seven years in front of a television set by age seventy, almost half of their leisure time.

Excessive television viewing is habit forming. Addiction is too strong a word and should be reserved for more physical forms of compulsive behavior. But excessive exposure to television can qualify as a producer of an altered state of consciousness due to extreme relaxation and numbness produced by passive activity. Many people tend to withdraw psychologically into the programming, and television viewers who watch excessively are more readily hypnotized. Because our metabolic rate drops while we're watching television, just as in sleep, the combination of TV watching and snacking has an obvious effect on obesity.

With the overload of information available by flipping from one cable channel to another, we eventually experience an overall saturation similar to museum fatigue, where we start off fresh and alert hoping to see the entire museum, but after an hour we have seen so many displays that we sit down feeling numb, not caring to see anymore. After experiencing so much television, we become satiated and the emotional effect is diminished.

Television distorts reality by overemphasizing crime, sex, glitz, and excessive material consumption. The effect of viewing this false world image can be profound in Third World villages as well as in impoverished communities in

North America, leading to disappointment and resentment. Real life in any country can never match the excitement and romance that fiction in television provides. Real life has no plot or background music. Our enemies never get their just deserts, and we rarely experience an ecstatic ending to our efforts. Real life is whimsical and has many jagged edges without solution, closure, or easy moral lessons.

Children now watch television three hours a day, observing many murders daily, which increases their threshold for excitement and desensitizes them to the consequences of violence. Saturday morning cartoons exhibit twenty-five violent acts per hour, including the coyote in the "Road Runner" cartoons getting blasted and flattened repeatedly, which makes violence funny and flip. Children who watch many violent programs tend to exhibit more aggressive behavior, because violence has been made an acceptable way to cope.

Cartoon scientists are portrayed as frizzy-haired eccentrics with foreign accents, doing dangerous things. Teachers are depicted as buffoons and ogres on MTV.

Children are pushed into accepting the values of consumerism and are barraged with thousands of commercials each year for products often not in the best interest of their health. When criticized, the responsible producers and sponsors run up the flag of free enterprise and freedom of speech. But the honest among them admit that the *raison d'être* of commercial television is to sell products, not to benefit people.

Many children watch old movies and reruns of old television shows such as "I Love Lucy" and "The Brady Bunch," which creates an obsolete view of a world of affluence in an intact suburban nuclear family which functions with gender roles unlike those of today.

Countless years before television, children's play had

been participatory, requiring the exercise of imagination and improvisational skills. Totally passive watching of television leaves no time for the development of these qualities. It is possible that the lack of stimulation throughout childhood could lead to permanent stunting of these active abilities. Of additional importance, the average of twenty-three hours of television watched per week essentially displaces reading as a leisure activity for older children, who consider reading boring compared to the hypnotically moving lights, color, and action of the electronic circus. Having ceased reading, younger viewers are deceived into believing that television images are more objective because they transmit the visual experience itself rather than words about it. For older children computer use has also added to the decline of participatory social interaction and reading.

Many feel that the television networks have become increasingly controlled by large corporations and government and are less likely to provide critical analysis of issues regarding the government and industry. Big corporations control television news, information, and entertainment. For instance, General Electric now owns NBC, which casts doubt on whether NBC will fully support unbiased coverage of attitudes toward nuclear energy and the military-industrial complex.

The overall amount of advertising on television has increased. I can remember when there were substantially more documentaries and public affairs debates on prime time than we have now. The trend now is toward triviality, with celebrities and sports taking precedence over more substantive issues.

An analysis of television writers and producers shows that they are predominantly highly educated and secularized urbanites, mostly white males, tending to be liberal. The increasing number of women journalists are even more dis-proportionately liberal. The current image of America cre-ated by these individuals tends to cause bias toward cultural diversity and cosmopolitan, trendy lifestyles. The leading female actresses tend to be significantly younger than the men. Among murderers depicted on television, blacks tend to be underrepresented and Hispanics overrepresented. Iron-ically, businessmen are shown as greedy, corrupt villains. In general, professionals like physicians, lawyers, teachers, and social workers are given beneficent roles but blue collar, unionized workers are seldom portrayed.

Television news panders to visual entertainment. Fires, athletic events, and helicopter rescues of stranded flood vic-tims are more popular than the discussion of the non-telegenic, mundane issues of government and social prob-lems. The magazine news shows such as "Prime Time Live" and "20/20," which feature human interest, sex, crime, and celebrities, have almost replaced the full-length network doc-umentary. Even more so than in the print media, television news comes in staccato segments. Medical news on televi-sion is usually given in ninety-second magic bullets, empha-sizing high-technology new breakthroughs, with time rarely given for a balanced report including expert testimony ques-tioning the validity or benefit of the new sensation.

Because politicians have learned that the way to get elected is to look good on television, the likes of a Lincoln couldn't be elected today. Politicians are advised to create a good visual image without really saying much and boring people with the facts. If you can look like a pleasant good guy, you've got it made. Oliver North showed this in the Iran-Contra hearings. The image of the good soldier that he conveyed gathered a huge mail support, which tended to influence the attitudes of the committee members investigating him. Robert Bork, erstwhile Supreme Court nominee, didn't come across as a good guy, because he looked and spoke like the intellectual he is.

Television political ads are now able to shape and distort debate and have increased the tendency for negative campaigning. People now don't ask if an ad is true, they question only if it is effective.

Particular television images can influence world opinion. As an example, prior to the Gulf War, a Kuwaiti girl gave emotional testimony to a congressional hearing about how Iraqi troops took babies from incubators and put them on the floor to die. Shown repeatedly on television, this testimony had a great effect on the American public and on Congress. President Bush mentioned it in his exhortations to go to war. Later investigations by Amnesty International revealed that these atrocities never happened. The girl was later found to be the daughter of a Kuwaiti official. Kuwait had paid a Washington public relations firm to orchestrate a "Free Kuwait" movement, and the girl's testimony was part of this.

There are many other unrecognized effects of media influence on our attitudes and ideas of propriety. Media content can be accepted or rejected depending upon the setting of its presentation. Producers and writers can get by with showing sexually explicit material if they present it as comedy. Imagine yourself casually changing cable channels and coming across "Saturday Night Live" with its raunchy skits. The men and women in the audience are seen laughing and clapping, in total acceptance. As we continue to flip through the channels, we come to a stand-up comedy theater where a female comic is enthusiastically shouting four-letter words to a cheering audience of men and women, black and white. On another channel, Dr. Ruth is holding forth in a humorous manner. If we continue to flip channels we might then encounter a retelecast of the Senate Judiciary Committee hearings, where a close-up of Anita Hill is seen with her face frowning in a hushed, somber mood. She says that then Judge Clarence Thomas spoke of pornographic movies he had seen, and once mentioned that there was a pubic hair in his soft drink. The committee members, all in serious, pained demeanor, tell Thomas that he has been accused of heinous, unspeakable behavior. The diverse attitude changes toward sex on television are striking; they require only the proper setting provided by television.

In the future, we will have a thousand choices of news and entertainment images emanating from receptors in entire walls of our homes, or presented in realistic holograms and/or virtual reality programs. Possibly some zealots will select only material that supports their narrow belief systems, whether it be far left, far right, or religious fanaticism. In this situation, they may never peruse broad opinions and hence go further afield. Will this voracious, addictive image consumption isolate us from the real world? Will we lose our ability to speak, read, and think effectively?

References

Brimelow, Peter. "TV's Killer Businessmen." *Forbes* (December 23, 1991): 38–40.

Centerwall, Brandon S. "Television and Violence." *Journal of the American Medical Association* (June 10, 1992): 3059–63.

Chomsky, Noam. *Necessary Illusions: Thought Control in Democratic Societies.* Boston: South End Press, 1989.

Donovan, Robert, and Ray Scherer. *Unsilent Revolution: Television News and American Public Life, 1948–1991*. New York: Woodrow Wilson International Center for Scholars/Cambridge University Press, 1992.

Eisenburg, Anne. "Scientists in the Movies." *Scientific American* (April 1993): 128.

Greider, William. *Who Will Tell the People: The Betrayal of American Democracy*. New York: Simon and Schuster, 1992.

Jamieson, Kathleen Hall. *Dirty Politics: Deception, Distraction, and Democracy*. New York: Oxford University Press, 1992.

Kellner, Douglas. *Television and the Crisis of Democracy*. Boulder, Colo.: Westview Press, 1990.

Koren, Gideon, and Naomi Klein. "Bias against Negative Studies in Newspaper Reports of Medical Research." *Journal of the American Medical Association* (October 2, 1991): 1824–26.

Kubey, Robert, and Mihaly Csikszentmihalyi. *Television and the Quality of Life: How Viewing Shapes Everyday Experience*. Hillsdale, N.J.: Lawrence Erlbaum Associates, 1990.

Mc Kibben, Bill. *The Age of Missing Information*. New York: Random House, 1992.

Mitchell, William. "When Is Seeing Believing?" *Scientific American* (February 1994): 68–73.

Postman, Neil. *Technopoly: The Surrender of Culture to Technology*. New York: Alfred A. Knopf, 1992.

Rennie, Drummond, and Annette Flanagin. "Publication Bias: The Triumph of Hope Over Experience." *Journal of the American Medical Association* (January 15, 1992): 411–12.

Schwitzer, Gary. "The Magical Medical Media Tour." *Journal of the American Medical Association* (April 8, 1992): 1969–71.

Weaver, Paul H. *News and the Culture of Lying*. New York: Free Press, 1994.

4

Negotiation, Selling, and Advertising

―――――――――∾∾―――――――――

When the attractive clothing saleslady coos, "You look fabulous in this suit," you have your doubts, but you buy it anyway, baggy pants and all. We are all gullible. We think we see through advertisements and believe we're not getting sold anything we don't need. But the fact is, we just don't know ourselves well enough.

Because we're usually oblivious to rhetorical and persuasive influences, advertisements in the form of billboards, television, radio, magazines, and newspapers all take their toll. We're hit by phone calls and other solicitations by charities and politicians, and receive countless catalogs and brochures. Even our immediate family members, in their own loving ways, try to manipulate us, and they do so more often than we like to admit. A teenage son is apt to wait until three minutes before his father's favorite television program starts before he asks to borrow the car, knowing that dad will likely capitulate quickly.

In knowing more about ourselves, we should be aware of the latest psychological techniques to control us. People in business and law, who have been well trained in rhetoric, accept persuasion as normal human activity, and don't consider it devious. Those educated in the more scientific disciplines supposedly based on logic and truth don't fully understand this, and they can be at quite a disadvantage by not understanding the large gray area between influence and deception.

To appreciate fully the various ways that others try to manipulate us, let's look at some of the techniques employed by negotiators and persuaders.

Negotiations and Meetings

Suppose you're trying to learn how to be a smooth negotiator. The following techniques might be taught to help you gain an advantage: Make sure that your manner and appearance reflect respect and power. Walk swiftly and purposefully. Others step aside for one who appears to know where he is going . . . even though he is lost! A college friend of mine saved time waiting in restaurants and at sporting events by the cocky use of only two words, "Coming through." The crowds parted like unzipping your jacket. Stand and sit erect. Never exhibit body language that would indicate insecurity, such as chewing on a pen, twiddling thumbs, slouching, or covering your face with your hand. Gestures of confidence include open hands and an unbuttoned coat. Dress a half step up from the others. Wearing a dark blue suit is effective, as are the uniformed ornaments and decorations of any profession, such as a white coat for a physician. Carrying the latest-model beeper further establishes you as busy and important. Have superior props such as expensive audiovisual aids and a first-class briefcase. Ordinarily, the individual with the most clout in a room is the one with the least body motion and also the one who says the least. Look people straight in the eye when you talk with them. Height gives a psychological edge. For this reason, J. Edgar Hoover, who for years headed the FBI, stood on a raised platform behind his desk when speaking to agents.

My brother once endured a most creative ploy used on him by a wholesale grocery buyer to gain an advantage in negotiating. He was offered a seat in a very large and well-cushioned chair in front of the buyer's desk. Almost imperceptibly, my brother soon noticed he was no longer face to face with the buyer but was looking up at him. The contract negotiations did not go well and it was only at the conclusion of the meeting that my brother realized that the sinking feeling he had experienced was, in fact, just that. At the end of the meeting my brother was sitting no more than nine inches off of the floor and he realized that the oversized seat cushion was designed specifically to put him at a psychological disadvantage.

If at all possible, have negotiating meetings on your home grounds, in a familiar setting. Also, try to have more people with you than the opposition has. At the meeting table sit at the control positions—the ends. More devious ploys involve catching your opponents when they are busy and under stress, or setting up a meeting for them on short notice after you've had plenty of time to prepare. The presence of lawyers and the use of all the trappings of any type of office or profession, such as government buildings, is valuable.

Plan the strategy of your meeting beforehand. Arrive at the meeting early—others may reveal their thoughts prematurely and you may be able to make a deal with someone. If your adversary happens to arrive late, a mild rebuke by glancing at your watch might give you an edge. Once the meeting starts, initiate the offensive by stating your case first; this shows confidence. Plan ahead to have a colleague promptly follow with his approval. Uncommitted people will then tend to side with you because they know they must oppose at least two people if they don't agree. This could start a domino or bandwagon effect and the meeting could easily proceed in your favor.

Don't underestimate the power of a superior knowledge of parliamentary procedure. If used with aplomb, you can bluff your way along and twist the rules of order to your advantage.

People respect strength. Don't ask permission to speak. Always speak deliberately, firmly, and slowly; make confident, bold declarations. Your tone of voice should be well modulated and of a slightly lower pitch than usual. Call others by their first names. Work at suppressing any outward signs of fear or intimidation. Say things only once; repeating them seems like you're overcompensating and defensive. Be polite, yet assertive. Skillful negotiators use all kinds of acts such as calculated displays of feigned anger that are timed with precision. Anger conveys that you are confident in your position and therefore can afford to express righteous indignation. When a group plans beforehand to vent anger at one individual, all, in unison, can show amazement at this person's dishonorable behavior ("We demand an apology from you!"). Have total confidence that you are being fair and reasonable while the opposition is not. Make it obvious that truth and justice are on your side.

Some dishonest negotiators employ people to give false information and act as shills to enter fake bids. Others have someone enter the meeting and say, "I'm sorry to interrupt, but the president would like to seek your advice for a minute on an important matter."

Another technique is to list a large number of things in favor of your case, overwhelming your opponent with the absolute number of items in your favor. Other ploys include purposely making a small error in the negotiations to distract the opposition and to make them think they have an advantage.

The psychological need to reciprocate a favor probably arises from our ancient methods of survival by sharing food and other goods. This deep-seated obligation to return a good deed is used by panhandlers who may first give passersby a flower or piece of candy, thus making the recipient feel guilt if something—namely money—isn't given in return. Contributors to political campaigns also know that they may, in turn, ultimately receive benefits. Other minor exploitations include the food samples given away at grocery stores and the personalized address labels mailed by charities.

In negotiations, granting a small favor to your opponents can often serve to soften them up. Throwing out a small item as a sacrifice can also be distracting and disarming. Giving up too much, however, can be perceived as weakness.

Sometimes the "bad guy, good guy" technique is effective. You can perhaps first use a lawyer to act as the extremely obnoxious, aggressive individual. The mild-mannered, personable "good guy" then goes in and tries to settle things "because of the lawyer's bad techniques." The affable guy wants to settle things immediately, "while the lawyer is out of the room."

Winning negotiators don't try to demolish their opponent's case, preferring to give the other side a face-saving residual. Winners, however, never agree to split a disputed point fifty-fifty, but always try for seventy-thirty before giving a little and being satisfied with sixty-forty, in your favor of course.

It is axiomatic that the negotiator who starts with the highest goals and sticks with them for the longest time will win. Some individuals simply enjoy the ancient sport of haggling. They have the advantage over those who don't relish this contest.

Selling Techniques

Your decision to buy this or that item is influenced covertly by smooth psychological techniques, which are usually not dependent on power or authority. Rather, the salesperson tries to be liked and adopts a relaxed, pleasant demeanor. We tend to prefer (and buy from) physically attractive people who are familiar and similar to us in social background and age. Effective salespersons smile warmly, make easy eye contact, and compliment their prospects by looking at them and listening intently to them. A salesman I once knew said, "Even if you don't mean it, always be *sincere*."

In persuasive situations, such as when closing a sale, always choose an unhurried time and comfortable place. People should not be hungry while they are deciding, and there should be no interruptions.

Salespersons use various euphemisms, such as saying *agreement* instead of *contract*; they prefer to *own* something rather than *buy* it.

Proven psychological techniques augment persuasion

and selling. The reciprocation technique is used indirectly when the price of an item is reduced. If you give someone a free brochure or small token, such as a sample of your product, the then-obligated person will tend to buy a larger item. When giving this freebie, the effective salesperson always hands it directly to the person and tries to touch him or her while doing so.

It's a good idea to keep people saying yes. Salesmen often ask questions that require only positive answers. It's a cold day, isn't it? You like to look at beautiful pictures, don't you? You want your children to have the best, don't you? This tends to make people feel good about themselves, and they tend to join the salesperson in subsequent leading questions aimed at pushing them in the direction of buying the product.

One technique is to "assume the sale." Take, for example, when salespeople ask, "What color car do you want to own?" or "What size dress do you wish to wear?" Any answer presumes a commitment to buy a car or dress. The salesperson tries to get prospective customers used to the idea that they will buy the product. The salesperson talks about how the customers will use the product and how each family member will be proud of it, acting as if they have already bought it.

Another psychological ploy is to ask a prospective buyer to buy an expensive item. The seller expects the buyer to refuse this, but when the salesperson acts surprised, hurt, and disappointed, this obligates the buyer to buy a smaller item.

People like to think of themselves as being correct when they have done a small thing, such as donating a small amount to a charity. They have a slight momentum in this direction, and when later asked to do something similar but larger they are more inclined because they want to justify their previous decision. When a salesperson induces a customer to commit to a small purchase, the salesperson then creates a need in the customer to be consistent with his own actions and thereby be more apt to make a larger purchase in the future. When a car salesperson lets us drive a car home and keep it over the weekend to try it out, he is attempting to create a personal commitment on our part, as well as doing us a favor for which we may then feel obligated.

Contrast can be used to advantage in sales. Real estate agents sometimes purposely show someone a shabby and overpriced house before they show them the one they are really trying to sell. The agent may also mention that there is another potential buyer, creating a feeling of competition and urgency. Clothing salespeople always sell the accessory items such as shirts and ties *after* selling the more expensive suit. The cost of a tie then seems trivial in comparison. The ensemble then also gives a sense of completion.

Some salespersons set up small "straw man" arguments that can easily be refuted, thus letting the potential customer win and feel good. They may also set up an obvious error in the arithmetic of the price. The potential buyer feels pleasantly smart about catching the mistake and therefore becomes more involved in the entire process.

Another ploy is to "reduce" the perceived cost of an item considerably by stating what it costs on a weekly or daily basis. Realtors know it is easier to sell a residential lot at $300 a month than at the price of $75,000.

If people are offered several options, most will pick an intermediate choice. If asked to pick between the numbers one, two, three, and four, a vast majority will pick numbers two or three. With this psychological knowledge in hand, the intermediate options set up as most favorable to the salesperson will be chosen by people who are unaware of this tendency.

Advertising Hokum

We are willing players in the advertising game that surrounds us. When we walk outside to get our mail and newspaper, which are both at least half advertisements, we see a delivery truck with a corporate logo or bumper sticker for a politician. As we return, we notice a grocery discount flyer stuck on our front door. Advertising fits the American psyche. In contrast to the older European cultures, Americans tend to be fickle and more easily manipulated to accept the latest idea and product. The current Generation X, which is highly conscious of material things, is even more subject to advertising influence than Americans in the past.

Although we know we are being conned by advertisements, we wink at the fun of it. We accept phony advertising because we constantly indulge ourselves in the borderlands of honesty, like believing in superstition, telling white lies, and embellishing stories for interest. Some ads are, however, now more honest than in the past because of the consumer protection movement, lawsuits, and regulatory bodies.

Many people today define themselves by their possessions, whether they admit it or not. Advertising hypes unnecessary material items as a road to happiness. Following this false goal creates eventual dependence and invariable dissatisfaction.

Many ads prey upon our need to find a sense of self. We're all searching for roles to play, and advertising helps us decide just who we are. Those who need to pose as rich and suave are compelled to buy a Ferrari and dark sunglasses. Those who want to play at being a "with-it," active teenager must have a red Jeep, wear a baseball cap backward, and listen to the latest music. Loose pants and untied Reeboks are essential. Those who want a more rugged, country look drive a pickup truck, have a baseball cap on frontward, and wear scruffy blue jeans, boots, and a plaid shirt.

Advertisements help establish behavior patterns. Some encourage us to take pills. Ads tell us that it's okay to be a glutton of spicy foods, because there's always quick relief with antacids. Some ads portray people in stressful situations, having interpersonal difficulty, but then their headaches are promptly cured by pills. An individual coping with the normal stresses of life—a busy mother or a rushed businessperson—takes a pill or a gelcap and is consequently made happy (relieved of pain). This fallacious model does its part in contributing to drug abuse.

Psychological needs play a large part in advertising. All ads are geared, often deceptively, to exploit these needs. Advertisers tell us that the car we choose makes a statement about our social status, our financial condition, and our sexual prowess. Life insurance salespeople gear their ads to those who need to create their own immortality and perpetual influence. Men in particular have a persistent desire to protect and control their families after death; therefore, a sizable insurance policy assures them of continual guidance of their families.

One ad for a station wagon implied by the use of models that women sitting in it appear thinner because it is so roomy, thereby exploiting women's preoccupation with being slim. Similarly, many cigarette ads portray slim, tall women. Though some people who quit smoking gain weight temporarily, this weight is certainly not as harmful as continuing to smoke. In addition to ravaging the health of young smoking women, nicotine addiction can also injure fetuses and the second-hand smoke can harm children within the household.

Teenage girls are led by ads to think that it is cool and sophisticated to smoke and be thin. They might even meet a handsome, tough Marlboro macho-man. The evidence concocted by the tobacco industry to lobby in support of smoking against the evidence compiled by the scientific community is pathetic and irrational.

Beer ads are replete with psychological ploys appealing to male adolescent needs. Male bonding is emphasized by the he-man in-group of fishermen relaxing around a campfire. Women are usually portrayed as convivial "serving wenches" or objects of sexual conquest—aided by drinking beer.

Since the 1950s, there have been claims that advertising exploits the subconscious by using subliminal techniques, such as the placement of subtle sexual symbols within the ice cubes of whiskey ads. These claims have never been proven, and more recent ads tend to spoof these claims. There are, however, obvious phallic symbols in many ads.

Some advertising ploys do need to be noticed, though. Be aware of the superhype that contains an overt untruth so big that even if it is deflated it is still untrue. We sometimes see automobile ads that say "unbelievable discounts," "absolutely no catch," "there has never been such a discount anywhere at any time." Most people who see such an ad will admit that it's overdone, but still, in spite of this, think that the dealer must have a better deal than most in order to justify the ad. Wrong, usually.

Another way advertisers deceive us is by camouflaging ads as news stories. We can be caught unaware by "infomercials," advertisements that masquerade as news or information. Often the actors and established personalities are seen in attractive surroundings, and, before we realize it, we have watched a commercial. These contrived formats, though criticized, probably will prevail. Recent program-length commercials on television and radio tend to be indistinguishable from regular programmed entertainment. We have to watch experts being interviewed on the nature and therapy of baldness for perhaps ten minutes before we realize it is an ad.

Advertisements now subtly insinuate themselves into more and more activities. Professional auto racers are speeding billboards for motor oil and professional sports figures wear specific lines of sportswear. Advertisements are placed within movies, with actors very obviously drinking specific soft drinks or beers. The list is endless.

Tricks at the supermarket include selling more goods based on people's tendency to buy packaged foods when they see a shelf loaded in massive quantity. Who wants to buy the last box of something? Items with a high profit margin are usually put at eye level so they will be big sellers. Because shoppers notice an increase in the price of goods, food marketers instead reduce the quantity of the product while retaining the price. Shoppers usually don't notice on the label's fine print that there are fewer diapers in a pack or that the jar of baby food now contains 4 ounces instead of 4.5 ounces. Another tactic is to maintain the same ounce content but make the container wider to gain more shelf space and enhance visibility. Since the supermarkets make more money on their private label brands, their items are positioned next to the leading national brands for price comparison and because the shopper is drawn to the location of the best-selling brands.

Labels on food items are sometimes misleading. Many food products now seem to promise nutritional perfection. The "low cholesterol" or "no cholesterol" labels misinform because many of these foods, such as potato chips, contain large amounts of vegetable fats that *have never had* cholesterol. The percentage of fat in the product is the most significant dietary concern, particularly for individuals with atherosclerotic heart disease, hypertension, or diabetes. Often the word "natural" is thrown into the ads and placed in product labels. In fact, only a tiny amount of fruit juice mixed with artificial flavoring and color fulfills the legal requirement for this half-truth.

Multiple gimmicks support advertisements. Consider these examples:

Pity and modesty: "We're not the biggest company, just the best, and we try to please even though we're a small company."

Getting on the band wagon: "More people use our brand than any other."

Long-standing tradition: "Our company has been in business since 1730."

Appeal to science: "Four out of five doctors agree . . ."

Overall authority of endorsement: "The American Dental Association recommends . . ."

Appeal by endorsement from celebrities: Michael Jordan and Bill Cosby endorse many different products.

Appeal to time deadline: "Special limited time offer."

Appeal to scarcity: "Get 'em while they last. Only a few left."

The commercialization of children's television exploits youngsters. Children watch about five hours of television commercials a week, with food and toys being the most frequently advertised products. Young children are unable to distinguish between programs and commercials, and are actually more attentive to the commercials, which employ smiling faces and snappy music. Even program-length commercials now exist for children who do not realize that these commercials are designed to make them want products that are not necessarily good for them. The breakfast cereals pushed are usually of the high-sugar, low-fiber type. Parents, rather than advertisers, should choose what children eat; unfortunately, many adults can be just as gullible as children regarding advertisements.

Sure, we can see through any of these shallow attempts to alter our judgment if we are asked specifically about any one ad. However, the sum total of the barrage of ads over the years undeniably affects the behavior of even the most rational and skeptical individuals.

References

Burns, David D. *The Feeling Good Handbook: Using the New Mood Therapy in Everyday Life*. New York: William Morrow, 1990.

Cialdini, Robert B. *Influence: Science and Practice*. New York: HarperCollins, 1988.

Gerrig, Richard. *The Life of the Mind: An Introduction to Psychology*, audiotapes. Springfield, Va.: The Teaching Company, 1991.

Hopkins, Tom. *The Art of Influencing People, Listen and Learn Series*. New York: TDM Caedmon Audio, 1987.

Key, Wilson Bryan. *Subliminal Seduction*. New York: Signet, 1973.

Levine, Joshua. "Search and Find." *Forbes* (September 2, 1991): 134–35.

Pacifico, Carl. *Think Better, Feel Better*. Libra Publication, 1990.

Packard, Vance. *The Hidden Persuaders*. New York: Pocket Books, 1963.

Savon, Leslie. *The Sponsored Life: Ads, TV, and the American Culture*. Philadelphia: Temple University, 1995.

Taylor, Shelly E. *Positive Illusions: Creative Self-Deception and the Healthy Mind*. New York: Basic Books, 1989.

5

Laws, Ethics, and Religion

W hen in doubt, do the right thing.
Many of our "honorable" actions and ideas that we
believe originate within us are based on societal pressures
which are so indirect that we are unaware of their influence.
Although our culture provides our conscience with a complex mix of "shoulds" and "oughts," we don't realize that we
are forced to do many things because of laws.

When I was a boy, I knew that abortion was wrong
because I had heard of a villainous doctor who had performed an abortion. I could imagine the townspeople hoist-
ing torches and ropes while marching to his office (as in the
old Frankenstein movies). I also assumed that it was right for
"colored people" to sit in the back of the bus. I didn't realize
that these beliefs I took for granted were all based on laws.

Civil order and rules naturally develop in a free society

regardless of whether they have been legislated and written down or are of a more informal variety. Laws as we know them had to await the advent of writing. Written law was first put to civil use in Mesopotamia, in the city of Ur, in 2100 B.C.E. Later, the Babylonians developed the famous code of Hammurabi. These laws began to create governments of men instead of gods and ushered in a secular system to stabilize society.

In the past (and in the present in some countries), ecclesiastical and state laws were entangled in such a way that religion determined the legal strictures on human behavior. Heretics—those who blasphemed against the established church—were burned at the stake, and, not insignificantly, their property went to the church.

Most laws are passed with the hope that they will benefit the entire society in the long run even if the group they help initially is relatively small. If you have trouble getting out on the main street from your little sidestreet and you document that there have been some auto accidents at this intersection, you and others on your street can push for and perhaps obtain a stoplight to control traffic flow. The problem is that the other 99.99 percent of citizens must stop at this light, even though it doesn't benefit them. So it is with all laws, too many being passed to rectify small problems. They all add up, and the total effect is that our entire system of civilization is "gummed up" by too many laws. These senseless regulatory obstacles often cause contempt for the law.

Our interpersonal relations are often affected by laws against real or imagined prejudice and exploitation. We don't dare appear to be a sexist, a racist, or an ageist society today. Recent court cases have ruled that even the appearance of sexuality in the workplace can be damaging to a woman. The slightest activity that could be interpreted as sexual harassment has been ruled to cause a hostile work environment. Such compliments to another worker as, "You have a great figure" may now be considered sexual harassment, and calling another worker of either sex "honey" could be deemed offensive. People now are much more inhibited in their conversations at work. A group of ten people, all on coffee break, are now held to the language of the most prudish person present. The Federal Age Discrimination in Employment Act and similar laws in each state protect workers who are forty and over from disparaging comments regarding age, such as calling someone "Pop." Such comments are illegal if they cause mental anguish and "loss of enjoyment in life."

The slightest ethnic comment is now considered out of order. Interpersonal relations are indeed complex, and what is considered appropriate behavior has been determined by countless small, interpersonal acts over thousands of years. Today, a simple law can render many physical and speech acts illegal. On some college campuses now, political correctness is operative, creating a tyrannical intolerance in itself and inhibiting free thought, rendering the climate for learning quite destructive.

I have seen fears of litigation prevent people from acting, even when basic common sense would dictate that action be taken. Often when someone is injured or seriously ill, people stand around not doing the obvious things to prevent bleeding or render aid, often because they are afraid they may do the wrong thing and be sued. Litigious pressures are gaining disproportionate influence on our behavior, which was previously determined by practical obligations of expediency, morality, and compassion. All my life I have seen thunderstorms come and go and have not been concerned, but in the past few years I have noticed that any time there is a thunder-

storm, if you turn on your television, you will see dire warn-
ings. The neighborhood sirens go off now with the slightest
provocation. The weather bureaus and television stations
don't want to take any chance of being late about informing
somebody of a serious storm or tornado. Because the whole
thing has been overdone, people may no longer pay attention
to the sirens when there is a real threat looming.

Many legal pressures are detrimental to American industry because it is difficult for companies to innovate and com-
pete internationally. The cost of product liability insurance in
the United States is much greater than in most European
countries. Frivolous lawsuits and arbitrary punitive damage
awards drive up the cost of production, for which consumers
eventually pay. Since 1950, court costs have grown at a much
greater rate than the economy as a whole. Much of the
money that claimants do win goes to pay lawyers, court
costs, and other administrative expenses.

Many of our major drug companies have been sued. This
litigation makes it extremely difficult to test new drugs and
use them. We are all aware of the defensive medicine doctors
practice. Many potentially unnecessary tests are performed
because doctors can't take any reasonable chances. The bill
for medical malpractice liability insurance is indirectly
passed on to the patients.

The idea that nations should be ruled by laws and not
men has been honored since the signing of the Magna Carta,
which took arbitrary and abusive power away from
medieval English kings. Today, in some ways, this idea has
been permitted to extend too far. Because personal intuitive
actions, relative to official laws, now gain no respect, personal responsibility and ethics have been relinquished by the
individual and given, like a hot potato, to the courts. We

seem to live under the motto: If it's legal, it's moral. We've become robots with laws as our batteries, expecting social problems to be cured immediately by external legislation instead of by internal self-directed effort over the long haul. We all have encountered the cold "organization man" who abides strictly by the rules instead of making more appropriate individual ethical decisions. Many bureaucrats are so "hung up" on the technical processes of law they forget to use their common sense.

Where do our laws come from anyway? Society now looks at laws, courts, and lawyers in a more analytical and critical way. In the past, the average citizen considered laws to be rock-solid rules to honor and obey because they satisfied our need for structure and order. We have taken refuge from our ambiguous world by making social rules like the Constitution and the Ten Commandments sacred. But the age-old American concept of holding "these truths to be self-evident" is now being viewed skeptically. Deconstruction by critical analysis is being applied to the entire legal system. We are now holding up the Supreme Court justices to lights that may be too bright. When we consider the difficulty of being nominated and confirmed by the Senate we are painfully aware that each of these justices has legs of sand; each has personal foibles that could be headlined by the media. More and more each decade, the Supreme Court is considered a political and social institution rather than a legal one, with its justices making policy rather than judicial decisions. The word is now out that the High Court's decisions are made after incorporating compromise and creating tactical alliances. Any nonunanimous decision would have to incorporate these factors.

Judges attempt to decide cases interpreting the Constitution, but actually they are trying to read the minds of the Founding Fathers, who were fallible eighteenth-century fellows who also based their ideas on political expediency and personal whims.

Some laws are forced on us by powerful politicians supported by monied or religious interests. It is obvious that many court cases are decided on the basis of the fact that people have money to defend themselves or to prosecute. We are becoming more aware of the many weak links in our chain of legal validity. Jury selection is too often the most crucial factor in the outcome of a race- or gender-sensitive case. Jurors may be selected specifically for their bias or lack of education. Often they are incompetent because their minds have long been saturated with escapist entertainment, and they may be easily caught up by an irrelevant detail. Our jury system is a disgrace for allowing this type of juror to perch in judgment of others. There are many laws against victimless crimes; however, many states have laws against private gambling but incongruently promote state-run lotteries.

The forces of political expediency tarnish the logic and value of many legal concepts. Affirmative action is really controlled reverse discrimination, and progressive taxation ("success" tax) offends the sense of fairness of many people, although these seemingly unfair concepts are generally supported on the basis of social practicality.

Lawyers are human, too, but they drape themselves in incomprehensible legal jargon and thus appear intimidating. Some may prolong and complicate legal proceedings by filing motions, taking depositions, and the like, because it is in their financial interest to do so.

Most people assume the basic purpose of a lawyer at trial is to help uncover the truth in the case. According to leading lawyers, this view is incorrect within our American system of adversarial jurisprudence. Instead, the purpose of lawyers is to win the case for the client. There are legally sanctioned limits on methods of uncovering the truth. One need only take note of the Fifth Amendment privilege against self-incrimination, or its rule against unreasonable searches. In addition, our courts honor privileged communication between doctor and patient, clergy and penitent, and lawyer and client.

Measured deception is generally accepted in handling a legal procedure. Witnesses can be coached to selectively omit information, or to emphasize the "wrong" truths. Many lawyers attempt to damage the credibility of a witness who they know is telling the truth. Lawyers have greater license to pursue such behavior within the courtroom than they would have outside it, where they might be accused of slander, obstruction of justice, or abetting criminals.

Case decisions are increasingly determined by technicalities rather than whether justice is served.

Ethics

We realize that laws often do not reflect moral and ethical values very well. On the other hand, there have been many failures to legislate morality. Philosophers throughout the ages have influenced legal thought. In Plato's *Republic*, Socrates accepts the state as the supreme authority and puts the individual below it. Plato viewed the state as basically beneficent and natural, which was a more reasonable idea at that time because Athens was a small city with close communications and a stable social structure.

In his Doctrine of the Mean, Plato's student Aristotle recommends observing moderation in all things and avoiding excess and deficiency. Aristotle and the Greeks defined goodness differently than the Christians. To them, a good person wasn't necessarily altruistic and self-effacing. The Greek ideal of a heroic man was a competent, well-rounded expert, like Odysseus, who was smart, strong, and able to lie without being caught.

The German philosopher Immanuel Kant (1724–1804) had a great influence on ethics. In his "categorical imperative" he recommended that we should always act as if our actions could be willed a universal law. That is, we should behave as if our actions would be good for everybody to copy—another form of the Golden Rule. If you live by this moral rule, there can be no exceptions. You can't individualize, and you should treat everybody equally. The problem with this rule is that it is dependent upon someone else's notion of what other people want to have done to them. Some people think that instead of doing unto others what *we* would have them do unto us, we should do unto others as *they* would have us do unto them. After all, what I want done to me may not be the same as what you want done to you. Remember, there are masochists among us. Kant believed that true morality comes from within each rational individual, not from coercion by laws or by other people. Some people feel this way about religion. If you act morally only because your religion dictates that you should, then you don't get any credit. Also, Kant's philosophy included the ascetic thread that if you get pleasure from doing good, you are not really behaving on a high moral plane.

John Stuart Mill (1806–1873) and Jeremy Bentham (1748–1832) espoused utilitarianism, the ethical concept of bringing the greatest good to the greatest number of people. By this philosophy, the morally right action is a calculation that weighs the different likely outcomes of how your behavior would affect other people. Much of today's public policy formulated by our politicians and economists is based on a utilitarian model, although we often call it a cost/benefit analysis. Actions based on this broad principle presume to treat all individuals similarly. No special treatment can be given to friends and family. A school teacher who is giving individual attention to a failing student may be neglecting the other students. With a strict utilitarian philosophy, society could not justify the cost of saving the life of a very prematurely born infant, or spending large sums of public money to save a child who has fallen into a well.

In trying to "do the right thing" we can't face the infinite complexity of defining a "good" course of action. If good is defined in the moral, altruistic sense, or in the sense of one's best interest, both still vary with *time*. What's good for the short term (sleeping late) is not good for the intermediate term (getting to work on time), but may be good again for the longer term (preventing you from getting sleepy at work, injuring yourself, and missing more work). For an even longer time frame, however, it may again not be good (not getting a pay raise at the end of the year because your boss noticed your tardiness).

The good can vary with *circumstance*. An action that may be good for you, such as taking a higher-paying job in another city, may not be good for the family, especially the children (if it disrupts their school year). Taking the job, however, may be good for the larger number of people in that city if your work on the job improves their overall standard of living.

The ethics involved in international trade become problematic because value systems vary between nations. Bribery is a time-honored method of business transaction in some parts of the world but is considered reprehensible in other parts.

Karl Marx emphasized how much our ethical behavior was influenced by our social and economic status. A poor person, by necessity, must prioritize his actions; doing far-reaching, charitable things is generally of low priority because basic survival must come first. Most loving, generous people have enough money and time to permit such charitable behavior.

Business ethics appears to have acquired a degree of isolation, since the ethical standards of our personal lives are often not applied to our business lives. An extreme example is the religious, family-loving Mafia chief brutally conducting "business." More common examples include respected citizens involved in deceptive advertising or pollution of the environment.

We are such prisoners of our culture that it is unusual to have to choose between good and bad. Most choices are between degrees of good or bad actions, or in mixtures of good and bad, such as in divorce, abortion, or military actions.

Religion

Even though Bertrand Russell considered anything taboo well worth discussing, frank conversations about religion remain prohibited in polite company.

Religion, because it historically has been the basis for ethics and laws, has a profound but variable influence on our behavior, depending upon one's particular religious convictions. A great many people accept religion on faith as a welcome respite from the uncertainty in their lives and from cold science and reason. Many psychiatrists categorize religious belief as a form of self-deceptive psychological defense mechanism that enables us to adapt to life's mental stresses. Religion can offer a metaphorical or poetic treatment of reality that enables many to express their deepest concerns.

Free thought (the questioning of the foundations and assumptions of religion) and religion have been at odds for a long time. Things can be tough on any philosopher who disagrees with the existing religion of his time. One of the crimes for which Socrates was sentenced to death was impiety toward the gods. Therefore, his student, Plato, went along with contemporary religious teachings because he thought this engendered peace. Aristotle fled Athens in part because his teachings were interpreted as antireligious. In the Roman Empire Christians were martyred for not believing in the Roman gods. Modern Islamic fundamentalists now also consider Christians to be infidels. Many religious people who view themselves individually as adhering to the "one true faith" consider other religions as exercises in heathen practice and blasphemous.

Augustine (354–430) and Thomas Aquinas (1224–1274) realized that they had better speak of God in a rather broad sense in order for their philosophy to be accepted. Thomas Aquinas defined God as an ineffable essence of being with no form. This loose definition, however, didn't stop him from recommending that heretics be killed. Some philosophers who were basically nonbelievers were able to avoid imprisonment or death because their language of religion and God was so generic. Baruch Spinoza (1632–1677) spoke of God as the "infinite and eternal first cause." William James (1842–1910) defined religion as the "feelings, acts and experiences of individuals in their solitude, in relation to whatever they may consider the divine."

With this definition, everyone is religious. Some claim to be religious because they believe in God even though they don't believe in *a* God of an organized religion. If religion is defined in a meaningful way, these people would not be considered religious. Carl Sagan said, "If by 'God' one means the set of physical laws that govern the universe, then clearly there is such a God." Many people tend to define God so broadly that virtually everyone can be said to believe: "God is everywhere." "God is love." From these definitions, God cannot be distinguished from Mother Nature or the laws of physics.

Most politicians know the exact role they must play regarding religion: going through the motions, speaking of God, occasionally going to church, but also showing that they are really not too serious about religion. In general, the behavior of most Americans is not altered by religion as much as they like to think. Most compartmentalize religion, think religious thoughts during church services once a week, then return to their secular lives. Church services have become a symbolic ritual, representing social respectability and fraternity, somewhat like the Thanksgiving dinner. To participate is considered to be in our best interest.

Most Americans really don't discuss what they truly believe, even within their immediate family. It is considered inappropriate to disclose what they really believe regarding God to their spouse, to their children, or even to themselves. Most people concede that the social and moral aspects of organized religion are beneficial to society, but beliefs in such things as hell and angels are simply not discussed. People joke about witches, fairies, and trolls, yet are reluctant to admit that they don't believe in angels, Lucifer, or Noah's ark. Rather than believing in God as a supreme being, many accept the social benefits of organized religion.

In reaction to our ambiguous, postmodern, secular world, many people desperately need simplicity and certitude. They want to find absolutes that will explain the world more clearly. The growth of religious fundamentalism worldwide attests to this need. Such early Christian leaders as Augustine and Thomas Aquinas considered much of the Bible to be allegory and didn't expect people to believe it word for word. It was not until the Inquisition that the Jesuits decided that free interpretation of Scripture was getting out of hand and that the words of the Bible were to be considered inerrant. The belief in the exact words of books written two thousand to three thousand years ago takes all of the decision and anxiety out of our modern life. Bumper stickers now say, "The Bible says it. I believe it. That settles it!" Biblical inerrantists hate the complexity and pluralism of today's world and opt for trading freedom of thought for the security of absolutes and dogma. Many of these people willingly relinquish their most precious gift of free thought and become a member of the "flock" that their television evangelist shepherds, using a pitiful way to cope with the modern chaos that has rendered their identity obscure. Laborer philosopher Eric Hoffer said, "Absolute faith corrupts as absolutely as absolute power." When pinned down, those advocating a universal return to moral absolutes have difficulty in declaring *whose* particular morals to obey.

The American pragmatic philosopher John Dewey (1859–1952) had an approach to religion that has profoundly influenced modern America. Dewey said that religion had lost itself in the supernatural and cults. He wanted to broaden the concept of religion, saying that all experience may have a religious quality if it gives security and stability. The exact way that this experience is religious depends on the individual, and can be a devotion to a cause, appreciation of art, or philosophical reflection.

Though Americans have a thread of skepticism running deep through their psyche, few admit to nonbelief. Some of our most eminent presidents, including Madison, Jefferson, and Lincoln, were freethinking deists. In Walter Truett Anderson's book *The Truth about the Truth*, Arthur Schlesinger, Jr., mentions that "the American mind is by nature and tradition skeptical, irreverent, pluralistic, and relativistic." Many popular and influential writers, such as Ralph Waldo Emerson, Mark Twain, William Faulkner, Ernest Hemingway, Carl Sagan, and Isaac Asimov, have reflected basic nonbelief in their writings. *The Wizard of Oz* has been beloved for many decades. Its basic theme is that we do not need a supernatural wizard, but that we have the capability within ourselves for intelligence, courage, and emotion. The movie is enduring for reasons people never admit. It's decidedly humanistic and debunks the spiritual, telling us that there is really no magic and our actions are all up to us. But alas, as we will emphasize in this book, our behavior is not simply just up to us, or even to our culture.

References

Anderson, Walter Truett. *Reality Isn't What It Used To Be*. New York: Harper and Row, 1990.
———. *The Truth about the Truth*. New York: Jeremy P. Tarcher.
Armstrong, Karen. *A History of God*. New York: Knopf, 1993.
Carter, Stephen L. "Conservatives' Faith, Liberals' Disdain." *New York Times*, op-ed (August 15, 1993): 15.
Glendon, Mary Ann. *A Nation Under Lawyers*. New York: Farrar, Straus and Giroux, 1994.

Goldberg, Martin A. "Ignoring These Laws Will Cause Big Head-aches." *Medical Economics* (February 17, 1992): 179–87.

Hadorn, David. "The Problem of Discrimination in Health Care Priority Setting." *Journal of the American Medical Association* (September 16, 1992): 1454–58.

Howard, Phillip K. *The Death of Common Sense: How Law Is Suffo-cating America.* New York: Random House, 1995.

Huber, Peter W. *Galileo's Revenge: Junk Science in the Courtroom.* New York: Basic Books, 1992.

Johnson, Mark. *Moral Imagination: Implications of Cognitive Science for Ethics.* Chicago: University of Chicago Press, 1993.

Lachs, John, and Michael Hassel, eds. *The Giants of Philosophy: Spinoza, Kant, Dewey,* audiotapes. Audio Classics Series narrated by Charlton Heston. Nashville, Tenn.: Knowledge Products, 1991.

Marty, Martin E., and R. Scott Appleby. *Fundamentalisms Observed.* Chicago: University of Chicago Press, 1991.

Roderick, Rick. *Philosophy and Human Values,* audiotape. Arlington, Va.: The Teaching Company, 1990.

Spencer, Leslie. "The Tort Tax." *Forbes* (February 17, 1992): 40–42.

Steiner, Franklin. *The Religious Beliefs of Our Presidents.* Amherst, N.Y.: Prometheus Books, 1995.

Todd, James S. "Must the Law Assure Ethical Behavior?" *Journal of the American Medical Association* (July 1, 1992): 98.

6

Language Effects

Speech is the mother, not the handmaid, of thought.

Karl Kraus

We are what words make us. We think we control language as a tool for communication, but words themselves, as our dominant form of communication, control our behavior covertly. Because we speak and write so often and effortlessly, we become oblivious of the history of language, its momentum, and the dominant role that language plays in our lives. We rarely appreciate the whimsical and faddish nature of the words that influence us, and we remain unaware that our speech is fettered by social convention.

Communication of Life Forms

Language is one of the more highly specialized methods of transferring information, communication being necessary for evolutionary adaptation. Even insects use language, communicating by visual, auditory (chirping), and smelling (pheromones) means. Ant species use many separate messages, with one pheromone meaning "beware" and another designating "follow me." Bees communicate by pheromones and tail wiggles. Primates have many ways to communicate and convey various emotions, and some monkey species make different sounds to identify different predators. Though primates make hand gestures and facial grimaces, they cannot verbalize as humans do because the anatomy of their larynx does not permit it.

Human Speech Development

Considering the broad definition of the word *language*, it is difficult to estimate when it actually began in humans. Some believe that human speech began after a lowering of the anatomical larynx position about a hundred thousand years ago, when primitive man developed a rounded tongue and a longer neck. Humans began to coin individual names for themselves about ten thousand years ago, when they started living in larger groups after the advent of agriculture. Written language began approximately six thousand years ago, which not only permitted an exchange of information between individuals distant in space and time, but also accelerated cultural evolution, which was later enhanced further by printing and telecommunications.

Brain and Language Centers

Because language centers within the brain reside in the left hemisphere, many think that consciousness is more fully governed by the left brain than the right. Since language involves the processing of sequence and structure, even sign language is thought to be handled predominantly by the left hemisphere. Deaf individuals who suffer focal (well localized) brain damage near these language centers may lose the ability to make or understand sign language.

Language is not only controlled by these structures in the left hemisphere, but also initially by a broader processing in both hemispheres. This generalized processing converts sensory input from eyes and ears to a broad concept of recognition. Because humans recognize an entity but have to collect a simple construct to symbolize it into a word, language is at first a cognitive process before it is communication. First, you must "gather your thoughts" and name something before you can tell someone about it. Wernicke's area in the left temporal lobe has connections to the auditory and visual areas, letting it mediate the comprehension of words.

A secondary processing for nouns takes place in the occipital and temporal lobes in the left hemisphere; verbs are probably handled predominantly by the left frontal and parietal areas. Only later do the more specific language centers provide the final grammar. Broca's area in the frontal lobe near the motor strip is responsible for the motor output of speech by coordinating the functions of the tongue and larynx.

The Unconscious and Language

Many feel that conscious awareness in primitive humans developed only after the advent of language. Both language and consciousness enable us to reduce a complex thought to a smaller, more workable symbol. Language reduces a broad thought to a single word, and consciousness narrows the vast unconscious nature of our minds down to one focus of attention. Language allows us to describe to ourselves how we feel and to show awareness of the outside world. Self-awareness becomes complete at about age seven, when our language has fully developed.

Besides being important in communications, language is necessary in conscious thinking. Unconscious thought is not tied as closely with speech as is conscious thought. We think to ourselves in words, and we think about thinking in words if we have enough time to do so. But our unconscious processes occur too quickly to be formulated into words to ourselves. When I play tennis and lunge for a wide forehand, I don't have time to verbalize the action in my mind. The mind is much faster than language. A speed reader can totally outstrip a speaker's ability to verbalize thoughts.

Acquiring Language Skills

Linguist Noam Chomsky feels that we have an innate genetic predisposition to grammar that enables children to acquire a language quickly and without formal instruction. Just as we are born with the ability eventually to walk or make sounds, we are also born with an ability to learn the structure of our own language in a sudden leap rather than by the prolonged task of learning and instruction. Even children with a low IQ readily learn to speak their first language. Newborns are suddenly put into a very informal version of the language of their culture, hearing imperfect and fragmented sentences. Children construct their grammar too quickly for it to have been derived by induction through experience.

Immanuel Kant and other philosophers have described what they called *a priori* knowledge, which is not dependent upon experience or instruction. Like animal instinct it is in us from birth. Grammar abilities are programmed into the mind by the information carried by the DNA in our genes.

The infant brain is innately able to categorize the sounds and orders of words, but it must be exercised by cooperative interaction with parents and siblings in gestures, voice tone, expression, and, later, formal language. Being deprived of such stimulus can cause irreparable damage. Rare documented cases describe children raised in an environment totally void of human speech. Some have been raised in the wild, and others kept in a silent closet by psychopaths. These children never learned to speak even after prolonged attempts to teach them.

A baby's early language experience is crucial to its overall development. Those who teach a child written and oral language teach a child to think. Optimal language development requires the give and take of a child with older individuals who speak well. Watching television does not fulfill this need, because the child is passive and does not interact with television verbally. The relative inexperience with language by a small child who has spent many hours watching television will eventually affect his social skills adversely. Because many mothers are now in the work force, babies are often left in the care of individuals with inferior language skills or even the inability to speak the native tongue. The consequences of these childrearing decisions may soon come to light.

Words Are Only Imperfect Symbols

We assume words represent a mirror image of real objects and concepts, but don't always realize that definitions in the dictionary depend upon the opinions of the dictionary's authors. Language is unstable because it has no bedrock extralinguistic reference. Just as a map is not the territory, words are only arbitrary symbols that do not depict independent reality. Ultimately, words are defined by giving examples (an ostensive definition). Definitions are not absolute and precise; they are eventually fuzzy on the periphery, becoming "kind of" or "sort of." Seemingly nonabstract words—simple nouns such as *horse*, for example, are still arbitrary. Is a Shetland pony a horse? What about a zebra? A saw horse? If language is incorrigibly imprecise, then so is thinking.

Some thoughts do not translate into language readily. Philosopher Arthur Schopenhauer (1788–1860) said, "Thoughts die the moment they are embodied by words," and Oliver Wendell Holmes (1809–1894) wrote, "The flowering moments of the mind drop half their petals in our speech." Mathematical thoughts are verbalized only after laborious search. Most mathematicians use visual thinking and geometric spatial thinking, which are mediated predominantly on the right side of the brain. With complicated mathematical principles, no words are available to express the thoughts; instead, thoughts are communicated by symbols and equations.

Language is a game of the particular culture that uses it, subject to all the pressures of group convention. Various in-groups and professions have their own jargon. Language is jostled by the whims of ideology, politics, fads, and esthetic fashions. Ninety percent of language is based on background knowledge; therefore, it must be interpreted in the context of other known cultural information. That is the reason automatic language interpretation machines don't work. A robot would not understand or be amused by hearing Mel McDaniel sing, "Smilin' Mona Lisa loaded up my Visa, then took a bartender home."

Misinterpretations and misperceptions of our language constantly affect us. Physicians experience this daily when a patient tries to repeat to relatives or friends what the doctor has said. When this account gets back to the doctor, it has often been distorted unbelievably. When I was a medical student, one of my patients had infectious hepatitis, a viral infection of the liver. I described the virus to him and told him how these organisms affected his liver function. Some weeks later, one of my classmates told me that I had frightened this patient terribly by telling him that he had "bugs in his liver."

I am wary of my own misinterpretations when I visit a lawyer, an insurance salesman, or a car repairman. When these experts tell me in a number of paragraphs what is wrong and what should be done to correct the problem, I realize that I am focusing on one or two words they say, trying in my mind to simplify their explanations into one bottom-line sentence that I can remember. This reduction in words always distorts the content.

A System Unto Itself That Changes Our World

Once a language is established, it becomes a force unto itself, having a living momentum to change reality and sway our thoughts. Since words are catalysts that generate ideas and emotions, the words we choose to verbalize internally about ourselves tend to structure our self-image and influence our behavior more than we realize. Sometimes we berate ourselves with bad names. When we create new words, we create a new world. I have seen terms such as *macho, burnout, gay, battered child, sociobiology,* and *political correctness* all come into our lives. These words, by their very existence, change our world and manipulate us. A word, like a label, is easy to stick on but hard to take off.

Our mental function is limited by the words that are available to us. Certain languages lack a word for an idea and, therefore, this idea does not exist for people who use those languages. Multilingual people sometimes skip between languages to express their ideas more precisely. Some isolated cultures have no word for *war* because the whole concept of war is foreign to them. Trobriand islanders have no word for *indecent* or *obscene,* so it never occurs to them that sex could be dirty or evil.

The force of language affects our behavior more than we realize. For many years, there have been endearing terms for drinking, such as *happy hour* or *partying.* These terms, used without much thought, actually contribute to the injudicious use of alcohol. After the term *hot flashes* entered our language, many menopausal females became aware of, or imagined, symptoms. The term *hot flashes* does not exist in the Japanese language, and menopause in Japan is not regarded as something that has much physiological import. Consider also the recent attitude change in describing someone as *homeless* rather than as a *tramp* or *bum*. The former term engenders sympathy and makes us feel responsible for this unfortunate. Some even prefer *underhoused*, but others say this term absolves such individuals from any personal responsibility for this situation.

Deconstruction and Linguistic Philosophy

Not only has language been deconstructed (disassembled critically) and debunked, since World War II it has been analyzed by philosophers and mathematicians. Ludwig Wittgenstein portrayed language as many different word games played according to their own rules and varying in commands, greetings, jokes, and narration. We are now skeptical of the ability of language to give true representation and information. Feminists say language has patriarchal bias embodied in such words as *mailman* and *chairman*. Anything you say now may possibly offend somebody. Older people are no longer *senior citizens* but *chronologically advantaged individuals*. Some say that *pet* is demeaning and should be *animal companion*. Our thoughts are influenced by our system of language and we are mainly unconscious of it. I have seen the terms regarding race change from *colored*, to *Negro*, to *Negroid*, to *black*, to *Afro-American*, to *African-American*, and back to *people of color*. I no longer *practice medicine* but, according to modern bureaucratic jargon, *deliver health services*.

Eminent twentieth-century philosophers such as Willard Quine and A. J. Ayer have employed linguistic analysis, which involves dry exercises and tedious constructs in logic and mathematics which have, in general, been considered uninteresting and isolated from the rest of philosophy and problems of the world. These analytic efforts do, however, increase awareness of language ambiguities and misusages. Wittgenstein mentioned that language can't be precise, either practically or theoretically. It is inherently fuzzy and uncertain. It is impossible to define accurately any word, because the very words used to develop the definition are themselves subject to debate. Thus, Wittgenstein spent much effort trying to define the word *definition*.

After World War I the logical positivists of philosophy wished to organize language and completely correct its ambiguity by using mathematical form. Most linguistic analysts believe that any abstract term such as justice and freedom is nonsensical. A statement such as "Does God exist?" is nonsensical because it is impossible to define *God* or *exist*. God is sometimes defined as "the essence of being." How do you define *essence* or *being*? Currently, the existentialists, skeptics who doubt anything is firmly rooted, accept the ambiguity of language as the only possibility and savor these murky definitions.

Words as Things and Ideals

We mistake words for simple "things." We confuse abstract symbols such as words or numbers with actual, unchanging, physical entities or events. Hostility and love are considered tangible things that we can measure and convey. Words are only labels on boxes, not their contents. To communicate a broad concept, it must be expressed concisely in a few words, or even one word. As an example, the word *democracy* represents a very broad concept. It would require a whole chapter or book to describe democracy adequately, but the need for brevity requires a compromise. Words also vary from culture to culture. We commonly hear statements such as "criminality is inherited." How is *criminality* to be defined? Criminality in a society of head hunters is defined in a much different way than in other cultures. Simple adjectives such as *good* or *bad* are only relative terms. Eating a worm is good for the robin but bad for the worm.

When abstract words are translated into other languages, they change immensely. A term like *reason*, after it has gone through several language translations, is totally distorted when it is translated into English again. How can we define *reason*? It is impossible. We can only use words to define it that are themselves impossible to define and which vary immensely from language to language and culture to culture. We can never condense or paraphrase language without changing its meaning. To say something "in other words" is to say something in other thoughts.

Many statements sound wonderful because they are so ambiguous that they mean only what the receiving individual wishes them to mean. "All men are created equal," is an example. In the Unitarian Universalist fellowship that I often attend, we recite a statement of purpose at the beginning of the meeting. "We come together in freedom, for the pursuit of truth, the service of humanity, and the fulfillment of self." This sounds great, but what are *freedom, truth, humanity,* and *self*?

Some entire disciplines and professions revolve around certain words. What would modern education be without *dyslexia* or education in general without *intelligence*? What would medicine be without *diagnosis*? People want to hear a word for their illness; they want a linguistic handle to hang onto, preferably one derived from Greek or Latin. What would religion be without the word *soul*? What would family life be without the word *love* or psychiatry without terms such as the *unconscious* or *paranoia*?

Many believe that if something has a name, it certainly must have an independent existence of its own. Once the word *witch* entered the language, it became a true entity in the minds of most people. We still hear about the Aryan race. Its contemporary racial connotation was invented by Nazi ideologists. The novelist George Orwell said, "If thought corrupts language, language can also corrupt thought."

Words as ideals create an undue influence on us. Tied into the entire fabric of human activity, the nuances of language regulate interpersonal relationships and status. How much foolhardy macho activity has been inspired by the worship of the word *courage*? How many unwanted children have been born due to being *in love*? Words can tend to distort reality by their very existence. The word *darkness* implies a tangible dark substance, when in fact, scientifically, darkness is actually the absence of light.

Words are sometimes idealized as sacred objects. Fundamentalists and biblical inerrantists believe that the words of the Bible are perfect and absolute, not subject to any error whatsoever. The words of the U.S. Constitution are similarly idealized. In literary criticism and deconstruction the main debate concerns the location of the real meaning of the body of literature. Does it reside in the mind of the author, in the text itself, or in the mind of the reader? Literary criticism has no final answer.

Word Changes—Flukes and Fads

Words change their meaning over time. In the seventeenth century, the word *skeptic* meant one dubious that life could be based on science and reason rather than religion. The term *bad* now often means hip, creative, and courageous. *Liberals* in the 1800s were free-market capitalists; today, they tend to be pro-government and even socialists. The word *nutritious* has changed its meaning through the years. Originally it meant calorie-laden to reflect its immediate life-sustaining nourishment, but now, in our modern Western world, *nutritious* refers to low-fat food containing fiber, minerals, and vitamins.

Certain words can mean their opposites. *Scan* can mean to study intensely, as one does with a CAT scanner, or to look at something in a hurried, perfunctory manner. *Cleave* can mean to divide or to adhere. *Flammable* and *inflammable* mean the same thing.

The meanings we give to words are often not dependable but paradoxical. For example, we park in a driveway and drive on a parkway.

Words often enjoy fad status. I can remember when the term *serendipity* suddenly became the word du jour. *State-of-the-art*, new to me twenty-five years ago, is now a cliché. *Egregious* and *segue* are also now in vogue. The word *like* has become ubiquitous and is used with many different meanings, particularly by teenagers. Like, they likely like a word like *like*.

Language is capricious and is influenced by literary style. A whimsical choice of words can influence our understanding. In trying to convey the idea that a friend is enthusiastic about computers, we may say that he is *into* computers, he is *involved* with computers, he is a *compulsive user* of computers, or he is *addicted to* computers. Sometimes people make a poor choice of words. Just as a tennis player must make a shot selection in a split second, we all are making word choices in split seconds, and rarely do we have unlimited time and a dictionary of synonyms available. After an important conference or argument, when we review the event, we can always think of a better word we could have chosen. We sometimes regret the use of a word that, in retrospect, we feel was too strong. Certain shadings of words influence attitudes. We may say *politician* instead of *congressman,* or we may say that an individual *snuck in* instead of *entered quietly,* or that a person is *rich* instead of *wealthy.* If witnesses to an automobile accident are asked to estimate the speed of the car as it *struck* the other car, their estimate will be slower than if asked about the car *smashing into* the other. Another example of how words can be used to persuade depending upon how they are said is given in a quote by Bertrand Russell. "The conjugation of firmness: I am firm, you are obstinate, he is pigheaded."

Social pressures often change the selection of words. With the political correctness movement, any form of racial slang is subject to severe criticism. Terms such as *wetback* or *snowbird* or even *Yankee* are considered now to be in poor taste. Many now take issue with the words *crazy, psycho,* or *looney bin* as being insensitive to the mentally ill. They feel these words, along with *schizo,* tend to perpetuate the stigma and reinforce the overestimated relation between violence and mental illness. We all speak in euphemisms—somebody *passed away,* or we have to *visit the men's room. Garbage collection* becomes *sanitation services,* which later becomes *environmental services.* Knowing the latest "in" term marks one as having read the proper magazines but unjustifiably hurts the status of those more remote people who don't happen to know that *Latino* is more politically correct than *Spanish-American*. Some females even prefer the feminine, *Latina*.

Word inflation is another vagary of our language. At a White House conference on the family in 1980, the term *family* was enlarged to include single-parent families, step families, and homosexual couples. The term *rape* has been expanded to include persuasive and sensuous language (seduction) that leads to sex. Such inflationary definitions distort the incidence of true rape. The term *addiction* likewise has been enlarged to include wealth addiction, food addiction, and love addiction, making almost everyone addicted to something. *Beating* now includes slapping, shoving, and spanking.

French words always convey a sophisticated atmosphere when they are used in English, examples being *debutante, hors d'oeuvres,* and *savoir faire*. After William the Conqueror invaded England, the French were the aristocracy and the Anglo-Saxons the common people, and to this day French terms seem aristocratic. Which sounds the most cultured: *cuisine* or *food, en masse* or *altogether, rendezvous* or *meeting, debris* or *trash*?

Other intellectual and sophisticated terms come from Latin. *Ad infinitum, alter ego,* and *vox populi* sound intellectual because the clergy guarded the knowledge of Latin throughout the Middle Ages. These terms were eventually transferred into the professions of law and medicine.

English is a complicated, rich language. Many of the shortest words are homonyms, words pronounced the same and sometimes spelled the same but with different meanings. Examples are *pain* and *pane,* and *sale* and *sail*. "Because of his twin daughters in the kindergarten ballet, the father's interest was not only directed to the twin's bonnets, but *to two tutus, too.*" "When he saw it on the chest films the radiologist *knew new pneu*monia was present." The word pronounced as *see* has many different meanings. Besides meaning to visualize it can mean a letter in the alphabet, a body of water, the musical note, *yes* in Spanish, or understanding. These confusing sounds and meanings in English can lead to misunderstandings and mistakes of which we are often not aware. Radiologists have to be careful to avoid errors in communication. I have learned to say the word *correct* instead of *right* because we are constantly dealing with the right side and left side of a patient and the word *right* has two different meanings.

Gender Differences in Language

Females tend to use language to establish and maintain personal rapport and to reinforce intimacy, whereas males tend to use it to protect their independence and report information.

Women complain that men don't talk to them; men complain that women talk too much. The sexes have different opinions about what is important. The female's friendship is directed toward talking and a more intimate sharing of the small events of one's life. Men, however, enjoy companionship with other men and communicate more through sports and hunting. A man doesn't tell the woman the details of his life because he really doesn't consider these details that important. The man who makes eloquent speeches at board meetings may talk little at dinner, because he doesn't feel the need to prove anything. The woman, though, wants him to share his intimate thoughts and often feels hurt if he doesn't.

Gender distinctions within the English language sometimes describe women in subtly demeaning ways. Newspaper reporters call Hillary Clinton *spunky* and *feisty*, terms used for a diminutive creature that they would not apply to a man. A *commanding* man would be a *demanding* woman. A *strategizing* man would be a *manipulating* woman, and a *persevering* man would be a *stubborn* woman.

Linguistic Differences Between Countries

Few people are aware of the varying styles of conversation among different countries and different ethic groups within a country. Among northern Europeans one person typically speaks at a time. In other cultures, people talk simultaneously; Hawaiian children do this often. What is considered to be interrupting and dominating in one country is considered participatory and involved in another. In Thailand and Japan, simultaneous conversation is also acceptable. In New York City, it is more common to have rapid conversation with frequent interruption than it is in other parts of the United States.

Within any language, there are subtle status implications in one's accent or dialect. The most notable is the Britisher's specific accent called Received Pronunciation (RP), which is the speech of the educated upper class in London and Southeast England. Britishers credit speakers of RP with qualities of intelligence and ambition. The Edinburgh Scottish and the Dublin Irish accents are also acceptable. The accents considered the worst are those of Cockney London and Liverpool. One may recall George Bernard Shaw's statement, "It is impossible for an Englishman to open his mouth without making some other Englishman despise him." Many American businesses seek receptionists with an RP British accent to convey upper-class status.*

Body Language

Ralph Waldo Emerson said, "When the eyes say one thing and the tongue another, a practiced man relies on the language of the first." For thousands of years before speaking evolved, humans used Cicero's *sermo corporis*, the language of the body. Nonverbal communication includes facial expressions, body postures, vocal intonations, and manual gestures. Even today these are mostly mediated on an unconscious level and constitute the majority of interpersonal communication. Postures in which arms and legs are open convey warmth and approachability. Crossed legs or arms folded in front of one's chest imply a closed, aloof attitude. We are all familiar with the woman who "lets her walkin' do her talkin'." Americans aspiring to be a "tough guy" assume a somewhat bow-legged stance, carry their arms away from their body as if they were carrying a barrel under each arm, and might wear only a T-shirt in the winter. I have noticed some teenage boys affecting a form of pseudoathletic walk, bobbing up and down on their toes.

We can't assume that our familiar body language, which is natural in our culture, is recognized anywhere else in the world. In Saudi Arabia, when a man holds your hand, it is a sign of respect. In many Middle Eastern countries it is proper

---

*Attitudes are changing in England, however, and it has more recently become "in" to affect a lower-class accent, because some think it is pretentious to have the perfect posh accent.

to stand very close to another and place your face as close as one foot. In Japan, sticking your hands in your pockets is considered a rude gesture. In America, we teach that a firm handshake is a confident, positive act, but in many countries it is considered aggressive and offensive.

The "okay" sign (a circle formed by the thumb and fore-finger with the three remaining fingers extended) is considered an obscene gesture in Australia and Russia, and the "V for victory" sign is obscene in Australia and England if the back of the hand is turned outward. In certain locales in India, moving your head up and down means no, rather than yes. When an individual changes oral language (from German to Italian, for instance) he may also change his body language to correspond to the facial expressions and gestures appropriate to that language.

Most of us are ignorant of these differences; we go through life oblivious of them, thinking that we know everything and are in full control. Martin, our Swedish exchange student, was chastised when he snapped his fingers at a waiter in a restaurant and at his high school teacher. In Sweden, this is an acceptably polite way to gain another's attention. When a black student sitting across from Martin said, "Give me five, man," with an outstretched hand, Martin obliged by handing him five sheets of notebook paper.

We are unaware of how much body language affects interpersonal relations. Often a slight touch at the right time and place can mean more than hundreds of words. A wink can do wonders for one's morale.

In general, our body language is complicated, being partly inherited, partly learned. All humans have an innate tendency to smile when they are happy and to frown when they are worried. Our time of eye contact is crucial. Each culture defines an appropriate time to look into somebody's eyes before looking away. If you maintain eye contact with somebody for too long this means that you have become too intimate. Americans maintain a proper distance when they converse standing, usually about three feet. The Japanese and the Arabs tend to stay closer to one another, and the Arab likes to touch his companion and even smell his breath.

Sometimes chronically used body language can become permanent. Someone who is constantly worried develops a frown that is always present, and a depressed person may develop a stooped appearance with slumped shoulders. A shrinking body posture, as if one is trying to hide himself, often means depression.

A natural leader's body language conveys confidence and maturity. This individual does not waste body motion, never scratching his head or shuffling his feet. He or she withholds words for the important summary or conclusion of a conversation.

Erotic body language is defined in both sexes by flashy dress and an arrogant gait. In the United States, a male sometimes encroaches on the normal three-foot space when talking to a female he is pursuing. Men in this preening stage tend to stand straight with their shoulders back and abdomen pulled in. Eye contact tends to be prolonged. Smiling more and often touching, the man tends to focus his attentions on one woman to make her feel special. The man often chooses his object of affection based on her receptive body language—a languorous gait or a hushed, breathless voice, a la Marilyn Monroe. Or, she may sit unusually close to a man or stroke her thighs. A casual touch on the man's arm can be a signal. She may adjust her skirt, cross and uncross her legs, and employ provocative dress and ample perfume. She may stroke her hair or repeatedly brush her hair away from her face. The flirting female might tilt her head sideways to expose her neck. Men and women interested in one another will arrange their bodies to face one another and lean slightly forward.

When women enter a room with table and chairs, they tend to sit facing one another and talk with ample eye contact, but men situate their chairs so that they do not look at one another. This is the natural way men would act to eliminate the possibility of a combative action. Women often complain that men don't make enough eye contact with them, saying that men are disengaged and not interested in them. These are female standards and not male standards, however. These standards demonstrate the woman's emphasis on openness and connectedness and the man's emphasis on hierarchy and independence.

Verbal language and body language work as a team. Usually, one's head goes up at the end of a question. When a speaker wants to continue talking, his voice holds the same pitch, and he may look away. But when he wants to indicate that he has finished his statement, his voice goes down at the end of the sentence, he returns eye contact, and his head tends to then go down. Many subtle eyelid movements and forehead creases indicate various emotions and nuances of meaning while speaking.

You who are suspected of lying use halting or evasive words in a strained, higher-pitched voice; make nervous unconscious gestures; and have an awkward smile.

Modern philosophers accept the fact that language stands between us and reality. Our thoughts can only be expressed by sounds, squiggles on paper, or gestures. Language, one of our most unrecognized covert masters, is filled with mistakes, stand-in metaphors, and anomalies—everything from typographical errors to misunderstandings of bodily gesture. Language, therefore, prevails as an unreliable determinant of our conscious sense of reality.

References

Anderson, Walter Truett. *Reality Isn't What It Used to Be*. New York: Harper and Row, 1990.

Bremmer, Jan. *A Cultural History of Gesture*. Ithaca, N.Y.: Cornell University Press, 1991.

Campbell, Jeremy. *Grammatical Man*. New York: Simon and Schuster, 1982.

Chomsky, Noam. *Language and Responsibility*. New York: Pantheon, 1979.

Claiborne, Robert. *Our Marvelous Native Tongue*. New York: Time Books, 1983.

Damasio, Antonio R., and Hanna Damasio. "Brain and Language." *Scientific American* (September 1992): 89–95.

Dewart, Leslie. *Evolution and Consciousness*. Toronto: University of Toronto Press, 1989.

Eckman, Paul. *Telling Lies: Clues to Deceit in the Marketplace, Politics and Marriage*. New York: W. W. Norton, 1994.

Elgin, Suzette Haden. *The Gentle Art of Verbal Self Defense*. New York: Dorset Press, 1980.

Fast, Julius. *Body Language*. New York: Pocket Books, 1970.

Fellows, Hugh P. *The Art and Skill of Talking With People*. Englewood Cliffs, N. J.: Prentice Hall, 1964.

Gazzaniga, Michael S. *Nature's Mind*. New York: Basic Books, 1992.

Gergen, Kenneth J. *The Saturated Self*. New York: Basic Books, 1991.

Gray, John. *Men Are From Mars, Women Are From Venus*. New York: HarperCollins, 1992.

Gregory, Bruce. *Inventing Reality.* New York: John Wiley and Sons, 1988.

Hayakawa, S. I. *Language in Thought and Action.* San Diego: Harcourt, Brace, Jovanovich, 1978.

Jaynes, Julian. *The Origin of Consciousness in the Breakdown of the Bicameral Mind.* Boston: Houghton Mifflin, 1976.

Leo, John. "The Words of the Culture War." *U.S. News and World Report* (October 28, 1991): 31.

McCrone, John. *The Ape That Spoke.* New York: William Morrow, 1991.

Mc Crum, Robert, William Cran, and Robert MacNeil. *The Story of English.* New York: Penguin Books, 1986.

Pease, Allan. *Signals.* New York: Bantam Books, 1981.

Penrose, Roger. *The Emperor's New Mind.* New York: Oxford University Press, 1989.

Pinker, Steven. *The Language Instinct.* New York: William Morrow, 1994.

———. "The Name of the Game." *New York Times,* op-ed (April 5, 1994).

Restak, Richard M. *The Mind.* New York: Bantam Books, 1988.

Russell, Bertrand. *Philosophical Essays.* New York: Simon and Schuster, 1966.

Russell, Peter. *The Global Brain.* Boston: Tarcher—Houghton Mifflin, 1983.

Rymer, Russ. *Genie: An Abused Child's Flight from Silence.* New York: HarperCollins, 1993.

Tannen, Deborah. *You Just Don't Understand.* New York: William Morrow, 1990.

———. *Gender and Discourse.* New York: Oxford University Press, 1994.

7

Psychosocial Illogic

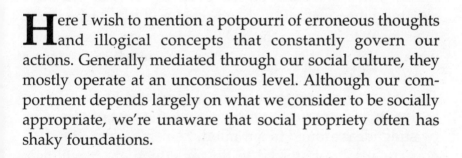

Here I wish to mention a potpourri of erroneous thoughts and illogical concepts that constantly govern our actions. Generally mediated through our social culture, they mostly operate at an unconscious level. Although our comportment depends largely on what we consider to be socially appropriate, we're unaware that social propriety often has shaky foundations.

Hearts and Minds Will Follow

A free mind is the most precious thing we have. It's amazing, though, how we pretend that we behave freely and with relish when actually our actions are limited because we have no reasonable alternative. We're "had by the neck" by our genes,

111

culture, and physical environment. To paraphrase an old Watergate hearings phrase, "If you've got 'em by the neck, their hearts and minds will follow." We love the English language and profess that it is the best language, not admitting that it is the only language we can speak. We praise our country, job, and family, not facing how difficult it would be to obtain others. On a trip to Russia during the 1970s, I talked with some of the people there and expressed sympathy for them because of their lack of freedom and the abuse they suffered at the hands of the state. Offended by this, they quickly told me that they were very happy in their situation.

Many of the American prisoners of war in Korea accepted the Communist viewpoint after only a minimal amount of brainwashing, learning to love their captors. Historically, this phenomenon has been reported in primitive societies when marauding bands captured women and took them away to live with them. After a few years these women were retaken by their native tribes, but, much to the men's surprise, the women did not want to leave their captors. This adaptability represents our way of enabling ourselves to live in an imperfect world, making the best of things by twisting ideas around in our mind. Remember the adage, "If you are absolutely forced to do something, do it willingly with a smile." Much of our satisfaction in life is based on "considering the alternatives." We're not altogether mindful of this, or at least we don't admit it. I've had the experience of shifting back and forth from the academic world of medicine to private practice. It's amazing how our reality changes depending upon which side of the fence we're on. When in academic life, I looked upon myself as an intellectual, caring person who was above seeking a large amount of money for my services. When in private practice, I looked upon myself as a gallant worker on the front line facing real problems head-on.

We always think the fraternity, sorority, or club we join is the best one, even if it was the only one that would have us. We do not choose our political views and religion freely because our occupation and our social status, and the location of our birth direct our decision. According to an old saying, "Our language and our religion we suck in with our milk." We tell ourselves that we vote for the politician who is the most noble and who will do the best for all citizens, but in reality we vote for the person who will most benefit us. We delude ourselves when we think our political leanings are not based on our existing traps and obligations.

Country music star Earl Thomas Conley sings about a woman in love: "What she's got is what she wants." This ability to love what we have, or at least to be satisfied with it, is inherent in humans of all ages. Children want to be with their parents even when they are being abused. Older people usually think that their nursing home is the best of all worlds.

We don't allow ourselves to be dissatisfied if we feel there is no way out. Many people claim satisfaction with their present job but actually can't change jobs because they are unable to obtain new health insurance at another job if they leave. This means that they must remain at a job that they dislike. These employees are often praised for their faithful service, but their loyalty exemplifies the aphorism, "Virtue is another name for lack of opportunity."

Karl Marx (1818–1883) was right about one thing: the need for economic security rules our actions to a larger extent than most of us will admit.

Our behavior is also controlled by previous decisions,

commitments and psychological adjustments. We become prisoners to our choice to enter a certain profession, marry a particular person, or have children. Even though we may no longer believe in certain principles, we act as if we do to protect our ego and our need to be consistent. We don't wish to appear fickle. Members of a professional group, such as lawyers or physicians, generally adhere to long-established group policies. It is difficult for a political activist to change beliefs. In the U.S. Congress, where you stand depends upon which side of the aisle you sit.

Herd Instinct

We are all bandwagon jumpers, having a fear of being left behind, or ostracized as different. We think if everyone is doing it, it must be right. People generally vote for likely winners, not underdogs. They tend to buy the most widely sold product and vote for the politician who inundates our lives with the greatest number of political ads. Somehow, they think that it is best for them to be on the side of those who crow the loudest and are able to buy the largest number of political ads and signs.

Everything is more acceptable if we are part of a large crowd. When watching television, we lose interest in a football game when the camera follows a high punt and we can then see that the stands are almost empty. We were interested in the game until we saw that there were few who shared our interest. We also want to go to the "in" restaurant that is crowded, regardless of the noise and slower service. The crowd is there and the crowd *must* have better judgment than we do. The effectiveness of a dubbed-in "laugh track" in television sitcoms attests to the force of the herd instinct. Some theaters pay people to applaud.

When starting up an office, young doctors know to schedule their few appointments close together so that patients will gain confidence in them by seeing others in the waiting room. Similarly with real estate agents trying to sell an unattractive house—it becomes more alluring when prospective buyers see others leaving the house as they enter it.

Children are not as individualistic as we sometimes think. They go with the crowd and all want the same type of clothing and toys. They tend to be led by classic advertisements which show them what other children wear and play with. If you want your child to try something new, such as playing tennis, just let him or her see other children enjoying the game.

Various manias and fads of our world are explained by people accepting, like sheep, what others do. Independent thinkers are rare; the old "Candid Camera" episodes prove this again and again. Pedestrians will step over a prone man on the sidewalk if they see others before them doing this, because they accept this as the correct behavior and assume that the man is drunk. In one "Candid Camera" episode, an aggressive waiter at a formal seated dinner swooped up the plates when the people were only half finished eating. Those who were "in on the act" (confederates) didn't protest, hence the unknowing subjects accepted this abuse placidly. Another episode showed subjects sitting in a diner reacting docilely when a man sitting beside them dunked his doughnut in their coffee. It was only after many flustered people left or moved away that one brave soul looked the dunker in the eye and said, "Buddy, one more dunk and it'll be your last dunk." Another memorable episode was based on psychological research in which a group of seated people in a waiting room see smoke coming under the door. If a subject is alone in the room, 70 percent will stand, walk, and investigate. If, however, there are also two confederates who do nothing but observe the smoke and look blasé, only 10 percent of the subjects rise to investigate. People behave like sheep in these circumstances because they unconsciously believe that the larger number of observers dilutes their individual responsibility. They don't want to be embarrassed, and most have such low self-confidence that they expect others to know more than they do.

On the other hand, we all know those who try too hard to be independent outsiders. These people are not necessarily correct and don't suspect that they are actually conforming to nonconformity. One truly liberated thinker, Thomas Jefferson, refused to join what he termed the "herd of independents."

All or None Mentality

For some people everything is black or white; there are no gray areas, no qualifying statements, no ambiguity. Like a light switch, a position is either on or off, bold decision is their modus operandi. They are either for or against euthanasia, either in love or not in love.

We acquire this habit of using simplifying absolutes early in life from our culture. In sports we either win or lose. We acquire a distorted idea of reality because of our concepts of arithmetic. We deal in whole numbers—either one, two, or three—and forget there are an infinite number of fractions between these. A court of law decides either guilt or innocence. Our religion is filled with absolutes; we go to either heaven or hell. A movie usually has a definite ending, and either the hero wins or troubles are resolved in a simple manner. We're all guilty of polarizing things into simplistic opposites. Most Americans have difficulty understanding politics in terms of anything other than liberal or conservative, and many hide from complex political choices by accepting the far right or far left position. Consider the statement, "He who is not a success is a failure." At some time in our lives we ask, "Does he or she love me?" We assume that love is established like picking petals from a daisy—"He loves me, he loves me not."

An old Johnny Mercer song goes, "You've got to accentuate the positive, eliminate the negative, latch on to the affirmative, and don't mess with Mr. In-between." The problem is, most things are in-between. There are no perfect choices, only choices among imperfect possibilities.

The popularity of motivational speakers again testifies to our penchant for oversimplification—most emphasize thinking and speaking positively, which can sometimes lead to mindless, puerile affirmations, or even self-delusion. Realistically, we must separate neutral facts and accuracy from overly hyped positive ideas, and not force ourselves into foolhardy superoptimism. We don't have unlimited abilities, and if we don't face our limiting circumstances, we can get into trouble. A sensibly optimistic mood is an asset, but it comes from deep within the psyche and cannot be turned on or off by superficial, short-term methods.

Expecting Happiness

Happiness eludes people because the definition of it eludes them. Happiness compared to what? For what period of time?—a minute? a year? One year later, lottery winners are no happier than they were before winning. Happiness can be a momentary escape from unhappiness.

Some unfortunate individuals are truly and justifiably unhappy, such as those with painful chronic illnesses. Many more, however, are frustrated by the constant expectation of happiness, assuming that its arrival will provide a "high" for them forever. In reality, we experience true ecstatic happiness only at rare moments, such as when our team wins on a long, three-point shot at the buzzer, or when we suddenly find a piece of lost jewelry for which we have long been searching.

Well-adjusted people are not on Cloud Nine. Psychologists have analyzed many highly successful people in all walks of life—business people, athletes, artists—who were healthy, had well-adjusted families, and had financial security. Rarely did these people say they were unusually happy. They generally had the same day-to-day worries and disappointments that the less successful have, and most considered themselves, overall, neutral in their degree of happiness.

Therefore, neutral is about the most we can expect for the majority of our lives. Sigmund Freud admitted that the best one could expect from psychotherapy was a return to "common unhappiness." A frantic search for rousing happiness only serves to disappoint us. My father told me that we all have to make our own happiness from within. No other person or job can make us happy. We are, however, made reasonably satisfied when we are striving for a meaningful goal and are able to receive and give love. The attainment of a particular goal will not make us happy for long, because it is the journey and not the arrival that satisfies us. After the arrival there may even be a letdown because of temporary loss of sense of direction.

Sexual happiness and exhilarating romance are also constantly sought after because lifelong media influence creates
unrealistic expectations. Contrary to many advisors, hard
work to keep romance alive and make a relationship exciting
is guaranteed to eventually douse any small flame that exists.
Striving to be sexy and intoxicating just creates tension in a
relationship. Any direct assault on pleasure leads promptly
to boredom, because making enjoyment a goal puts a burden
of obligation on each activity. Currently, interest in psychology to "get in touch with our feelings" has made us too intro-
spectively aware of our lack of sheer enjoyment in life and
has fostered unattainable expectations. The intense passion
of a romance will fade in time, always, but there remains a
residual contentment and companionship that we should
savor. Expecting endless, blissful love is illogical. The heady
rapture of new romance depends on a biologic process
dependent upon brain chemistry (see chapter 13). Sheer happiness involving sexual ecstasy is a momentary thing much
like a "cocaine rush," and must have an obligatory ending
because the continuous "high" would deplete our neurochemical transmitter resources. Many cultures even today
are afraid of romantic love and consider it inimical to the
long-term welfare of marriage and family.

Whenever there is an admitted, conscious happiness,
there almost must be a corresponding downside. When we
attain happiness, we soon become satiated and dissatisfied,
which propels a further search for happiness. Not only is
there a physiological letdown based on brain chemistry functions, but there is a psychological letdown based on the comparison between the previous high and the routine of day-to-
day life. We derive some pleasure of anticipation from this
overall search for greater happiness and we may purposefully

delay gratification in order to prolong this pleasure. Where this natural tendency blends into masochism is debatable.

How much do we actually want to be happy all the time? If we could enter a virtual reality machine using cerebral electrodes and drugs to create eternal happiness for the rest of our lives, how many of us would wish to do this forever, if we knew we could not return to the former natural state of reality? Probably the struggles of mundane life constitute a part of our happiness.

Happiness is relative and exists only in contrast to its opposite—pain, sadness, dissatisfaction. The movie *Shadowlands* portrays the romance of author C. S. Lewis and Joy Gresham. Both knowing that she was in a temporary remission from advanced cancer, the couple experienced profound happiness on an idyllic vacation to the English countryside. During a moment of insight she remarked about her impending death and the subsequent sorrow, "The pain then is part of the happiness now. That's the deal." We could never experience the exhilaration of winning a close tennis match if we had not felt the pain of losing. I recall a "Twilight Zone" episode where a criminal, after being shot in a holdup, awakened to find himself in a luxurious bar where he could enjoy endless indulgence in food, wine, women, and gambling successes. He couldn't lose. After several days, boredom set in and he went to the proprietor of the bar and requested to leave. Only then did the viewer see the proprietor's Devil's tail.

Fairness Hangup

Many people are frustrated by having an overdeveloped sense of justice; they assume the world is and should be fair.

This concept is inculcated early in life. We are taught that sports rules are fair, that the courts of law are unbiased and just, and that that is the way the world should be. Historically, the notion of fairness was also generated by democracy, with each person's vote being completely equal. This concept of egalitarianism was also supported by Darwin's idea that we all are fundamentally animals, having a common genetic origin and no valid royalty or "blue bloods." This idea of fairness is a product of humanity's wish to simplify life.

But injustice in nature is here to stay. Each person is born different; some are mentally deficient and others are geniuses. When she hears about all men being created equal, I am sure Mother Nature has to hold back a chuckle. Earthquakes kill unfairly. Darling little three-year-olds get leukemia. Undeserving, rich cads win lotteries. Devious, unjust creatures abound in nature. The praying mantis disguises itself as a twig so that it can grab other insects. The angler fish has a wormlike extension hanging down in front of its face. Smaller fish that fall for this deceptive bait get eaten by the unfair angler fish. Inequitable big lions eat little antelopes.

The expectation of fairness, engendered by current pervasive, though misguided egalitarianism, leads to the notion that everything should be equal for everyone in a perfect manner—not only equal opportunity but equal rewards. This idea leads to frustration when we look around and realize that people do not have equal homes, equal education, or equal athletic trophies. Equality of goods can be gained only at the expense of liberty, by one party forcing another to give some of his goods to someone else. When government assumes this role, it is often necessary to suppress excellence. The progressive taxation policies that redistribute income emphasize enhancing equality rather than productivity. We have been taught that people are equal before God and that they are also equal under the law. But Winston Churchill mentioned that we are entitled to equality at the starting blocks only, not at the finish line. Fairness in society means that someone may lose. Fairness also means someone wins, even though it may be a privileged white male. Even after removing all unfair privilege to make the playing field level, those with superior talent and drive overtake the mediocre and then become the privileged to be envied and to be torn down. Constantly comparing our own lot in life with others and assuming that things are wrong because they are not equal can result not only in disillusionment but even in self-destructive envy or even violent retaliation. Expecting absolute parity leads to "get evenism" implemented by reverse discrimination—women getting even with men, blacks getting even with whites, and the poor getting even with the wealthy. Some people can actually be disgruntled because Queen Elizabeth lives in Buckingham Palace, and their home doesn't have as many rooms.

A spin-off of the fairness hang-up involves an inflation of the call for "rights." Addicts should have the right to treatment, derelicts should have rights for housing. Children should have rights against their parents or teachers. When carried to extremes, the underlying moral basis for these claims becomes ridiculous. Claims for entitlement based on victimization by society only erode the sense of personal responsibility to improve one's life. Unfortunately, to resist these unrealistic notions invites accusations of elitism.

Another aspect of the rigid application of fairness involves going to extremes to avoid stereotyping individuals by virtue of their appearance, gender, race, or social class. Sometimes politically correct idealists become foolish in the opposite direction, assuming (hoping) everyone is equal, and not facing the vestiges of truth in all stereotypes. We all have to live in the real world in which each day we make many quick judgments of others without thorough analysis, rating them on their appearance, title, and associates. We don't have time to interview and attain the resume of each person we happen to meet. If we're walking down the sidewalk and see, in the distance coming our way, an individual that fits the commonsense profile of a mugger, we have to use measured stereotyping, play the odds, and alter our walking route.

Illogical Cultural Bias

We are oblivious to many of our culture's controls on us. We have a penchant to overly respect uniforms, titles, and trappings of authority. The policeman's badge and squad car are among the first to come to mind, along with the doctor's long white coat, then the security guard's braids and holster. We're apt to forget that these trappings and positions do not guarantee that the person so dressed is competent. We need to be wary of letting a symbol prevent us from analyzing the content of a situation. Some shoe salesmen are ignorant about shoes and feet. I know a young lady who got a job as a tour guide in Alaska one week after she arrived there.

Because psychological tests have shown that we attribute all sorts of unjustified positive factors to physically attractive people, in a school admission interview such people have an advantage in being admitted regardless of their previous academic accomplishments.

We are inclined to like someone whose name is familiar, like Bob, Bill, or Mike, and to distrust someone with an unusual name. If your name is John King or Bill King you may be viewed with extra respect. The familiar first name is generally accepted and the idea of you being a King is meaningful based on hearing the nursery rhymes during formative years. If you're tall and attractive, you're additionally lucky.

We have many illogical ideas that are rarely questioned. Certain insects are considered wonderful, benign creatures, such as ladybugs and crickets (Jimminy). Rats are terrible, but squirrels are likable little animals, even though they are very similar to rats except for their bushy tails. Besides wine being deemed upper class and beer middle class, even vegetables are subject to cultural prejudice, with artichokes and asparagus thought to be high-class vegetables, and mashed potatoes and black-eyed peas low class. Whoever long ago decided that fruit juices should be served in small glasses and iced tea in large glasses? This certainly influences the amount we drink. For some reason, Ireland and the Irish are considered warm and endearing. What other ethnic group is given a national celebration such as St. Patrick's Day?

People tend to anthropomorphize inanimate things, looking upon their hospital, their company, or their city as thinking, breathing entities. Some talk about their hospital "liking" them for working hard for many years, or their company "taking good care" of them after they retire. They speak of being "loyal" to their city or school, or having faith in them, and hopefully assume that if you love them, then they will love you.

We accept our social milieu as rational because we can't completely escape it. Nevertheless, we follow it down illogical paths. In chapter 10, on culture, we will have more to say about its whimsical, ambiguous influence.

References

Gerrig, Richard. *The Life of the Mind: An Introduction to Psychology,* audiotape. Springfield, Va.: The Teaching Company, 1991.

Henry, William A., III. *In Defense of Elitism.* New York: Doubleday, 1994.

Leo, John. "The Spread of Rights Babble." *U.S. News and World Report* (June 28, 1993): 17.

Mapp, Alf J. *Thomas Jefferson: Passionate Pilgrim.* Lanham, Md.: Madison Books, 1992.

Myers, David G. *The Pursuit of Happiness: Who Is Happy and Why.* New York: William Morrow, 1992.

Stone, Mark, John Lachs, and Mike Hassell, eds. *Giants of Philosophy—Arthur Schopenhauer,* audiotape narrated by Charlton Heston. Nashville, Tenn.: Knowledge Products, 1991.

8

Compulsions and Psychological Defense Mechanisms

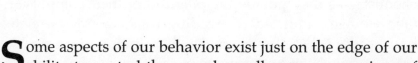

Some aspects of our behavior exist just on the edge of our ability to control them, and usually we are conscious of this borderline status of self-control. An overlap exists in the meaning of the words we use to describe undesirable human behavior. From the least to the most severe: habits, compulsions, behavior disorders, addictions, severe mental illness.

Words get overused, as mentioned in the chapter on language. Language inflation dilutes them until they become meaningless. *Addiction* is one of these words. Originally used to connote the medicophysiologic effects of drugs and alcohol, the term *addiction* has been stretched to include almost all compulsions and habits. We now hear of antique addicts, those who are unable to drive past an antique store. As they enter the store, their hearts begin to pound. First they fill their home with antiques, then the garage, then the attic.

A large industry has arisen to serve the dysfunctional, including self-help books, treatment centers, and drugs. Buzz words, such as "twelve steps" and "inner child," abound: it seems that everyone is now either in recovery or in denial, and all are codependents. Support groups, such as Gamblers Anonymous, Overeaters Anonymous, Sexaholics Anonymous, and Shoplifters Anonymous surround us.

I reserve discussion of the term *addiction* for the chapter on medicine and physiology. True addiction actually is related to physiological response, such as significant withdrawal symptoms. Some compulsions or habits, however, often have mild physiological responses. Gambling addicts and sex addicts actually experience some alteration of brain chemistry as they pursue the pleasure of their compulsion. One woman "addicted" to reading romance novels relates how reading these novels makes her "pulse speed up like crack cocaine," and other women say they get headaches if they can't pursue such reading.

Clearly all forms of improper behavior cannot be called addiction or disease. To use our language in this way removes the obligation for self-control and gives ethical immunity to the responsible party.

Compulsions

Some individuals are predisposed to an overall addictive personality. The heavy smoker is also apt to be a heavy coffee drinker, to gamble compulsively, and to be an alcoholic.

Others may be compelled to play chess, or to do church work to excess (a churchaholic). One can become obsessed with exercise and sports, devoting every moment to these pursuits to the point of harming others and / or oneself. This latter aspect of any habit or compulsion distinguishes it from merely enthusiastic advocacy.

Many people become "TV bugs." Watching television is easy to do, since it is so inexpensive and passive. With it there is such a low level of cerebral cortical arousal that people become so relaxed that they continue watching even after natural satiation comes about. There have been reports of so-called withdrawal symptoms after a family's television set breaks. Family arguing and violence have ensued because the families became bored and irritated. One such family mentioned that they walked around like "chickens with their heads cut off."

Some may not appreciate that they are becoming hooked on television. Since television viewing is a major factor in most of our lives, grade school education should address this problem and actually train children to become more discriminating television viewers. Few people read books now, but instead watch television, which stays on incessantly in many homes. Children who don't have enough self-confidence are in trouble if they have never seen the example of an adult turning off the television set. Children who are never taught to draw, make pleasant conversation, or play in a creative way, are also unable to take the initiative to turn off the television set.

The number of compulsive gamblers is increasing, now that many states have legalized gambling. The pathologic gambler experiences a short-lived euphoric rush regardless of whether he or she wins or loses. With time, the gambler has to take a greater and greater degree of risk in order to get the same thrill. An estimated one out of twenty gamblers becomes compulsive to a harmful degree, and 80 percent of these are male. The line between fun and addiction is a thin one. Compulsive gamblers have a high suicide rate due, in part, to the huge debt they accumulate. Many are also drug and alcohol addicts.

Workaholism is very common and easy to drift into, being, like religion addiction, a socially acceptable form of compulsive behavior. We have always been taught to work hard, for work provides financial security, but many work so hard at making a living that they don't have a life outside their jobs. Many professionals are workaholics without knowing it. Not only do they pride themselves on never taking vacations and constantly working, they justify this lifestyle as being altruistic and beneficent. When they withdraw into their work, it becomes the path of least resistance, making broader family and community decisions more difficult to the workaholic than staying at work. People who work excessively create the illusion that they are indispensable, elevating their status in their own eyes at least. Such people can find many excuses for such immoderate work, such as imagining that they are financially insecure, or that their children or grandchildren depend on their excessive work to be financially secure. In their final days facing death, aged people often gain insight about the totality of their lives. Many sadly say, "I wish I'd spent less time at the office."

There is a thin line between workaholism and masochism. In the past, this perversion was called self-denial and had religious and ascetic connotations. The puritan work ethic teaches that pursuing pleasure is sinful and only leads to feelings of guilt, and that suffering brings us true pleasure, for it is by suffering that we enter the kingdom of God. Perhaps H. L. Mencken was not altogether wrong when he defined Puritanism as the fear that somewhere, somebody is having a good time. Workaholics can always find another workaholic with whom to compare themselves; doing so with any other such individual who may be making more money, an entirely different game can come into play: *competition compulsion*.

Akin to the martyr complex and mild masochism is the habit of *delay of gratification of pleasure*. Many people say they will be happy when they finish school, or get married, or make a lot of money. The bliss never seems to arrive. In doctors, the habit develops slowly in high school, where they have to study hard and deny themselves many things for the rewards that will come much later. It continues in college. During medical school and residency it remains a way of life; things will always be better in the future. When working to establish a practice, this concept still prevails, living life with pleasure on the installment plan. If these people are not careful, an entire life will tick away while they unconsciously delay gratification, never realizing that this can be a form of masochism, deriving perverse pleasure from delaying pleasure.

Visit a museum of medieval culture and you will learn that for many centuries people were overly preoccupied with religion. I'm sure someday there will be a museum of twentieth-century America, and visitors will think that we were overly hung-up on material possessions. Our culture teems with superfluous gadgets and goods which advertising compels us to work excessively to possess. We live in an overly competitive age when status-seeking is much more instrumental in our motivation than we are aware. Often we waste money by indulging in self-esteem-enhancing behavior such as shopping in expensive stores and impulsively buying on credit the latest name brands and labels. Our industry produces many products to create wants and imagined needs.

We didn't want our music on CDs *before* they were advertised, because we thought that our stereo was just fine.

For many, leisure and interpersonal relations have become of secondary importance to owning things. Some parents are apt to express their love for their children not with time and interest, but by giving them complicated toys. Similarly with couples; diamonds are forever, but relaxed, loving conversation is limited. *Acquisition compulsion* tends to escalate into illusory "needs." We imagine we need more expensive and more complicated cars, and more electronic gadgets that encroach on our freedom and infringe on our personal relationships. In order to drive a status car, listen to music on a CD, and play with multiple electronic phones and recorders, we must necessarily forego time for travel or more meaningful interpersonal relations. Increasingly, our possessions are becoming burdens.

Sometimes acquisition compulsion can take the form of working purely for money—miserliness. *Wealth addicts* slave diligently to have multiple financial investments, stocks, and bonds. They drop the names of these assets to peers and derive great pleasure in savoring their net worth in great detail. They may have an impoverished life except for their bank account, but they justify this by imagining that they will be stronger and more secure when the inevitable financial holocaust comes. Deluding themselves into believing that they are being a savior for their children, they don't realize that acquiring a large inheritance at a young age is often destructive. Wealth addicts defend their actions by overstating how much tax they pay and how tough it is to meet their great expenses. Having their lives totally revolve around making money is the path of least resistance, a rut from which it takes too much energy to emerge. It takes initiative and creativity to get out into the real world and make new decisions about community, family, friends, personal health, politics, and fulfillment as a human being. The Roman philosopher Seneca summed it up well. "Money has never yet made anyone rich."

Psychological Defense Mechanisms

Many illogical behavior patterns are never analyzed completely. The psychological defense mechanisms, which employ minor distortions of reality, serve to soften the blows of reality—to disguise and lubricate. It has been said that if we could see reality as it really is, we would go mad instantly. These mechanisms are grounded in measured self-deception, but we cannot function without them. Mediated through emotions, these mechanisms provide an easy way to enhance self-esteem. As an example, we optimistically "psych ourselves up" for a big event. Like a medical placebo, this behavior often becomes self-fulfilling. Naturalist and writer Joseph Wood Krutch said, "The most important aspect of our lives—our sensations, emotions, desires, aspirations—takes place in a universe of illusions which science can attenuate or destroy, but which it is powerless to enrich." The tenets of religion—faith, hope, and charity layered with emotion and ritual—lie outside the dictates of science and logic.

Rationalization involves rhetorically justifying or making excuses for improper behavior. We use avoidance or *denial* to adapt to painful emotion, much as we do in response to severe illness. *Sublimation* is the transformation of a socially unacceptable desire into motivation for a more acceptable one, the classic example being diversion of high sexual drives into psychic energy to excel in some other endeavor, such as sports, work, or art. Rationalization and sublimation are mechanisms that are sometimes helpful; other mental mechanisms are less helpful.

Anger is a coping defense mechanism used by primitive man to enhance his chance of survival. Personal threats stimulated his sympathetic nervous system and activated a fight-or-flight response, which increases the flow of adrenalin from the adrenal gland and speeds up the heart and breathing rate. We modern humans no longer need these basic emotions to assure our survival, but our brains still have the residue of the primitive anger system—the limbic system. On occasion, a show of anger, if calculated and controlled, can be effective in relieving tension and getting things done. Aristotle taught that anyone who doesn't demonstrate an appropriate degree of anger at the appropriate time is a fool. In general, however, it tends to be destructive to the angry person as well as to others. We all regret things we say in extreme anger, a form of temporary insanity that usually impedes logical thinking. Most often, anger only makes the person to whom it is directed brace up for further offense. "How much more grievous are the consequences of anger than the causes of it," Marcus Aurelius said.

Envy, one of the most damaging emotions of humanity, results from illogical thought processes. It is based on the notion that every person should be equal and that fairness demands that each person should be as talented as anyone else and have the same rewards. The envier seems to derive pleasure from witnessing the destruction of another person who is in better circumstances. Commonly used by politicians to win votes, this resentment of another's success is the recurring theme of communism, where the egalitarian concept of equal distribution of income is foremost. Being pro-mediocrity and also antifreedom, envy aims to pull down those who have earned their good fortune.

Guilt is another mental mechanism that frequently hurts us. This painful emotion is based on past actions, which no longer exist, so dwelling upon them cannot be helpful. While remembering the past and learning from mistakes is benefi-cial, experiencing excessive pain because of them is harmful. This worrying about the past can take many forms; we can worry about having done something bad in our childhood, and we can also remember having made an error while play-ing some sport. This error could have occurred just five min-utes previously but it still occupies our thoughts with need-less guilt. In tennis, I have long learned that when I decide a close line call in my favor, I will usually punish myself uncon-sciously by missing shots soon after my petty crime. Guilt-ridden people are apt to have been raised in overly strict, puritanical homes. Parents and teachers often instill guilt in a vulnerable child's mind, which can result in serious, subcon-scious, self-punishing behavior by children. Religion can sometimes serve to promote an abnormal sense of guilt.

To some extent we all adhere to the further illogical con-cept that if we feel guilty enough and suffer enough, other people aware of the situation will have sympathy for us, and "somebody up there," such as God, will also look upon us in a more favorable light. The problem is that all of our emo-tional energy is going into the suffering rather than into changing the things that we can do today to improve our-selves. Needless suffering does not, cannot, change the past.

Worry is a painful emotion caused by an excessive projec-tion into the future. We waste emotional breath worrying about things that do not yet exist. With our minds so occupied we are apt to make a mistake in the present that prepares the way for the bad event to happen. Excessive worriers procrastinate and never take chances. Because there is always something that may go wrong, they do nothing in the present. When worry is directed toward others' welfare, it can be considered a mark of a caring individual, with attendant social approval. Most of our worries are about events that never happen; therefore, the majority of effort spent on worrying is wasted.

We continuously use these defense mechanisms to cope with anxiety by unconsciously distorting reality. We must always try to use these in moderation, so bringing them into our conscious awareness and facing their effects on our behavior is beneficial. All emotions can be thought of as coping defense mechanisms that help to alleviate stress. A proper emotional response first depends on a rational and correct interpretation of reality. With faulty evaluation, one can get angry at the rain or fall in love with an inappropriate person. Although we are constantly admonished to "keep cool," we should not dismiss emotions as undesirable, neurotic lapses. Evolution has provided these useful strategies for survival because they give us motivation on a conscious level. Some emotions, such as love and joy, are unsurpassed at making our lives worthwhile.

References

Brothers, Joyce. "Do You Have Enough Fun?" *Parade Magazine* (February 2, 1992).

Kaminer, Wendy. *I'm Dysfunctional, You're Dysfunctional.* Reading, Mass.: Addison-Wesley, 1992.

Kubey, Robert, and Mihaly Csikszentmihalyi. *Television and the Quality of Life: How Viewing Shapes Everyday Experience.* Hillsdale, N.J.: Lawrence Erlbaum Associates, 1990.

Murray, Kathleen. "Linking Personalities and Stress." *New York Times* (September 12, 1993).

Neill, John R. " 'Addiction' Phenomenon." *Southern Medical Journal* 84 (August 1991): 1003–1005.

Rappaport, Herbert. *Marking Time.* New York: Simon and Schuster, 1990.

Rappaport, Judith L. *The Boy Who Couldn't Stop Washing.* New York: E. P. Dutton, 1989.

Solomon, Robert J. *Clinical Practice Management.* Gaithersburg, Md.: Aspen Publishers, 1992.

Waters, David. "Focus Is Growing on Religion Addiction." *Memphis Commercial Appeal* (September 5, 1993).

Zois, Christ. *Think Like a Shrink: Solve Your Problems Yourself with Short-Term Therapy Techniques.* New York: Warner Books, 1991.

9

Handling Time

Time

An illusive concept.
At its essence mortals guess.
But we spend it,
And waste it,
And save it.
And wish we had
More, or less.

Ward Parsons

You *are* time. In Einstein's space-time continuum, time is your fourth dimension. Our behavior is regulated by time because in making most decisions we unconsciously weigh time expenditure against benefit. These choices are made in different time frames, from microseconds to hours to decades. Our unconscious mind judges in a split second whether we have enough time to take a full back swing on a served tennis ball or whether we must only block it back. We determine if we have enough minutes in the morning rush for another piece of toast. Consciously and more deliberately, we decide in later life whether it is worthwhile to go back to college for three years.

We act as if time were a thing because we've made a word for it, but it is really an intracranial concept. Nobody knows what time looks like, and we can't comfortably define it. Augustine said that time did not always exist, since before the creation of the universe there was nothing, and God created the universe and time is part of that creation.

In Isaac Newton's orderly world it was assumed that time was stable throughout the universe; an hour in England was the same as an hour in the far reaches of space. Both space and time were regarded as even more fundamental than actual events. The concept of simultaneity meant that any two events that were simultaneous for one observer were simultaneous for all other observers in the universe, regardless of their state of motion.

Albert Einstein's theory of relativity, however, concludes that space-time depends on the state of motion of the observer. Each observer's time is the same only if all are traveling at the same speed. If at different speeds, they have different estimates of the time and space they observe between two events. There is no uniform, absolute "now." The faster an observer speeds away from a clock, the slower the clock runs. If you were rushing away from a clock face at the speed of light you would be keeping up with the light waves entering your eyes, and therefore the hands of the clock would not move. These concepts of time, however, are of significance only at tremendous speeds, not in everyday life.

Einstein concluded that the whole of space-time was constant. It's all there in the total fabric—past, present, future, which exist simultaneously. Space-time is fixed and doesn't move forward the way we humans perceive. All equations of physics are symmetrical in time and can go in any direction. If a movie film of a planet's revolutions and orbits were run backward or forward, we wouldn't know the difference. Einstein wrote, "The distinction between past, present and future is an illusion, although a persistent one." The laws of physics give no support to the idea that the present or past determines the future. Every process that occurs in one direction is also possible in the reverse direction. From scientific facts that we know in the present and also in the past, we can predict future events such as solar eclipses. From information that we have in the near past and present we can retrodict events in the more distant past such as solar eclipses, or the Big Bang.

The present is such an infinitely small moment, it actually doesn't exist any more than does the past or future. But from the perspective of conscious awareness, the present is the only thing that exists. Our memories of the past and our visions of the future can happen only in our conscious minds "at present." Zen Buddhist philosophy makes much of gaining enlightenment from being totally and only "in the now." With relativity, "now" depends on the motion of the observer; there is no constant present.

The perception of time is based on certain events only. If there were no events there would be no time. If you were in a room without windows or clocks, you would not be able to tell for how many days, weeks, or months you were in that room. Time would become meaningless.

Our present concepts of time are not the last word. Undoubtedly in one hundred years physicists will look back and smile at our concepts. Even today, many maintain that time, along with everything else, is an illusion within the mind of each different human. We really can't say that the stars we see exist, since each of these stars may have disappeared thousands of years ago, because of the number of years it takes for their light to reach our eyes. We see them only as they were in the past.

Gravity alters both time and space. Your watch runs slower when you are on the surface of the earth than it does high in space because on the earth you are subjected to a stronger pull of gravity. Gravity can become so strong as to destroy time or distort the reality of time as we know it. A star massive enough to collapse under its own gravity and shrink to zero size would bend light rays one hundred eighty degrees and light would be unable to leave the star. This region of space-time is called a black hole. Everything is dragged back by a black hole's gravitational field. It would be the end of time for any astronaut or superman flying into this black hole. If an astronaut was lucky enough to miss the black hole and instead fall through a "worm hole," a tear in the fabric of space-time, he might exit in another region or time of the universe. In order to play around with this concept, one hypothesis must be convoluted upon another. Thinking about time travel is full of paradoxes. If you were able to travel into the past, it is then theoretically possible for you to do something that would prevent your own birth generations later. Is it impossible to exist and not exist simultaneously?

Our sense of time is relative. To a snail a turtle is a speed demon. We try to communicate with putative extraterrestrial life forms, assuming that their time frame is similar. Their thought processes could move much more slowly or quickly than ours. Our central nervous systems may respond to something in about two seconds, whereas their response might take two million years, or two nanoseconds.

Historical Development of Time

Primitive humans probably had very little conscious understanding of time, moseying around with only the concept of day and night and the seasons to give them a rough sense. People didn't even have ages. It was not until civilization progressed to invent containers for storage of food that the concept of time began, because people could then plan for future droughts and protect against famine. When humans were able to have some effect on their future, they became more aware of its existence. We need to remind ourselves that early in the Middle Ages people had no conscious awareness of hours, minutes, and seconds. The Benedictine monks first gonged bells to designate an hour. Later, they invented the mechanical clock, which put punctuality on a pedestal. The human mind was then conditioned to regard time as an external, exacting entity. The clockwork universe of Isaac Newton was accepted by the Western world, with the Christians endorsing it completely and teaching that it was the duty of all to be punctual and to know their place like the parts of a clock.

When clocks were introduced into factories during the industrial revolution, each worker was expected to surrender his autonomy to the new time control system. The time clock, documenting arrival and departure of employees, was instituted in about 1800. The word *efficiency* became the instrument of the slave drivers of the factories, and today the concept of efficiency remains overrated.

Schedules and sophisticated motion-time studies are used now to regulate workers' activities like automatons. Their tasks can be timed and geared to optimum efficiency. Worker time can now be measured in seconds per unit of production or service. Time sheets are used to ensure discipline and accountability.

The movie *The Gods Must Be Crazy* compares the lives of modern workers to the lives of bushmen of the Kalahari Desert, where there are no laws, bosses, or days of the week. In the Kalahari there are no clocks or calendars to tell you when to do this or that. In the cities civilized humans invented labor-saving devices but didn't know when to stop, because the more we improved our surroundings to make life easier, the more complicated we made it. Eight o'clock in the morning means that everyone has to look busy. At ten o'clock the clock says that everyone can stop looking busy for fifteen minutes. The peaceful, natural day is chopped up into little pieces, with each changing increment ordering you to adapt to a new set of circumstances.

We assume that certain man-made time symbols are natural and have always existed, such as the International Date Line and Greenwich world time. We don't realize these things are artificial products of modern human scheduling. Why isn't a week three days, or twenty days? By using artificial symbols and standards we can even create such false realities as seeing our broken, stopped wrist watch keep correct time if we fly from Paris to Los Angeles across nine time zones in nine hours. In 1993, the people on Kwajalein, one of the Marshall Islands, decided to change their time base to the other side of the International Date Line. As a result, they went to sleep Friday night and awakened Sunday morning.

The author Thomas Mann said, "Time has no divisions to mark its passage. There is never a thunderstorm or blare of trumpets to announce the beginning of a new month or year. Even when a new century begins it is only we mortals who ring bells and fire off pistols." Time has found such exalted priority that we now speak in terms of time for activities rather than distance—a forty minute commute, or, "San Francisco is now only two hours away."

The concept of time developed differently in China, with religion fostering the idea that history and time are circular and tend to repeat themselves. Consequently, the Chinese revered tradition and the past because they thought these past events would eventually again become the future. Regarding time as predestined and cyclical, they had little interest in innovation, but worshiped ancient authority. The Japanese were running in a different gear. With their Shinto religion regarding time as a linear process, they adopted the accelerated pace of Western culture, and now consider time a precious resource not to be wasted.

On a scale similar to what the clock did to mankind's thoughts about time in the thirteenth century, the computer is running our lives today. In *Time Wars*, Jeremy Rifkin sums up the present situation. "Now with the clock and the schedule joined by an even more powerful time technology, the computer and the program, efficiency has assumed an unchallenged position in the social scheme of things, becoming the premier value of our age." Working on a nanosecond basis, the computer has certainly speeded up our concept of time. Our time is now organized into the future by the computer program. Computer time is foreign to the natural rhythms of our known seasons and circadian rhythms. Computers engineer a type of social control because the workers' future is now programmed in nanoseconds.

Computer programming can rob us of our freedom to change our minds, to "play it by ear." Computer programs mandate exact activity in the future. In the stock market crash of October 1987, the computers did their thing automatically. They had been programmed in the past to respond and respond they did. We may be facing computers in space that will take all of the human intellect out of the decisions about whether to launch a nuclear holocaust in a matter of nanoseconds. Should we preprogram World War III?

The rapid transfer of information by computers has altered the timeframe of communication between humans. We now have become impatient with language because we can transmit huge amounts of information by computers instantaneously. Talking is comparatively slow, and writing out language by hand is even slower. Some long-term "computer nerds" have become socially inept because they have lost their sense of conventional time that other people take for granted and become irritated with normal conversation which naturally includes pauses and uncertainty.

Time Obsession

> *Time is a storm in which we are all lost.*
>
> William Carlos Williams

Our culture's increasingly fast pace affects our conduct in many subtle ways. Most people maintain that they have little, if any, free time. Predictions thirty years ago called for much more free time, but this has not happened. In today's high-technology world, with our microwave ovens, expressways, and fax machines, we do everything much faster, but the time saved by these inventions is taken up by other life-complicating conveniences of consumption such as car phones, VCRs, and video cameras. Our surfeit of time-saving "stuff" has decimated our time. We now have many more choices for activities and we don't want to delete any of them. We are compelled to jam them all—requiring them all to be done quickly. Like one of Murphy's laws, the more time we have to do things, the more things we find to do. We read articles on how to budget time and we even attend seminars, but these actually make us worry about time even more. Experts advise us to listen to tapes while we drive, make a priority list each day, keep a time log for a week, and use our lunch hour for specific activities. We make out priority lists and boil down the possibilities to absolute musts, but then we can't find time to perform the musts. We take videotapes of our family and no one ever has time to view them. We tape meaningful television programs on our VCR, and the tapes gather dust. We buy a new telephone answering machine or digital wristwatch yet don't have time to read the four-page instruction pamphlets that come with them. We're doing more but enjoying it less. It seems that, as singer and songwriter Jim Croce tells us in his "Time in a Bottle," "But there never seems to be enough time to do the things you want to do once you find them."

Our whole life has speeded up. We once wrote leisurely with quills, then faster with fountain pens, then ballpoints, then typewriters, then word processors, now e-mail. You can now watch your taped television on a speeded-up monitor.

When watching a recorded ball game, you can speed through all of the time-outs and advertising breaks and reduce the game down to half the regular time. With "computer treatment" the chipmunk tone of a speeded up audiotape can be removed but the sound comes at such a rapid pace that the playing time is halved.

The hectic pace of our lives allows very little thoughtful communication between family members. I remember the pleasant times in our family as a child when we made "pull candy." We put butter on our fingers and pulled out the taffy, seemingly for hours. Similarly, we made homemade ice cream, churning slow and easy. Recall the lyrics of "Cats in the Cradle," sung by Harry Chapin. After neglecting his son, the father, now an older man, seeks his son's attention, only to be told, "I'd love to, Dad, if I could find the time. And as I hung up the phone it occurred to me, my boy was just like me."

Without question, our society accepts this frantic obsession with deadlines, timetables, and expiration dates. We now pack our calendars with tiny writing to fill in the squares of each day. With some political leaders now scheduling appointments every five minutes, it's easy to see how they can miss the big picture. Overly structured time management (micromanagement they call it) in an office may go unrecognized as an inhibiting system. The detailed schedules and memos may be accepted by the insecure and passive as welcome order and efficiency because the smallest decisions about what to do and when to do it are made for them. At work, stress is created by the corporate timeline that businesses place upon employees, who are expected to reach certain points of achievement in a fixed sequence or they are removed from the growth ladder.

We all feel as if we are oppressed by the "tyranny of the

urgent," because some immediate crisis always takes priority over something more meaningful. We are forced to extinguish an emergency fire now, therefore never gaining time to relax, go back, and build a better fire engine.

Some people are unable to handle this accelerated time-frame, eventually becoming overwhelmed and succumbing to "hurry sickness." They may lose orientation to the past or future, trying only to pack in as much in the immediate present as they possibly can. The classic type A personality is thus mind-rushed, inaccessible, and driven. In his book *Busy Bodies*, Lee Burns mentions "those among us who are dervishly whirling, cramming and ramming activity into a fixed time allotment." The vibes they give off indicate that they are "busier than thou," drumming their fingers, looking at their watch, finishing your sentences for you, or darting their eyes over your shoulder at something else to which they have to hurry. They listen to tapes via their Walkman while jogging in place (weights on ankles and wrists), waiting outside a fast-food outlet. They bolt breakfast down while driving fast to work, watch television while eating dinner, and read the newspaper with the radio on while on the commode. These "urgency addicts" actually look for problems in order to entertain more "busy-ness." The lyrics of a song by Alabama say it well. "I'm in a hurry to get things done. I rush and rush until life's no fun. All I really gotta do is live and die, but I'm in a hurry and don't know why." Frequently, the ones who are the least sure of what they want are the ones chugging the fastest to get it.

Rushing becomes a way of life, and many become unable to relax and slow down because when they stop for a moment, as with prolonged highway driving, they feel that they are going backward. Even a vacation creates anxiety. Our sex lives are certainly affected by being rushed all the time. Rushed young couples with overly complex lives, with children, and both working, just don't have the time for sex.

Feeling compelled to produce and consume at a frenzied pace, we are less able to enjoy the present and savor the past. Expected social behavior patterns have shortened many activities. In the past, people mourned the death of a close relative for months or years, but now the acceptable period of mourning has been reduced to weeks or days, depending upon the closeness of the family member. Increasingly, much telephone use today is limited to leaving and receiving messages on answering machines. This impersonal shortcut is more time efficient, eliminating obligatory salutations and small talk. With quick out-patient surgery, you can now have your cataract removed and be back home within one day. Many small decisions hang on time constraints. We buy ready-to-drink orange juice rather than mixing up the frozen concentrate, or taking the time to squeeze fresh oranges. We get a cat rather than a dog because we don't have to spend time walking a cat. We use time-saving mail-order catalogues instead of going to a department store. Swallowing the delusion that time-shortening "things" benefit us, we don't realize that we are just ratcheting up the speed of the treadmill. Perhaps the appeal of the *Indiana Jones* or *Die Hard* movie series, which have nonstop sequences of rousing episodes, is based on a model of our frenetic lives. Most Americans opt to be on the fast track, but because they must set their schedule to the pace that track demands, they are unable to stoop to smell the roses.

Time awareness differs among national cultures. In many areas of the developing world people still are not compelled to be punctual and obey the precise deadlines that control those in the more developed nations. Japan's clocks are the most accurate in the world, and pedestrians in Tokyo walk the fastest. The Scandinavians and Germans tend to be very punctual. For them, an invitation for dinner at 7:00 P.M. means right on the dot. In Italy, Greece, and South America, arrival any time before 8:00 P.M. is acceptable.

Time Distortion

We probably acquire our basic perception of time passage while in utero by the rate of our mother's heart beat. When we have fever or an overactive thyroid our heart rate is faster and time seems to pass more quickly. Similarly, when listening to fast music, we overestimate the time lapse of an actual minute. Television and movies also tend to distort our time-frame because we seldom see mundane activities like people eating, sleeping, or driving to work. Only the important and exciting events are included and, with epics, such as *The God-father* episodes, decades go by in a matter of two hours.

Awareness of time changes with age. Time passes more slowly as a young child and during old age but in the middle years of life time races past. The estimation of time elapse also depends upon how many events occur during a given time interval. Personally, I find time passes the most rapidly when I am doing the same thing each day. I can slow time down by taking a trip and having many varied experiences. I get back from my five-day vacation and ask, "What happened?" I've imagined that momentous events have occurred in this seemingly long length of time, but others say, "Nothing. Have you been gone?" The hour in which you have an automobile accident and are taken to the hospital is recalled to be longer than the previous hour in which you were driving uneventfully on the highway. Sensory deprivation (flotation tanks, solitary confinement) also causes a variably altered sense of time lapse.

Since time sequencing (differentiating past, present, and future) is thought to be handled mainly by the left cerebral hemisphere, organic disease in this part of the brain may have greater effect on one's sense of time. Following epileptic seizures arising in the temporal lobes patients may temporarily lose sense of time. With Korsakoff psychosis, caused by chronic alcoholism, patients may lose their sense of short-term memory, and hence time.

We generally tend to underestimate time passage. If I think something happened two years ago, it probably happened four years ago. Time and age estimation are distorted by fame. Boris Becker, still a young man, seems like the grand old man of tennis because he has been famous since winning Wimbledon at age seventeen.

A child's idea of time is unique. Children regard someone they have talked with three times and played with one Saturday afternoon to be a close friend because this association is a relatively large part of their total life experience. Older individuals can work with acquaintances in the same office for thirty years and not consider them friends at all. Small children have a poorly developed understanding of time. The young live on first impressions. The first time a child plays tennis he may mention that he plays poorly because he has a bad backhand, having no concept that with time and practice he will be able to overcome any such early imperfection. I can remember as a sixteen-year-old playing a thirty-year-old opponent in a tennis tournament. I considered him an old man and tried to keep the ball in play so that I would tire him. I lost—exhausted.

We all notice that our early life experiences are "frozen in time" in our minds. We return to our hometown or our grade school and are disillusioned to find everything has changed. Based on our memory of one spat we had with a classmate in the sixth grade, we will glibly offer the opinion forty years later that that person is a jerk.

The conscious appreciation of time below one second and beyond one thousand years eludes us. We cannot think in terms of geologic time. That is why the theory of evolution had to await the appreciation of the earth's age in billions of years instead of the Western concept of biblical creation of about six thousand years. It is easy to see why primitive man failed to associate the birth of babies with sexual activity—the babies came nine and a half months later. And people lose their appreciation of time when they invest. Over a period of thirty-five years, compounding can do some miraculous things. If an investor invests a thousand dollars each year for ten years and then does not invest any more, after thirty-five years he will be worth more than his brother who invested (with equal annual gain) a thousand dollars each year from his eleventh through his thirty-fifth years (twenty-four years).

Herbert Rappaport studies our ability to cope with the passage of time in his book *Marking Time*. Time seems to come at us from the future, enter our present, and then become our past. We must be able to handle this temporal sequence appropriately. We should know where we are in the ball game, whether in the first quarter or at the two-minute warning signal. Those who do not handle time well are not as mentally healthy as those who do. Those who dwell on the past and neglect the future are prone to becoming depressed and to adopting addictive behavior. Because ghetto children are inclined to have no plans for the future, they live only in the immediate present, believing they can have no effect on the future.

We need a good sense of time perception and the ability to organize the sequence of events in our lives temporally, particularly with a healthy sense of the future. Not only should we take the time to stroll through the forest leisurely, but we should also take the time to plant trees and expect to eventually enjoy these. Rappaport finds that in our contemporary Western culture most of us have a better perspective of the past or present than we do of our future possibilities. Mental health depends upon facing the future, which people naturally resist. As Alvin Toffler mentions in *Future Shock*, we need to stress the importance of future analysis in our educational system to a greater degree, instead of ignoring it and overemphasizing ancient history.

Older individuals sometimes have a problem handling time perception, often becoming depressed by realistically facing their limited future and dwelling upon the past. Human nature being what it is, we cannot live contentedly in the absence of goals for the future. In our waning years we have to utilize psychological defense mechanisms, such as denial, and mentally block out the constant threat of death.

By overorganizing our lives with schedules and programs in ever-decreasing increments of time we become so inhibited that we lose our creative initiative and our ability to see the big picture in terms of history. Like language, time-keeping is something we take for granted, forgetting that it is a manmade practice that tends to enslave us as well as provide order in our lives. Only now are we beginning to question the benefits of efficiency and speed that have been implicitly worshiped too long.

Slowing Down One's Lifestyle

We should all take charge of *our* life's time to a greater extent. We don't have to watch television at all times, answer the phone, or respond to letters and surveys by solicitors. We can forget the idea of "always making good time" and utilizing every minute. Rushing becomes addictive. We're so busy doing that we don't have a chance to ponder what we're doing or where it's leading us. The poet Wordsworth warned us of this danger: "Getting and spending, we lay waste our powers."

We should reduce our accelerating awareness of time. We don't need to know exactly what time it is as much as we think we do. We can take the time to take the stairs instead of the elevator, or walk to the restaurant rather than drive. We can go to a baseball game on Sunday afternoon, get a beer and hot dog, accept the relatively slow pace, and enjoy it. At a cocktail party, we can calm down and chat with one person long enough to say something meaningful, instead of being compelled to lurch from person to person at ten-second intervals.

I have found beekeeping an excellent hobby for relaxation. Contrary to their reputation, bees spend most of their time "goofing off"—just hanging in and around the hive. The whole idea of inspecting bees is to slow down. I move deliberately in slow motion. I pick a placid Saturday afternoon to slowly get on my protective clothing, slowly light my smoker, and gently puff the smoke in the proximity of the hive. I slowly check each frame for disease and brood activity. This way the bees stay calm, but if they sense my jitters they respond accordingly.

To establish a more ecological, natural, temporal orientation for ourselves means changing many areas of our lives. In today's primitive hunter-gatherer cultures, from which we have inherited our natural psyche, individuals spend about half of their days in leisure. Consider your long-term health by taking time to eat right, sleep right, and get exercise. With education, take the attitude that you will live forever, so learn for the remote future. Economically, we should invest for the long term rather than the short term.

In future chapters we will touch upon the medical and physiological aspects of time perception in the natural biological circadian rhythms, and the nebulous nature of time itself will again be mentioned in the chapter on philosophy.

References

Burns, Lee. *Busy Bodies: Why Our Time-Obsessed Society Keeps Us Running in Place*. W. W. Norton, 1993.

Compton, John, John Lachs, and Mike Hassell. *The Giants of Philosophy—Jean-Paul Sartre*, audiotape. Nashville, Tenn.: Knowledge Products.

Cornish, Edward. "How Americans Use Time, An Interview With Sociologist John P. Robinson." *The Futurist* (September-October 1991): 23–27.

Deutsch, David, and Michael Lockwood. "The Quantum Physics of Time Travel." *Scientific American* (March 1994): 68–74.

Durning, Alan Thein. "Are We Happy Yet? How the Pursuit of Happiness is Failing." *The Futurist* (January-February 1993): 20–23.

Gregory, Richard L., ed. *The Oxford Companion to the Mind*. New York: Oxford University Press, 1987.

Hawking, Stephen. *A Brief History of Time*. New York: Bantam Books, 1988.

James, Everette A. "Micro-Management Yields Micro-Accomplishments." *Applied Radiology* (July 1993): 15–16.

Leggett, A. J. *The 'Arrow of Time' and Quantum Mechanics—The Encyclopedia of Ignorance*, edited by Ronald Duncan and Miranda Weston-Smith. New York: Pocket Books.

Mole, John. *When In Rome . . . A Business Guide to Cultures and Customs in Twelve European Nations*. New York: Amacom Books, 1991.

Ornstein, Robert E. *The Psychology of Consciousness*. New York: Harcourt Brace Jovanovich, 1977.

Penrose, Roger. *The Emperor's New Mind*. New York: Oxford University Press, 1989.

Priestly, J. B. *Man and Time*. New York: Crescent Books, 1989.

Rappaport, Herbert. *Marking Time*. New York: Simon and Schuster, 1990.

Russell, Peter. *The White Hole in Time*. New York: HarperCollins, 1992.

Rifkin, Jeremy. *Time Wars*. New York: Simon and Schuster, 1987.

Schor, Juliet B. *The Overworked American: The Unexpected Decline of Leisure*. New York: Basic Books, 1991.

Tassi, Nina. *Urgency Addiction: How to Slow Down Without Sacrificing Success*. Dallas, Tex.: Taylor Publishing, 1991.

Thorne, Kip S. *Black Holes and Time Warps*. New York: Norton, 1994.

10

Bindings of Culture

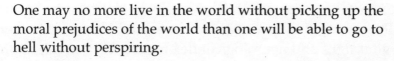

One may no more live in the world without picking up the moral prejudices of the world than one will be able to go to hell without perspiring.

H. L. Mencken

This chapter concerns the changes in us impelled by our ambiguous and rapidly shifting culture, which tends to overwhelm us with social and high-technology influences and models.

From preconception to postmortem, our culture plans, measures, educates, controls, and judges us. So tightly bound in the wrappings of our culture, we can barely give an authentic wiggle. In this book, I define culture not in its more narrow meaning of refined artistic taste (opera and poetry), but in its broader sense used by anthropologists and sociologists—all our nongenetic, socially transmitted behavior. To some extent your parents choose your genetic makeup by choosing each other—on the basis of present-day fashions of physical attractiveness, mental capability, and ability to be an acceptable parent. Most parents today are more inclined to plan the conception of their child to some degree.

Once pregnancy is recognized, ultrasound measures you and the exact date of your birth is predicted. Amniocentesis can reveal your genetic makeup and those who don't measure up may even be aborted. Expectations of the child's behavior are begun after quickening; the fetus is judged to be either a rambunctious or placid baby. The developing fetus may even be subjected to hearing music or various tapes transabdominally to give it a head start.

Moments after your birth, your behavior is more specifically measured by your Apgar Score (a tabulated assessment of vital signs and neurologic reflex responses) that might predict problems later on. As an infant, your milestones are carefully monitored—your first smile, your first step, your first word. Once in school, once immersed in the influence of birth order, words, and once in front of the television, your domination by culture prevails inexorably. IQ tests, SATs, and interviews determine your future course of study and put you on appropriate educational tracks. These evaluations can just as easily destroy your self-esteem and close opportunities. The media crudely provides you with its own sense of distorted reality. Throughout your childhood, the pressure of school social peers molds you. Your religion provides color to your ethical philosophy and the overly structured law of the land holds you to it.

Our culture in middle life is centered predominantly

around status, occupation, and financial security. We measure ourselves against the standards of our culture, which provides incentives, obligations, and force. It might even cause death by sending us to the battlefield, or to the electric chair. Even after death, our life's reputation is left to the whims of some bored news reporter assigned to the obituary desk, or perhaps some exploitative biographer. We may get autopsied or exhumed.

If you're now dejected after being reminded that your all-pervasive culture undermines the dignity of your imagined personal autonomy, just wait until you see how demanding the god of culture really is. Are we free? Are we self-determined? Are we in control? Less than we suppose.

Our Ambiguous, Open-ended, Postmodern World

A person's self-image depends upon comparing individual behavior to the perceived reality of the surrounding world. You are successful compared to whom? Your temper is labile compared to whose? Currently, in both our inner selves and the outer world, we encounter a jumbled assemblage. Unable to say which came first, each determines the other. All genres are now blurred. The term *postmodern* is arguably defined as a jaded, but open-ended skepticism and agnosticism, skeptical even of its own value. The postmodern world is eclectic, indeterminate, and celebrates maximum diversity. Its major characteristic is a disbelief in belief systems, whether they be religious, scientific, or political. The feeling is that there is no true thing in itself out there, and we are now free to make reality anything we wish. Postmodernists Jean-François

Lyotard, Jacques Derrida, and Michel Foucault carry the banner of deconstruction and discensus. Jean Baudrillard enjoys acknowledging the murky area where reality stops and media image begins.

Though ambiguity has always been present, scientific advancements and philosophical strides in the 1920s increased everyone's sense of disorder. Freud had described a powerful, irrational unconscious, and, to some, Einstein's theories and quantum mechanics just didn't comport with Newtonian physics. The whole idea of objective truth was in doubt, and even the doubters were subject to the whims of their ulterior motives and cultural pressures.

Modern art is often suffused with ambiguity. According to Pablo Picasso, "The world doesn't make sense, so why should I paint pictures that do?" M. C. Escher created drawings that defy logic. Modernism became too formal and yielded to postmodernism, which tends to change between media and is socially engaged. We now have paintings mixed in a pastiche manner with oil, watercolor, and objects pasted onto the canvas.

Our current architecture is a motley hybrid. The Stockholm town hall, built at the turn of the century, tended to reflect architecture of both the East and the West. Combinations are often now a mishmash, with a little of this and a little of that. Buildings may now have classical Greek columns with Asian touches. Robert Venturi is the architect credited with starting this postmodernism trend in the 1960s, by making outlandish combinations, with facades of buildings being brightly colored and of an indescribable genre (neoclassical kitsch).

Writing is now variegated and indefinite. Existentialist writings, such as *Waiting for Godot*, by Samuel Beckett, can be interpreted in many ways. Some novels contain a mixture of fact and fiction; the setting may jump in time and space indiscriminately, and plots are highly convoluted. Autobiography gets mixed with allegory. Few authors want to say it straight, and some play mockingly with traditional writing forms. It is now chic to be unable to tell what a book is about by its title. *What Color Is Your Parachute?* has been a big seller on selecting one's career.

Clothing designers such as postmodernist Karl Lagerfeld are leading the way out of our "dress for success" mode. You will find people who say anything goes—miniskirts one day and long peasant dresses the next. We can mix all sorts of colors and wear any width necktie. For protest and humor, which creates some status for certain individuals, one may wear a coat and tie plus tennis shorts, or a tuxedo along with sneakers. Now purple t-shirts can change color depending upon temperature and moisture, becoming various shades of blue and red.

Some movies exemplify the postmodern trend, utilizing many flashbacks and convoluted chronology. The *Back to the Future* (1985) science fiction film series plays havoc with traditional chronological order. In the movie titled *The French Lieutenant's Woman* (1981), near the end, we learn that everybody was actually acting during the first part of the movie. The plot is disclosed as a movie being filmed. In *The Purple Rose of Cairo* (1985), the actors come into the audience. Oliver Stone's movies *JFK* (1991) and *Nixon* (1995) are a controversial mixture of fact and fiction. One of the more popular television shows, "Seinfeld," is a postmodern hash of irreverent humor, satire, and philosophy. On Music Television (MTV) there is a confused mixture of surreal activity. Despite its shifting melange, the viewer is often not satisfied and flips the channels indiscriminately, perhaps turning to the comedians who use nonsequiturs in their delivery.

Our music is now a multivaried hodgepodge. Some of George Gershwin's work, such as "Rhapsody in Blue," tried to combine blues and classical forms. It is hard to define popular music—the Grammy Awards have multiple categories. Popular music is a medley of rap, classical, jazz, and country. Elvis Presley combined blues with country, and Hank Williams, Jr., combines pop with country. Concerts may now have an incongruous mix of Latin music, reggae, jazz, and religious rock.

The same admixture applies to the food we eat. Our cuisine now often mixes international flavors. We can eat a stand-up chili dog at a Le Snac in the airport. Many chefs do their own thing, mixing Mexican with French and Creole, all on the same plate.

Name changes have become more frequent among athletes and actors. The married hyphenated name, which blurs individuality and gender, emphasizing relatedness, is becoming increasingly popular.

Even bumper stickers have succumbed to enigmatic or nonsensical meanings. "No matter where you go, there you are." "I love bumper stickers." "The weather is here, wish you were beautiful."

Yogi Berra quotes, equivocal and cryptic, are relished. "The future ain't what it used to be." "I don't want to make the wrong mistake." "It gets late early out there." "If you don't know where you're going, you're not going to get there."

It is tempting to compare the bizarre paradoxes and dualities of our postmodern culture with the thought processes of schizophrenia. Both tend to deconstruct the world and portray it in contradiction to objective reality.

High-Tech Influences

> Men have become the tools of their tools.
>
> Henry David Thoreau, 1854

As you drive to the airport, you listen to a cassette on using persuasive techniques to sell. When you tire of this, you have fifteen different radio stations from which to choose music, news, or weather. From your car phone, you call your mother and tell her you're going to Europe. To monitor auto traffic, you might contact another motorist on your citizens band radio. At the airport terminal, you find myriad choices along the corridors. An ice cream vendor has fifty-seven flavors; the popcorn vendor has twelve. At the newsstand, a dozen newspapers and twenty magazines beckon. On your flight over the Atlantic Ocean, you watch an Indiana Jones movie that has settings in eight locations around the world. You think it would be cute to make a phone call as you pass over Iceland, so you phone a friend. The meeting you're attending in Brussels concerns planning the future. Participants from eighty-seven countries all have something influential to say and you can purchase audio- or videotapes of the different speakers if you don't have time to attend the sessions during the meeting.

After the meeting, you arrive home in the United States to find ten calls on your answering machine and dozens of e-mail messages on your computer. Your mailbox is full, including two videotapes from friends in different cities, four different newsletters from various organizations, and some Christmas newsletters from friends who describe their family activities. You then realize that you feel obligated to send out a similar newsletter about your family to close friends. Would three hundred suffice?

You go into the den, where you had programmed your VCR to tape three programs while you were away. Frustrated because you don't have time to watch them, you flop into a chair and start flipping the remote control, switching among the thirty-seven channels. You're interrupted by a telephone call announcing an upcoming conference call of the other six state professional society officers. While you're talking, the conversation is interrupted by call waiting. Much to your dismay, it's an automatic recording pushing a political candidate. Soon, the doorbell buzzes; it's the next door neighbor informing you that while you were gone, your neighbor on the other side died. You didn't know him at all.

How can a "true self" withstand this constant bombardment of a thousand points of view and social interactions? We have become slaves to our wants and needs, which have recently multiplied. The wants create needs and the needs create obligations. Our number of social obligations escalates with the number of social contacts we have. We spend time with hordes of people, and digest huge amounts of information. All of these people and pursuits influence us a little, some a lot. We have thousands of possible selves tumbling about inside us, any one of which can be brought out at the right time and place.

Personal Models

We have a multiplicity of role models. The heavy influences of media personalities such as singers, actors, and athletes have a disproportionate effect on our personalities. We can't watch David Letterman's late night talk show year after year and not adopt some of his mannerisms. A woman who exists on a steady diet of soap operas and romance novels can't help incorporating some of the ideas she sees there into her life.

Privacy is under siege, which undermines individualism. Our personal information regarding income, marital status, and shopping habits is all on file and for sale by many sources. Led by celebrities in their exposé autobiographies and by exhibitionists on television talk shows, people feel free to air the personal travails of their lives. Not only is our privacy voluntarily relinquished, it is taken from us also; the personal lives of political candidates merit no respect from media hounds.

Beneath it all we still feel a sense of self-contempt, and we often describe ourselves with words like superficial, plastic, spineless, and wishy-washy. Forget it. If we are all superficial—and we are—then no one is superficial.

Changing Fundamental Institutions

In the past, individuals modeled their concept of self and behavior on certain absolutes and stabilities upon which they could depend, especially institutions like family, science, religion, history, and government. Today, we are constantly reminded that all of these institutions are wobbly. There no longer remains a valid worldview, or "big picture." The deconstruction of our institutions and belief systems consequently deconstructs our cherished concepts of soul and self.

The typical family is changing, as the traditional two-parent family falls into the minority. This has been caused by later marriage and childbirth, divorce, and individual longevity. In the last forty years the role model for mothers has changed rapidly, with many mothers working and many more caught up in all sorts of charitable, social, or political movements. An example of postmodern family problems: a racially mixed couple adopt an HIV-positive, mixed-race child and then divorce, creating a problem of child custody.

Science no longer provides simple answers. Today, scientists can't decide whether global warming exists, and, if it does, whether it's harmful. Many people blame scientific advances for overpopulation, pollution, nuclear weapons, and the near-tragedy at Three Mile Island. Currently, computerized information processing and robotics have eliminated many jobs and produced rising worldwide unemployment. With quantum mechanics resting on probability, not certainty, which seems contrary to Newtonian physics, we now doubt everything. There is no unchanging truth in science, only shifting paradigms. Werner Heisenberg's uncertainty principle and Gödel's theorem, showing that scientific measurement and even arithmetic are incomplete and cannot be proven consistent, have shaken the most fundamental underpinnings of science. Chaos theory now tells us that we can't predict events completely. Scientific understanding is controlled by fickle convention and fashionable language. The laws of physics are man-made. Compared with the overwhelming moral dilemmas facing us, detailed scientific findings can appear ineffective or irrelevant. Science has been dethroned as the final seat of intellectual authority, and nothing has taken its place. Into this void many irrational ideas have entered: romanticized New Age buncombe, many forms of now politically correct alternative medicine, and overblown antiscience rhetoric voiced by environmentalists and neo-Luddites.

Reason itself is no longer untouchable, even by scientists. Besides being impossible to define, logicians can't differentiate between reason, faith, sanity, or insanity, because reason itself, the subject in question, must be used to perform the differentiation.

Religion retains a large and devoted following. However, religious wars, the scandals of television evangelists, and the inability of faith to deal with pressing modern problems like potential nuclear holocaust or juvenile crime have turned many away from the faith of their fathers. People now change religions frequently and are increasingly apathetic about their faith, because there is more and more religious intermarriage and increased mobility. For many, situation ethics and moral pluralism have supplanted religion's moral absolutes.

History is subject to political whimsy and is today considered basically opinion, art rather than science. After all, only the winners of wars live to write history books. History is manipulated by the existing power, as we saw in the Soviet Union for many years. Whose version of history do you believe? We now have black history, and feminist history. Writers and publishers of history textbooks vouch for the pressures inflicted by those who push for their own ethnic, ideological, or gender social engineering. Historians now disagree about the causes of the American Revolution. All of the heroes of 1776 have been dissected and some scandalized. Even the story of Christopher Columbus is being constantly revised. Since most people don't care much about the accuracy of scholarly history, they're more interested in the movie and television miniseries portrayal—the media's history becomes the reality. We will more likely remember the mood of the post–Civil War era from *Gone with the Wind* than from more objective records of that war. Visitors to England want to see Robin Hood's Sherwood Forest, and those touring Notre Dame Cathedral are most intrigued by where the Hunchback lived.

In the past, we have derived a significant proportion of our self-identity from our nationality. Many have been proud to volunteer for war, only to return in flag-draped coffins. Today, with the demise of the Communist bloc and economic globalization, national zeal in most countries has moderated. Some exceptions are obvious, as in Bosnia, where ethnic differences have heightened and become politicized.

All of the once-revered institutions have been thoroughly dissected, including law, government, medicine, and religion. Lawyer jokes abound. The dirty linen of our star athletes as well as our leading politicians and government officials is aired. Debunked, all heroes have been damaged as role models. Multiculturists say that our education, which has been defined and determined by white males, is blemished.

Because we have no stable role models and no solid support for any of our belief systems, our sense of self is thrown into a blurred jumble. Since we can't use history or our popular cultural institutions to anchor us in time and space relative to our own self-image, we try to fall back on our understanding of the more basic facts of human life, which we will pursue in the next chapter.

Our ephemeral, chaotic culture dominates us as we try in vain to deny its influence. The plot becomes more convoluted in the remaining chapters, which conclude that our genes and physiology actually determine our behavior more than culture. Furthermore, our scientific culture is now able to tamper with our genetic makeup, and reciprocally, the tampering scientists' zeal is regulated by both their genes and their capricious culture.

References

Andersen, Kurt. "Pioneer's Vindication—Postmodern Architecture." *Time* (February 17, 1992).

Anderson, Walter Truett. *Reality Isn't What It Used to Be*. New York: Harper and Row, 1990.

Angell, Marcia. *Science on Trial*. New York: W. W. Norton, 1996.

Appleby, Joyce, Lynn Hunt, and Margaret Jacob. *Telling the Truth About History*. New York: W. W. Norton, 1993.

Borgmann, Albert. *Crossing the Postmodern Divide*. Chicago: University of Chicago Press, 1992.

Danto, Arthur C. *Beyond the Brillo Box: The Visual Arts in Post-Historical Perspective*. New York: Farrar, Straus, and Giroux, 1992.

Gergen, Kenneth J. *The Saturated Self: Dilemmas of Identity in Contemporary Life*. New York: Basic Books, 1991.

Hanson, F. Allan. *Testing, Testing: Social Consequences of the Examined Life*. Berkeley: University of California Press, 1992.

Kammen, Michael. *Mystic Chords of Memory: The Transformation of Tradition in American Culture*. New York: Alfred A. Knopf, 1991.

Kors, Alan Charles. *The Origin of the Modern Mind*, audiotape. Springfield, Va.: The Teaching Company.

Malone, Michael S. "Tethered to the Office Only by Technology." *New York Times* (November 1993).

Postman, Neil. *Technopoly: The Surrender of Culture to Technology*. New York: Alfred A. Knopf, 1992.

Roderick, Rick. *Philosophy and Human Values*, audiotape. Springfield, Va.: The Teaching Company.

Said, Edward W. *Culture and Imperialism*. New York: Alfred A. Knopf, 1992.

Sass, Louis A. *Madness and Modernism: Insanity in the Light of Modern Art, Literature, and Thought*. New York: Basic Books, 1992.

Trucco, Terry. "The State of the Art in Travel." *New York Times* (January 12, 1992): 15–19.

Yardley, Jonathan. "'Social Engineers' Rebuild History." *Memphis Commercial Appeal* (April 3, 1994).

11

What Is a Self?

It's hard to remain true to a changing self.

Ashleigh Brilliant

Since this book concerns *your behavior*, words that imply responsibility of a unique self, we should discuss this crucial word, *self*. Your self-image is a vital determinant of your behavior. But what actually is *yourself*, anyway? Is it your genetic makeup, your mind, your actions, your free choices, or a combination of these?

We've all had the experience of nervously facing an interview and having a relative or friend advise, "Just be yourself." You think to yourself, "Gosh, what the heck is my true self? Which one of my many possible selves should I *act* like?" In this chapter we will explore the meaning of *self* and the ways that our modern world confuses and contradicts our self-image, which is established by comparing ourselves with others and by our interpretations of the world around us. No attempt will be made to convince anyone of any particular position. The absence of conclusions, judgments, or recommendations may bring discomfort. The reality of our modern self is neither good nor bad. It just is—constantly changing.

Freud's contributions to the ideas of self (the unconscious mind) and the Zen Buddhist concept of no self will be mentioned in later chapters, as will the genetic aspects of self.

As will be discussed in the chapter on philosophy, the manifestations of the self exist only in the minds of different conscious beings, each one of us perceiving our self and others in our own, unique way. To a large degree, who you are depends upon the perspective of others. From an airplane you are a dot, when babies view the world from their crib you are a virtual god, from across the breakfast table you are sleepy but lovable, from the radiologist's fluoroscope you are moving shadows, and from the physicist's blackboard you are quarks and leptons. An acquaintance may think you are a bozo while someone else may consider you a hero.

I remember as a small child asking my mother about going to heaven. I wondered, "When we die and our souls go to heaven, what will we be like? Will we be kids or grownups, healthy or sick? Could we choose?" Even a child finds it tricky to define his or her self.

One year after a diving accident rendered him quadriplegic, a young athlete decided his life was not worth living and told his caretakers to cease feeding him. His family and doctors ignored the pleas of their patient/prisoner and began abdominal tube feedings. Others maintained that his dignity as a human being to make rational, free choices should be respected. The court eventually decided not to honor the young man's wishes, but instead mandated psychiatric consultation. After antidepressant medication, he no longer wanted to die, and derived reasonable enjoyment from watching television and dictating poetry. In retrospect, some erroneously assumed that this man had only one, unchanging self to respect.

Individuals who think they know their real selves just don't understand the problem. Trying to find the true self is like trying to find the true patterns in a rotating kaleidoscope. The truth is, we are incorrigible chameleons. There is a you, but, like everything else in our postmodern, existentialist world, it is constantly in flux. Acknowledging his past and future self, the existentialist philosopher Jean Paul Sartre said, "I am not what I am, and I am what I am not." Self not only shifts with time, but with physiology, culture, and personality-altering drugs, such as Prozac and Ritalin.

The Historical Self

The concept of self that we understand today has not always existed. When did it start? I arbitrarily think of natural humans as the hunter-gatherers of fifty thousand years ago. Those people had basically the same genetic makeup that we have today, but their culture had not yet been changed drastically by farming and, later, industrialization. Essentially, in hundreds of thousands of years, evolution had, up until that point, prepared humans for a hunter-gatherer life.

These natural people didn't have the constant need for encouragement with respect to self-recognition the way we modern humans have. Being part of a nomadic group that

worked as a team, the men fulfilled roles of hunting and protecting the family, while the women gathered additional
food, cooked, and cared for the children. Existing mainly in
relation to their family and tribe, these people saw no change
from generation to generation and weren't bombarded by
thousands of different social interactions, advertisements,
and rhetoric by media and politicians. They did not know
about individual rights and hadn't read Ayn Rand's *Atlas
Shrugged* (published in 1957), which lionizes independence.

Anthropologists say that many of today's tribal cultures
don't include the concept of the individual that is widespread in the Western world. Their life is group life, with
activities of hunting and harvesting requiring mutual cooperation and obedience to tribal customs. For example, in Bali,
the language expressing a unique self is minimal because the
individual is considered part of a broad social complex.

Concerned more with the cosmos than the individual,
early Greek thinkers made great scientific strides in geometry and astronomy. It was the oracle at Delphi that codified
an awareness of the individual ("Know thyself"), a concept
that inspired Plato, Aristotle, and Augustine much later.

For centuries, we have been ambivalent about the concept
of self. The religious-romantic concept of soul or spirit has
been with us at least from the time of the ancient Greek
philosophers. Plato actually mentioned the soul of an individual. However, he also thought that since individuals
derived their language and values from the surrounding
society, they were subservient to the society and state. The
Greeks, however, introduced the concept of democracy controlled by individual citizens.

After the barbarian invasions, Greek thought was lost to
Western culture for several centuries. In the early Middle

Ages, philosophers taught that individuals were worthless in the sight of an all-powerful God. Names didn't really designate individuality; rather, they described class, religion, occupation, or locale: the Earl of Bath, Friar Tuck, William the Barber, or Anne of Coventry. Being part of a caste, people had expectations that limited their individuality. They dressed according to their class and wore appropriate social attire. The architecture of most homes did not reflect respect for the individual, for there were no individual rooms for privacy.

The medieval guild system suppressed individual competition in business; capitalism and concepts of private property were insignificant until the Renaissance, beginning in the fourteenth century. Economic arrangements were chiefly under political and ecclesiastical domination, with little individual enterprise. Those living during medieval times accepted authority for security and protection. The communal life provided by the manorial system suppressed individuality in the serfs (peasant class). To be self-centered was considered sinful and indulgent. Marriages were arranged and behavior was controlled by rigid religious constraints.

In the twelfth century the concept of individual romantic love, at first considered heretical and counterculture, arose. In the Tristan and Isolde romance, Tristan insists on loving Isolde despite condemnation by the church and the threat of everlasting punishment in hell. Romantic love now meant people were unique and could make a choice. During the thirteenth century, the works of Aristotle and other Greek thinkers, which had been preserved by the Moors in what is now Spain, filtered into Europe. An appreciation of the individual self began to appear in several ways. People adopted last names, created wills, and prepared individual tombs. The increasing division of labor in the workplace also fostered individualism, as occupational specialization encouraged greater differentiation among people. During the Renaissance, Machiavelli's *The Prince* acknowledged that politics was based on individual human activity. According to the *Oxford English Dictionary*, it wasn't until the middle of the seventeenth century that the word *self* was used in its modern context, along with other derivations like selfish and self-deception. During the eighteenth century's Enlightenment, individualism was voiced more clearly by the philosopher Immanuel Kant: "Dare to use *your own* reason." The self now bore the burden of individual responsibility.

The religious concept of the soul, mixed with emotion and romanticism, prevailed in the nineteenth century, when an inner, mystical being was exalted. Abiding love and devotion were praised. Character and personal morality were considered of great value, which developed the idea of the genuine hero and altruist.

Although they had been present since the days of Aristotle, in the eighteenth and nineteenth centuries other parallel concepts began to gain influence: reason and science. When Isaac Newton described a mechanistic universe, the supremacy of the soul began to be doubted. Later Charles Darwin's work diminished humans further, by placing us among animals in an unfeeling, competitive world. The work of Gregor Mendel (1822–1884) in genetics added to Darwin's theory. Bertrand Russell claimed that the social sciences would produce an understanding of human behavior as precise as mathematics. Utilitarian ethical concepts (the greatest good for the largest number) offered a simplified calculation for deciding ethical behavior. Psychologists thought they could measure the self with personality and IQ tests. With the prominence of the twentieth-century behaviorists, such as

B. F. Skinner, the idea grew that you could create your own child through behavior modification, just as you would build a machine. This scientific, modernist concept was upbeat and promised a self that we could understand, control, and fix. Among many, the mystical soul of the individual was "out."

In the last few decades, individualism has been "in." Such books as Ayn Rand's *The Virtue of Selfishness* (1961) and *The Fountainhead* (1952) promoted egoism and individual action. Robert Ringer's *Looking Out for Number One* (1977) and Wayne Dyer's *Pulling Your Own Strings* (1978) were best-sellers. We were all encouraged to "do our own thing." Abraham Maslow's hierarchical approach to psychology emphasized self-actualization as the highest form of human behavior. "Be all that you can be" and "I did it my way" were popular slogans. Feminism, which encourages the revision of societal roles to release the potential of the individual woman, flourished. Existentialism, a very influential philosophical movement during this century, extols the individual who stands heroically alone in a meaningless, impersonal world and makes his or her own decisions, thereby creating meaning to his or her own life. There is much interest now in the psychiatric concepts of self, concerning addiction and depression. The interest du jour is codependency, which warns us not to get wrapped up in others at the expense of ourselves. We are told that since we can't change, control, or be responsible for others, we should simply take care of ourselves.

Frustration in the Search for Self

We are encouraged to be our true selves. Polonius warns us in *Hamlet*, "To thine own self be true." We are told to be genuine, unadulterated, to put on no acts or affectations, to speak our own minds, to be intellectually independent. It is considered a disgrace to lead an inauthentic life and to act contrary to the true self. Forget it. If you're living, you're changing. Even after you are dead, the memory of you in others' minds is subtly shifting. Considering the rapid change in our minds caused by education, travel, and media bombardment, an attempt to live as a pure individual is frustrating. Who are you, anyway? Rapid cultural alterations assure no stability or constant image with which we can model and judge ourselves.

We still cling to the idea that the natural person is more deserving than people who have artificially produced themselves. The person of natural beauty is awarded a greater status than one who uses cosmetics and plastic surgery. We applaud the natural, precocious athlete more than one who has trained long and diligently or the one who has used steroids to attain the same achievement. We enjoy the idea of natural genius of an Einstein or a Newton, both of whom gained fame in their twenties. The composer Mozart, Elvis Presley, and Stevie Wonder are considered natural because they were nonacculturated and performed using their innate capabilities at a young age. Genuine folk artists also enjoy this elevated status. Rev. Howard Finster is celebrated for seeing religious visions and painting them in a totally unaffected way.

In the late nineteenth century, Friedrich Nietzsche (1844–1900) mentioned that there is no immutable self behind our many masks. None of us can become an authentic self, but only the best and most interesting self that we can create, like painting our life. But, as we have already explored, our modern mass culture splashes on too much paint.

Changes in Life's Basics

We all think we know the basic facts: we are alive, we are male or female, and we have the rights of a human being, which we consider preeminent. Our self-image is constructed by bouncing it off of these apparent verities. However, all of these fundamentals are now being questioned scientifically and legally.

The legal and moral definitions of life are now debatable. Does a fertilized ovum in a test tube or a frozen embryo have rights? Is it alive? Does life begin at fertilization? At quickening? Life has no scientific definition, only changing legal ones. We read that scientists will soon be able to produce primitive forms of life in the organic chemistry laboratory. Even now, some computer programs qualify, since they are able to replicate themselves and to evolve over generations into more advanced types; they explore the Internet and find information; they learn and adapt like the beaks of Darwin's finches. Artificial intelligence advocates predict that a robot will eventually become so competent that humans will be unable to tell by written language whether they are corresponding with a computer or a human. If we can't recognize the fake, what difference does it make?

Definitions of death become nebulous, too. We now have varying legal definitions of brain death. Is a brain-absent anencephalic infant brain-dead? We even know that certain cells in the hair and fingernails continue to live and function months after we die. Cryonics, the process of freezing a corpse in the hope of thawing it at a more advantageous later date, is still not taken seriously by the scientific community. It is watched with hopeful interest, however. Of more immediate impact is the recent ability to freeze testicular sperm-producing stem cells, thus preserving an individual's genetic line indefinitely ("biological immortality").

Further, regarding basic concepts of life, self, and mind, there is the problem of the split-brain personality. Individuals who have had accidental or surgical severing of the midline corpus callosum of the brain, creating two separate hemispheres, sometimes respond neurologically like two different individuals with unique personalities.

The definition of functional life gets murky. We now see plastic security guards standing in doorways who are impossible to distinguish from real ones. We might sit down next to one in a museum and strike up a conversation with this silent creature. Department store mannequins look extremely realistic. People actually admit to being turned on by buxom cartoon character Jessica Rabbit in the movie *Who Framed Roger Rabbit* (1988). What constitutes a true human being is further complicated by people with changes in their anatomy, such as those with kidney and heart transplants, breast implants, and artificial limbs.

Even gender is not always definite now. We can't assume someone is simply male or female, thanks to transvestites and sex-change operations. There are also androgynous characters, such as Boy George or Prince. Michael Jackson, with his multiple plastic surgical procedures and skin alteration, represents ambiguity in both gender and race. Female body builders have drifted more toward the male image. Some feminists encourage androgynous clothing and manner. We now have unisex cologne with names like "Deceived" and "Ricochet." Science cannot provide a simple answer as to who is male and who is female in terms of cellular sex chromatin microscopic analysis. Hormonally, and in physical appearance, many individuals fit somewhere between male and female. The medical committee of the International

Amateur Athletic Federation has recommended that to determine gender, the complicated genetic tests be abandoned in favor of simply looking at the athletes' genitals; the thinking is that it is unfair to single out X and Y chromosomes as sole determinants of gender.

The line between humans and other animal life is not as easily drawn as we have thought. We have always felt assured that as human beings we are the highest form of life and should enjoy the privilege of such. Animal rights activists question this, however, particularly concerning primates with IQs much higher than severely retarded humans. In 1992, a flap occurred in the news about Timmy, a Cleveland zoo gorilla, being shipped to New York for stud duty and being made to leave his steady mate, Kribi Kate, whom he cuddles and has sex with. The veterinarian president of the Defense of Animals actually hired an attorney to protect Timmy's rights as an emotional individual. Primates can think, emote, speak by signing, and use tools. There is no definitive qualitative difference between humans and primates. The human genetic code is more than 98 percent identical to the chimpanzee code, which is one of the reasons chimpanzee and baboon hearts and livers have been transplanted into humans. We like to exaggerate the differences between humans and other higher life forms to salve our guilt feelings when we enslave them, eat them, or wear their fur/hide.

Human intelligence, self-awareness, and speech have set us apart from the other animals, but we may need to reexamine this belief in our natural superiority. Whales, dolphins, and porpoises have brains complex enough to suggest that their intelligence may equal that of humans and that they are self-aware. Whales, for example, communicate through song and have definite social interactions.

We are now having to consider the effects on individual human autonomy of recent biologic manipulations such as germ-line gene therapy, in which injected genetic material actually becomes part of an individual's genetic makeup and can be passed on to offspring.

All of these concerns impugn our simple notions of human life, the mind, and the relation of self to them.

Personal Relations

Describing a person is like describing a hole in a piece of wood. The hole can only be described in terms of what surrounds it, its very existence being derived from the shape, texture, and color of the wood. People likewise are defined by their culture and their roles in personal relations. It is impossible to be a star football player without lesser players, to be a senator without a senate, or to be a human without being a child with a mother and father. When asked to describe ourselves, we usually approach this in the familiar resume format, emphasizing our education, family, and work history— all parameters of our interaction with others. As we will discuss in the chapter on philosophy, the Asian concept of humans is more grounded in relations to the entire universe—when we dance, the entire universe dances. In Asian philosophy, the idea of the self is considered beyond description, and the cultivated absence of self-awareness is pursued. In the ultimate analysis, the self and all things in the universe are one. We are, at our cores, united. A healthy mental attitude includes identifying with humanity as a whole as well as with other individuals, such as family members and friends.

With the increasing superficial social interaction and disruption of family life in our modern world, we play so many roles and enter and leave so many others' lives that our relational self has become indeterminate. We strategically manipulate ourselves, depending upon those with whom we interact. It is normal to modify our actions in appropriate social circumstances, but it is difficult to determine when this practice becomes excessive. When role-playing gets out of hand, becoming unconscious, the person may suffer from a psychiatric condition known as multiple personality disorder. Our mobile world, with its shallow, calculated, impersonal relationships, dilutes the pleasure we derive from deeper human connectedness. Nevertheless, relations continue to be important in forming our self-image. Since we are all playing different roles, the role we play depends upon the specific type of audience. Are we acting in front of our boss, our children, or a foreign visitor? We engage in such rapid changes in interpersonal relations that we are like actors with twenty different roles in one play.

We mistakenly fancy ourselves as being somehow separate from the rest of nature, being oblivious to the many connections with our surroundings and our unconscious mind. The philosopher Alan Watts said we think of ourselves as "an island of consciousness locked up in a bag of skin." Such an independent creature is as mythical as a unicorn. An isolated individual is helpless. Like honeybees, we are social entities cared for and defined by countless social interdependencies, whether they be family, education, occupation, or country. Our identity depends on our relations with others—and these others change. For instance, we would change drastically if our spouse became a drug addict, or died. Our reputations also depend on the fickle opinion of others.

A woman's concept of self has been anchored in personal

relations; she sees herself as part of the family. However, some confusion exists about women's role because they are now encouraged to be independent, frontline soldiers and fire fighters, but at the same time they are expected to report any minimal sexual harassment as if they were frail, helpless flowers.

A man's self-image is more centered around occupation. Men have learned from their culture to have their self-esteem revolve around their ability to provide financially for the family. This is partially biological in nature because the genetic endowment to provide for one's family assured the propagation of the genes that did so. A place at work is critical for establishing a place in larger society. At cocktail parties, people ask, "What do you do?" A man totally involved in his work who neglects other areas of his life eventually realizes that his work means nothing without relating to others who can appreciate it.

The overall image of American men today is at a low ebb. Because all heroes have been debunked, young men have few worthy role models. Television sitcoms usually portray the father figure as a fool. The proud image of man as warrior and king is now fashionably passé. A son often sees his father as a detached, irritable creature preoccupied with television sports. Men are now encouraged to participate more in domestic household duties and child care, which produces a further blurring of their traditional role and self-image.

Constructing One's Mask

Today, we are more inclined to change our behavior in a conscious way with respect to interpersonal relations and to force others to change. Employers mold their employees' behavior by evaluating them constantly. In my hospital I once had to make quarterly reports on radiology department employees, filling out pages of itemized categories and rating employees from one to ten on appearance, cleanliness, speech, and phone etiquette. These reports were intended to encourage employees to alter their behavior to fit the hospital model. Many employees in fast food restaurants apparently memorize a specific number of words to say to each customer, like living robots.

There are numerous devices for self-marketing. We can take the Dale Carnegie course on how to be popular, or read a book on how to train our voice for success. We now consider it acceptable to enhance our image by having cosmetic surgery. Changing our personality and ideology is also more respectable; it's not considered superficial and deceitful but flexible and versatile. Personal image consultants give us advice on clothing, tell us what colors we look best in, and even give instructions on table manners, such as recommending that when asked to pass the salt we should pass the pepper as well.

If the produced image of a woman or man is better than the actual man or woman, what difference does it make? As flashy-dressing tennis star Andre Agassi has said on a television commercial, "Image is everything." One of the basic ideas espoused in the "success" books is that looking prosperous not only changes others' responses to you, but also changes your own self-image, consequently creating success from within. If your dress influences your personal self-image, then multiplying such disguises can establish a self-image that is incoherent, sometimes leading to confusion and depression.

Leading U.S. political candidates set the example by

unabashedly surrendering themselves to image consultants, political strategists, and speech writers who often effect a total remake of the candidates, even if this means reversing the candidates' long standing positions on major issues such as taxation and abortion. These sometimes disreputable advisors have no allegiance to political ideology but their role gives them an inordinate covert influence on the country. Image consultants today feel that our created and perceived image is not phony, that it is the ultimate reality. Apparently, the national psyche is such that we accept the way image-makers exploit the practical reality that there is no authentic, enduring self. People want a figurehead who dresses and acts in the approved manner. Our politicians are just playing the right game for the modern world, and winning elections. The wise politician today does not take truth and reality very seriously, realizing that both are created.

Leaders are now expected to change their acts with the times. Any leader who tries to be his or her true self, with unwavering and deep beliefs, is suspected of being a rigid and neurotic egomaniac who might put his own bias into major decisions. Leaders who compromise and do the politically expedient and diplomatic thing are accepted more comfortably by the populace.

Throughout all of this, we are still made uneasy by the struggles within us. The modern world tells us to be mobile and change with the winds to make ourselves over into the appropriately packaged entity. Other philosophies teach us to be true to ourselves and to loathe phonies. These two competing desires are like two donkeys tied tail to tail. Mental health authorities have long advised us to have a stable integrated personality and they have labeled as mentally ill those having a "split personality" or an "identity crisis." But for effective coping in today's world it is mandatory for us to be versatile and innovative.

Facing Up to the Self

The self is socially determined. We are *only* our momentarily constructed, evanescent selves. We tend to deny this because it's hard to live with. The actor in us has won out in the world, de facto.

We no longer have a stable foundation for socially approved methods of behavior and beliefs. The present belief systems are too obscure and diverse, and the old systems are stale. Our self only mirrors the state of society, which is chaotic and uncertain. Even our opinion of ourselves carries the faulty judgment borrowed from our fallible culture.

Dr. Walter Truett Anderson, in his insightful review of our changing world, *Reality Isn't What It Used to Be* (1990), mentions this predicament. "When we step out of a reality to examine it, we step into a reality in which it is possible to examine realities, and that wider terrain is itself a culture, a custom. The idea of the social construction of reality is itself an SCR, and this book is a story. Learning about such things, continually reexamining beliefs, becomes the most important learning task of all the others needed for survival in our time."

But we shouldn't necessarily be depressed by the lack of support for our self. Many consider it a liberating concept that opens all sorts of possibilities, both good and bad. In *The Saturated Self* (1991), Kenneth Gergen writes a fitting summary of our postmodern consciousness: "We see the demise of personal definition, reason, authority, commitment, trust, the sense of authenticity, sincerity, belief in leadership, depth of feeling, and faith in progress. In their stead, an open slate emerges on which persons may inscribe, erase, and rewrite their identities as the ever-shifting, ever-expanding, and incoherent network of relationships invites or permits."

As we become more aware of the complexities of the changing self, we agonize in deciding whether someone is truly guilty of a crime. Which, of many selves, is to blame—the victim of society? the previously abused child? the temporarily insane?

In the future, there will be an increase in our present superenculturization. With more and more elaborate television exposure leading to continuous virtual reality stimulation, designer drugs controlling our emotions, and cyborgs "thinking" for us, will the space for our conscious self be squeezed to naught? Is conscious self-awareness a mere temporary, failed trial in human evolution?

References

Anderson, Walter Truett. *Reality Isn't What It Used to Be*. New York: Harper and Row, 1990.

Bandow, Doug. "A President in Need of a Vision." *New York Times* (January 12, 1992).

Cavalieri, Paola, and Peter Singer. *The Great Ape Project*. New York: St. Martin's Press, 1993.

Cooper, Morton. *Change Your Voice, Change Your Life*. New York: Harper and Row, 1984.

Csikszentmihalyi, Mihaly. *The Evolving Self*. New York: Harper-Collins, 1993.

Dyer, Wayne W. *Pulling Your Own Strings*. Thomas Y. Crowell Co., 1978.

Eaton, S. Boyd, Marjori Shostak, and M. Konner. *The Paleolithic Prescription*. New York: Harper and Row, 1988.

Elster, Jon. *The Multiple Self: Studies in Rationality and Social Change*. Cambridge: Cambridge University Press, 1987.

Gergen, Kenneth J. *The Saturated Self: Dilemmas of Identity in Contemporary Life*. New York: Basic Books, 1991.

Greenwald, Jerry. *Be the Person You Were Meant to Be*. New York: Dell, 1973.

Hewitt, John P. *Dilemmas of the American Self*. Philadelphia: Temple University Press, 1989.

Kripalani, Manjeet. "The Image Merchants." *Forbes* (November 25, 1991): 212.

Linkemer, Bobbi. *Polishing Your Professional Image*. Amacom, American Management Associations, 1987.

Lifton, Robert Jay. *The Protean Self: Human Resilience in an Age of Fragmentation*. New York: Basic Books, 1993.

Ljungqvist, Arne, and Joe Leight Simpson. "Medical Examination for Health of All Athletes Replacing the Need for Gender Verification in International Sports." *Journal of the American Medical Association* 26 (1992): 850.

Molloy, John T. *The Woman's Dress for Success Book*. Warner Books, 1977.

Ornstein, Robert. *The Roots of the Self: Unraveling the Mystery of Who We Are*. San Francisco: HarperCollins, 1993.

Peterson, Dale, and Jane Goodall. *Visions of Caliban: On Chimpanzees and People*. Boston: Houghton Mifflin, 1992.

Rand, Ayn. *The Virtue of Selfishness: A New Concept of Egoism*. New York: Signet Book, New American Library, 1961.

Ringer, Robert J. *Looking Out for Number One*. Funk and Wagnalls, 1977.

Roderick, Rick. *Philosophy and Human Values*, audiotape. Springfield, Va.: The Teaching Company.

Rosenberg, Jay F. *The Thinking Self*. New York: Temple University Press, 1986.

Shweder, Richard A. "What Do Men Want? A Reading List for the Male Identity Crisis." *New York Times* (January 9, 1994).

Smith, John E., John Lachs, and Mike Hassell, eds. *The Giants of Philosophy: George William Friedrich Hegel*, Audio Classics Series narrated by Charlton Heston. Nashville, Tenn.: Knowledge Products.

Storr, Anthony. *Solitude: A Return to the Self.* New York: Free Press/Macmillan, 1988.

Taylor, Charles. *The Ethics of Authenticity.* Cambridge, Mass.: Harvard University Press, 1992.

12

Unconscious Mandates

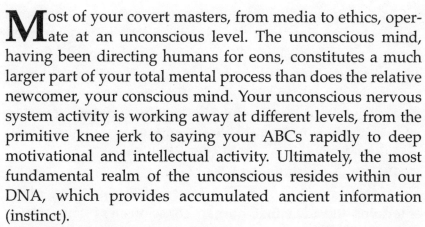

Most of your covert masters, from media to ethics, operate at an unconscious level. The unconscious mind, having been directing humans for eons, constitutes a much larger part of your total mental process than does the relative newcomer, your conscious mind. Your unconscious nervous system activity is working away at different levels, from the primitive knee jerk to saying your ABCs rapidly to deep motivational and intellectual activity. Ultimately, the most fundamental realm of the unconscious resides within our DNA, which provides accumulated ancient information (instinct).

Consciousness means attentive awareness of a specific thought, such as an admitted emotion, or noticing some form of sensory stimulus, such as hearing or seeing. We are all able to designate the point at which a headache finally reaches the conscious stage, or when an emotion, such as happiness, is verbalized to ourselves. Consciousness also implies an ability to differentiate ourselves from others in time and space and also entails being reflectively conscious of our own consciousness (metaconsciousness).

Most authorities agree that consciousness and language are interrelated and interdependent. A child starts to develop consciousness after age two, at about the same time that language skills develop. So it was with prehistoric man—consciousness developed along with language. Both entail selecting one specific item for attention from a large, complex source. We have a huge amount of information that is accessible in our memories. In this regard, conscious thinking is analogous to using a tiny pen light to read when there has been a power outage in a huge library.

At some point during evolution, consciousness developed to handle new decisions that were not already programmed into our nervous system. We acquired consciousness, which is a small, specific focus of our total mind, so that we could communicate with others more efficiently. Consciousness had survival value. In order to reduce the massive volume of material in our minds to a workable amount, we shortened a complex thought to one punctuated symbol, a word.

Princeton psychologist Julian Jaynes, in his book *The Origin of Consciousness in the Breakdown of the Bicameral Mind*, entertains the idea that human consciousness came much later in history than most people assume and that we were able to reason without it. In *Evolution and Consciousness*, philosophy professor Leslie Dewart makes the case for speech preceding and generating consciousness in the development of primitive man. He also believes this sequence is the same in the small child, because when the child begins to speak he differentiates himself from the rest of reality and becomes consciously self-aware.

Scientists remain puzzled by the physics and chemistry of consciousness in the brain. Roger Penrose, in *The Emperor's New Mind*, says that consciousness is related somehow with quantum mechanics and will never be produced in a robot (in contrast to unconscious processes, which may be algorithmic). Today, many people are so impressed by computers that they compare the brain to a computer, but most scientists maintain that machines are a poor metaphor for our brains and our minds. Imagine asking a computer cyborg how it feels to be a computer or if it is happy.

Neurosurgeons and anatomists are also unsure whether there exists a specific location in the brain that mediates consciousness. The cerebral cortex (the outer layers of the hemispheres) and the hippocampus (fibers extending into the temporal lobes), among others, have both been given the honor. Nobel laureate Francis Crick now believes that connections between the thalamus (the deep midbrain) and the cerebral cortex are crucial to consciousness. Since language and consciousness are interrelated, and since language is handled mainly by the left side of the brain, the left side is now getting more credit for handling consciousness.

The concept of mind is much broader than consciousness, since the latter is not the same thing as perception. An insect perceives a flower by its vision and smell, but it is not aware that it resides on a flower. Humans can perceive quite a bit through their senses without being conscious of these perceptions. We can drive a car, all the while seeing surrounding cars and traffic lights, and actually be consciously aware only of the news on the radio. We can run down a basketball court and be oblivious on a conscious level to pressure on the soles of our feet or a cheering crowd. Consciousness involves the separation of one particular aspect from our sensory input of multiple stimuli. We can, for instance, become aware of the pressure of the chair upon our left buttock. We can call forth and concentrate on a specific item from our unconscious mind, such as the visual image of a loved one or a song that we enjoy. Often, we notice one specific emotion on a conscious awareness level, but moods and attitudes remain unconscious functions, as do imagination, tact, taste, and common sense.

We can be conscious of only one thing at a time. Try thinking of a polar bear and the taste of pepperoni pizza at the same time. During their first tennis lesson, people get frustrated when told to concentrate on bending their knees, taking a full backswing, focusing on the ball, and making a full follow-through swing. When the ball is speeding toward them, they must choose only one of these things to be aware of, and only after much practice can they submerge all of the others (and more) into their unconscious. When attempting complex somersaults and twists, competitive divers rely predominantly on their unconscious.

Upon reaching full consciousness, a child develops language sufficiently to represent past, present, and future, and is then fully subject to the constraints of time-bound, conscious life. She is then able to worry about the future and about herself and to eventually realize that she will someday die.

History of the Unconscious

Plato mentioned certain aspects of our mental activity that are automatic, saying that we are not aware of each step that we take. In the seventeenth century, Spinoza, a philosopher with an interest in psychology, believed that many of our passions are caused by anxieties of which we are not aware. He warned us to understand the cause of our emotions. G. W. F. Hegel (1770–1831) discussed our inability to think of two things consciously at once. Specifically, we are unable to think of our simple conscious self and our complex changing self simultaneously. Before Freud, Schopenhauer noted the distinctness of the unconscious, saying, "Consciousness is the mere surface of our mind. We do not know the interior." He maintained that we can have a desire for years without admitting it to ourselves or even letting it come to clear consciousness. Also before Freud, Anton Mesmer (1734–1815) studied the unconscious by hypnosis, seeking to uncover deep emotional forces of which the individual is unaware. Freud was merely the first to popularize the concept that the unconscious mind motivates us. He discarded hypnosis as a tool to study the unconscious, which he felt was inaccessible if certain memories had been too deeply repressed due to early trauma. Freud also posited a level of our minds called the "preconscious," which permits easy access to the unconscious (such as when we need to recall someone's name).

Unconscious Reflexes

Flashing a word like *pain* on a screen for a thousandth of a second happens too quickly for us to perceive it consciously, but our brainwaves are altered almost immediately. Later, if the same word is flashed in a slower manner that is easily seen, it registers in the conscious mind, but alteration of brainwaves occurs somewhat later. This demonstrates that the unconscious mind perceives things more rapidly than the conscious mind. Flashing a word subliminally (very fast) will not register in the conscious mind of the subject but will affect our choice of words subsequent to our unconscious perception of the word.

Subliminally flashed "dirty" words are less likely to be seen in the conscious mind than are neutral words like *book*. Our unconscious apparently feels guilty about seeing such taboo words and doesn't admit them to our consciousness.

Are subliminal messages effective teachers and motivators? If you listen to commercial tapes designed to help you lose weight, all you hear is soothing music or ocean waves, because the suggestions are placed at decibel levels that are perceived only unconsciously. Some controversy exists about the effectiveness of subliminal advertising and subliminal tapes for learning and motivation. Although you can, indeed, process information subliminally, there is no guarantee that your behavior will change. Most advertising experts have abandoned subliminal efforts because they have been shown to be ineffective and possibly illegal.

Positron emission tomography scans can now provide real-time images of changes in particular areas of the brain caused by thinking. These show that unconscious processes precede or parallel conscious ones. If your brainwaves are measured when you consciously decide to move your thumb, they are recorded as changing a full second before your thumb moves. But if you have been conditioned to move your thumb at the flash of a light, the unconscious reaction time is about one-fifth of a second. When you must choose between red or blue lights in order to react, the reaction time is about two-fifths of a second.

A voluntary act actually begins in the unconscious mind,

contrary to our commonsense impression that we first decide to do something in our conscious mind, and then actions follow. That the unconscious mind is ahead of the conscious mind indicates that the unconscious controls the conscious.

Consider the "simple" act of running. In fact, running requires a vastly complicated set of reflexes sustained by constant sensory receptions of pressure in the feet and appropriate motor responses. For instance, the forward movement of your leg stimulates receptors in the leg that cause it to move back again. You have many such reflexes: swallowing, pupil contraction, coughing, and the like.

Since a simple spinal cord reflex (as occurs with touching a hot stove) requires no conscious action, it happens very fast. We're all familiar with how the knee jerks when someone taps on the tendon below the knee cap. That reflex happens in one-fiftieth of a second, because it bypasses the higher cerebral decision centers. You can inhibit the knee jerk, however, if you consciously concentrate on trying to do so. With conscious thought, impulses from the cerebral cortex extend down and inhibit the automatic spinal cord reaction.

Just as our breathing is controlled by a center in the medulla (the brain stem), many other activities are purely unconscious and reflexive in nature. While eating fish, suddenly you sense that there is a bone in the bite you are chewing and, automatically, a tiny bone appears between your lips that you pluck out with your thumb and index finger. This is performed without sight of the bone—a truly amazing feat of athletic ability by the tongue and lips!

Screening Our Environment

Most of our mental activity is, by necessity, unconscious. The unconscious screens out the huge amount of chaotic, irrelevant information that constantly bombards our senses, thus protecting us from being overwhelmed and confused by the mass of sensory input. For example, we notice only occasionally that we are uncomfortable sitting in a certain position and need to change. Likewise, at a level of stimulation that exceeds the threshold selected by our unconscious, we decide to use the bathroom; lower levels of bladder discomfort have been kept in the unconscious. When we walk, we don't decide to put one foot in front of the other because this information is too routine for the conscious mind. Since only one thing at a time can be presented to the conscious mind, the unconscious prioritizes and selects.

There are many examples of how the unconscious screens vast amounts of sensory perception, like hearing your name mentioned at a cocktail party in a crowded room, or quickly seeing your name on a page in the newspaper. Since you can think of only one thing at a time, the unconscious filters out the other thousand words on the page and points out your name. At the hospital, doctors hear their name paged while remaining oblivious to other names being paged. A mother can hear her baby cry over all sorts of extraneous sounds. Speed readers can grasp the essence of an entire page, as hundreds of words get submerged into the unconscious and only the gist of the meaning of the page registers in the conscious mind. We are continuously discarding extraneous information that our unconscious deems unimportant, but, when it suddenly becomes important, we perceive it consciously.

Try this experiment: Turn on several radios, tune them to different stations, close your eyes, and try to listen to only one radio. It's easier than you think. It is as if you made all the other radio programs disappear. The only station that exists in your consciousness is the one you have selected to hear.

If you suddenly received a free trip to Bulgaria, you might be hesitant to go because you probably know nothing about Bulgaria. While planning your trip, as you read newspapers and magazines over the next few days, items about Bulgaria will amazingly begin to jump out at you. You'll notice news about political turmoil in Bulgaria, or about a Bulgarian athlete. While shopping, Bulgarian buttermilk will draw your attention. Since you now need to know something about Bulgaria, your unconscious mind selects these things from the array of information that had always been there, but had previously been screened out of your consciousness.

Superiority of the Unconscious

Most people live their entire lives with a mistaken idea about a very important aspect of themselves—namely the unconscious mind. Many people think it is an unreliable second-class citizen in the brain. Many tend to associate our unconscious with primitive reflex actions and regard the conscious mind as the superior mental state. However, since we can unconsciously carry out highly intellectual tasks and make plans for the future, our unconscious mind is probably superior to our conscious mind and may even lead it. When an idea pops into our minds, where does it come from? Our unconscious has been giving it thorough consideration.

Nietzsche said that in relation to the vastness and multiplicity of the life of every organism, the conscious world of feelings and valuations is a small section. It is a mistake to posit our consciousness as the aim and purpose of the total phenomenon of life. He also wrote, "A thought comes when it will, not when I will."

Facts dwell in our unconscious that surprise us. For example, when a trivia question is presented to us, sometimes an answer comes into our minds out of the blue. I recall the question, "Who was the backup singing group for Roy Rogers?" I thought I had no idea, but amazingly the correct words, "Sons of the Pioneers," emerged from my lips. We must not underestimate the accuracy of our unconscious depths. We can suddenly realize that we have driven a car for two miles and have been driving unconsciously and safely the entire time.

Intuition, creative flashes, and momentary insights are all manifestations of the unconscious. Jean Jacques Rousseau (1712–1778) mentioned intuition as being "the sovereign intelligence which sees in a twinkle of an eye the truth in all things, in contradistinction to vain and deceptive knowledge."

We often diminish the accuracy of the unconscious by exerting conscious effort. Typists or pianists might be performing flawlessly on an unconscious level, but when somebody looks over their shoulder and makes them conscious of what they are doing, they become inhibited and make mistakes. In sports, when we are too self-conscious and think about some detail of our movements, we are apt to play poorly. The wise coach calls a time out before an important field goal or free throw attempt by the opposing team. This allows more time for inhibitory conscious thoughts to "ice" a player. When we try too hard to go to sleep, we can't. We have all been asked a question such as, "What's that man's name over there?" and replied, "If you hadn't asked me, I could have told you." This is an example of *preconscious material* becoming temporarily inaccessible because of resistances made by inhibiting conscious effort. If you can't remember someone's name, but it's on the "tip of your tongue," trying hard to remember it is usually fruitless. It will come to you later when you're no longer trying.

Certain areas of recall are inaccessible to consciousness. You should seriously respect your hunches or gut feelings, because they often represent your unconscious mind telling you the truth. For example, we may, for some unknown reason, sense that a person is excited. Our unconscious mind perceives that this person's pupils are dilated, but this fact never enters our conscious awareness.

We perform many mundane tasks, such as tying shoelaces, on an unconscious level, and do a good job of it. If we try to explain how we tie them, we become so inhibited that we have difficulty doing so. We brush our teeth while thinking of something else, going from the uppers to the lowers and including cheek surfaces and tongue surfaces according to lifetime habits. We write unconsciously, actually thinking several words ahead of what we are writing.

First impressions, such as on multiple choice tests, are often correct when compared with later deliberation. At times, I have to trust my unconscious gestalt when interpreting X-rays. A gestalt is a unified psychological perception having properties that cannot be derived from its parts. Too much measuring can lead me astray or inhibit my diagnosis—"paralysis through analysis."

We all tend to trust our head over our heart, not appreciating that our heart (metaphorically, our unconscious) may be more accurate and rational. Blaise Pascal (1623–1662) said,

"The heart has reasons which the reason cannot understand." We often wrongly ignore our intuitive thoughts, placing the superficial rules and teachings of our culture above them. Maxims, laws, and theological absolutes are often absurd when you try to apply them to your particular moral dilemma. Respect your heart when it warns you that highblown, universal moral principles do not apply to your specific personal problems. Experienced physicians know when to let their intuitive judgment override accepted medical-textbook teaching in order to benefit a particular patient.

Art

Plato taught that poets compose because they are inspired and possessed. In his work, *Io*, he says, "There is no invention in him until he has been inspired and is out of his senses and the mind is no longer in him." Most art gives free expression to the unconscious mind. The more that art is free of the contaminations of conscious preconceptions, the better it is, in theory. Modern art aims to delete the traditional conscious forces that would thwart imaginative expression. What many artists try to create is a spontaneous, primordial manifestation of their deeper mental states. Because art should not be affected by such inhibiting forces as critics and market considerations, we prize art such as that created by prehistoric man on the walls of the caves at Lascaux, France. Free-form art by folk artists like Grandma Moses, and outsider artists like Adolfi Wolfi or Myrtice West, tend to produce this natural free association of our unconscious. The unaffected flow of rap music, songs by the illiterate, and drawings by children or the mentally ill all reflect a truer picture of the uncon-

scious. There are few social distortions or acculturated prejudices in this type of "naive" art.

If you ask young children to draw a person, they usually
draw their own image taken from their unconscious. A child
with a poor self-image will draw a tiny, sticklike figure,
whereas a confident child will make more elaborate and
larger drawings, including more body parts and clothing.

Hypnosis

Hypnosis provides another method of gaining insight into
the unconscious aspects of our behavior. Though hypnosis
evokes an image of mystery and even evil, it really is a natural state of consciousness that has been explored since the
ancient Egyptians used it to treat disease. Under hypnosis,
the electrical brain pattern reveals relaxation of alpha and
theta rhythms. The limbic system, deep in the brain, is apparently stimulated, which can actually alter physiology. A large
overlap with psychological placebo effect occurs, however.
Your physiology can be altered in surprising ways under
hypnosis. If you are told that your right hand is submerged
in warm water, the blood vessels in your skin will dilate,
making you believe your hand is warm. Your skin temperature will increase. The reverse (blanching) occurs if you are
told that your hand is in ice water. The placebo effect and
physiology will be discussed further in the chapter on medicine and physiology.

Hypnosis is produced with the subject's cooperation in
first undergoing a drowsy state of altered consciousness, creating a heightened sense of awareness and suggestibility.
The American Society of Clinical Hypnosis maintains that

hypnosis can provide benefit in smoking cessation and weight loss. Susceptibility to hypnosis usually peaks about age nine and declines thereafter. Hypnosis is generally more effective in a group or audience situation, where there is a "collective expectancy." Certain conscious inhibitions are alleviated under hypnosis, forgotten experiences may be revived, and the retrieval of information is often enhanced. However, the popular idea that you never forget anything is an exaggeration. Indeed, the memories recalled under hypnosis may be quite unreliable. Medical use of hypnosis is based upon the patient's own secondary gain; that is, the patient knows that he or she will benefit by a successful program. One cannot induce behavior in the hypnotized against the subject's own morals or personal wishes, because the unconscious is too clever to be led astray.

Although hypnosis can help alleviate the pain in some medical procedures, such as changing burn bandages, its efficacy is limited. Hypnosis has been around a long time, and if it were incredibly helpful, doctors would use it far more than they do now. Hypnosis for pain relief has several overlapping explanations. For the procedure to be successful, the patient must usually respect and like the hypnotist and want the procedure to succeed for his or her own benefit—and also to please the hypnotist. This is basic to the placebo effect of any doctor/patient relationship. A patient who is paying money for the procedure feels a further obligation to make the treatment work. The individual is made more comfortable and anxiety is relieved, which, in itself, has been shown to relieve pain. In addition, some backup premedication or anesthesia is given. (Successful surgical operations using only hypnosis are very unusual and highly publicized in relation to the vast majority of cases in which hypnosis alone is not successful.) Hypnosis is sometimes useful in patients suffering from chronic pain, such as from cancer or arthritis. Patients taught self-hypnosis can put the pain perception at a different level of their consciousness, similar to filtering out unimportant background noise.

Therapists also use hypnosis to explore the personalities of a patient with multiple personality disorder, often the result of traumatic experiences early in life. Sufferers depend on their different individual personalities to handle the pain associated with the trauma. Under hypnosis, the different personae emerge, and sometimes the various personalities are unaware of each other.

Sports

The unconscious component of sports activity is larger than most of us suspect. Athletes playing their best game will often mention that they were "unconscious," "on a roll," or "in the zone," a relaxed state where their unfettered unconscious mind does the job. Floyd Patterson, former world heavyweight boxing champ, decided to retire in 1972 because he realized his reflexes were not "coming on instinct," and that he had to "think more and more." Anatomically, much of this unconscious activity is mediated through the lower centers of the cerebellum (the hind brain) and midbrain, rather than by the cerebral cortex. Too much higher-level thinking creates worry and distraction, inhibiting the optimal function of the lower centers. When a basketball player dribbles down the court, he or she is not thinking about pushing the ball forward with the right hand, then stepping off on the left foot, then moving the right thigh forward. The player is trying to become aware of the position of fellow players and whether or not a shot can be taken.

Similarly, experienced tennis players respond unconsciously to a muffled sound of the ball from their opponent's racquet, which means a softly hit, short ball that will barely clear the net. Automatically, they lunge forward for the return shot.

Not only are immediate body movements controlled by unconscious reflex centers, but broader aspects of sports, including winning and losing, are also conducted on an unconscious level. In the 1991 U.S. Open tennis tournament, Patrick McEnroe, the younger brother of John McEnroe, was playing the popular veteran Jimmy Connors. Connors has always had the reputation of a comeback fighter. McEnroe was far ahead, having won the first two sets and the first three games of the third set. But once Connors started making his comeback, it became almost automatic. The legendary hero was *supposed* to win. The fans wanted him to win, Connors knew he would win, and McEnroe's unconscious told him to lose. We go where we think we *should* go. The match became an *enactment*, with the two players acting in appropriate roles with the fans. It was no surprise to anyone when the white-faced McEnroe met defeat.

I believe that basketball often gives examples of team unconscious effects. In February 1992, the St. Louis University Billikens, playing at home, were trailing the Memphis State Tigers by twelve points with two and a half minutes left to play. A long three-pointer by St. Louis flipped on a psychological switch, the hometown crowd immediately coming alive for their team. In desperation, the St. Louis players began purposely fouling. The Memphis State players would miss the free throws and St. Louis would get the rebound and promptly hit a three-pointer. They did this four times to tie the score in the last seconds and put the game into over-time. It was a perfect unconscious orchestration, with the psyche of the home team Billikens saying they should tie the game, and Memphis State unconsciously knowing they were obligated to the St. Louis fans to hand the ball over to St. Louis. Unconsciously, they thought they should surrender to this team for its gallant comeback. In the overtime, however, the spell was broken; the Tigers no longer felt obligated to play poorly, and won the game by two points.

Physiological factors, prompted by higher unconscious forces, are involved in these examples, however. The tennis player's pulse rate increases when making a comeback, but as soon as he completes his comeback and the score is tied, his pulse rate then falls, as he breathes a sigh of relief, pats himself on the back, and tends to relax slightly.

Athletes can train themselves to create a calm, thoughtless mental state, free from calculations and worry. Self-critical judgments are harmful because they are apt to become self-fulfilling prophecies. Athletes often perform better if the reac-tion is one of quick, unconscious reflex rather than concen-trated cerebral cortical thinking. Often, with a high, floating lob in tennis, the player has too much time to think about how, where, and when to hit the ball. "You can't play and think at the same time," is an adage tennis players appreciate.

There are other, broader, unconscious factors in winning and losing. Drawing from my own family experience, I have found that it is difficult for my three sons to beat their father. I have been far behind in both tennis and chess with my sons, and find that they have trouble closing the match against me. This may represent some natural biological fear that it is harmful to their well-being to best someone upon whom they have depended for their very survival. Other complex unconscious motives might also apply to playing your boss or spouse in any sport. Many people unconsciously engineer their own defeat because they fear making a speech after receiving the trophy.

Probing the Unconscious

Social scientists, including psychologists, psychiatrists, and educators, use thousands of different psychological tests today. Businesses use these for employment screening, relocations, and detection of insider crime. These tests evaluate personality, anxiety levels, and job reliability.

Psychiatrists and psychologists may use the assessment projective techniques, and since these don't actually measure things specifically, most are not called tests. The Rorschach technique evaluates the full response to symmetrical ink blot designs. The Thematic Apperception Test utilizes pictures of open-ended interpersonal relations and has the patient describe a story about each picture. Free word association involves having the patient speak or write the first word that comes to mind after being given a stimulus word. A sentence completion test is also used in the free-association techniques.

Conscious self-evaluations often state opposite results from those revealed by psychoanalytic techniques. For instance, an individual may say that he is independent, strong, and has a low need for intimacy, but the tests reveal high need for intimacy and insecurity. People tend to consciously *compensate* for their unconscious state. This explains why overt "tough guys" may faint at the sight of blood and may be unable to shoot someone on the battlefield, or why some fervently homophobic males may have unconscious homosexual fantasies.

Techniques related to physiology mediated by the unconscious involve the polygraph lie detector test, which utilizes multiple physiological responses such as pulse, breathing, and electrical activity of the skin. A polygraph does reveal aspects of the unconscious mind, but its results are not sufficiently reliable to be admissible as evidence in court.

Freud discontinued the use of hypnosis and depended upon other techniques, such as free association, and sought to uncover elements in the unconscious such as repressed events that are too painful to be dealt with in the present, conscious state. There are many books and movies that play upon this concept of repressed events. *The Prince of Tides* (published 1986) is one involving a traumatic experience (an episode of sex abuse) under repression. Hollywood psychodramas tend to simplify mental problems down to one repressed event. When it is finally admitted to consciousness, suddenly everything is perfect, everyone is happy, and the movie ends. The concept of "recovered memory" has become faddish and much overused. Some psychological therapists have "created," rather than "recovered," memories of childhood sexual abuse.

Freudian slips of the tongue ("queer old dean" for "dear old queen") are verbal mistakes that betray our unconscious leanings. Purposeful accidents also fall into this category. Guilty people often punish themselves with such an accident. We often read about a thief leaving an obvious clue at the scene of the crime. Of course, the crime itself may well have been caused partly by unconscious forces.

Other manifestations of unconscious activity involve hysterical dissociations. These include somnambulism (sleep-walking), posthypnotic suggestions, and fugues, in which a patient may be found wandering in another part of the city in total amnesia. Some fugue states can be long lasting, with a person living an apparently normal life and sometimes changing personality and occupation.

Hysteria is also a form of unconscious dissociation, or conversion reaction, and classically is more often expressed in younger, egocentric, and petulant individuals. In a hysterical illness, often the symptoms are impossible to explain from a scientific, anatomical standpoint, there being no organic disease to explain them. For instance, the hysteric may have numbness of both hands that extends only up to the wrists, in glovelike distribution, which is anatomically impossible since the nerves that supply the hands course down from the shoulders along both sides of the arms. Hysterical deafness or blindness can be a manifestation of a severe psychiatric problem. Often there is some obvious secondary gain or ulterior motive, and, in some cases, there is a combination of conscious and unconscious factors, so that the psychiatrist struggles to differentiate between actual malingering, which is on a conscious level, and hysteria. The overlap between hysterical psychosomatic problems and hypochondriasis is great.

There have been documented cases of mass hysteria where many students in the same school became ill and had similar, bizarre symptoms, such as vomiting or fainting. Episodes of "dancing mania" have occurred in both medieval and contemporary Europe, with many people simultaneously running out into the streets and dancing with emotional fervor.

Dreams are a very controversial subject. Some feel that dreams are merely chaotic flukes of our minds with no meaningful connection with the unconscious, but others believe they do have some significance if the same type of dream is often repeated. Freud considered dreams a temporary form of mild psychosis, but thought they were very important in analyzing of the unconscious. Dreaming occurs during the rapid eye movement phase of sleep, the most restful part of sleep, which we cannot live without. No doubt all of us, on occasion, have awakened in the middle of the night, after dreaming, and recognize additional insights into some problems we have faced. This phenomenon has been mentioned throughout science, when someone awakens and immediately writes down the answer to previous mental struggles. The most famous example of this was when the chemist Friedrich Kekule awoke from a dream knowing the chemical structure of the benzene ring. Thomas Edison had an unusual sleep-work routine, taking many short catnaps and relying on these refreshing interludes to solve questions posed by his experiments.

Sometimes the unconscious mind can be assigned a task and it will do the job on its own. This is the idea behind the work of Dr. Maxwell Maltz, the author of *Psycho-Cybernetics* (1960), who maintained that the secret of natural behavior and the success mechanism lies in the unconscious. If one consciously tries to become successful, it is painful and jams the automatic, unconscious creative mechanism.

Creative ideas and the solutions to many problems sometimes arise suddenly, when the conscious mind is not straining to solve them. Bertrand Russell mentioned that he would give orders to his mind to proceed underground and then, after some months, consciously return to a problem and find that he could handle it successfully. We don't have to be great inventors or artists in order to use our unconscious mechanisms in this way in our daily work.

Sex

Freud emphasized the importance of unconscious sexual urges motivating one's behavior and he also thought neurosis was caused by stressful sexual experiences early in life, even in infancy. He contended that sublimation of abnormal sex urges into socially acceptable channels was curative. Most psychiatrists and psychologists today feel that unconscious sex drives play an important, but variable, role in all human behavior. Possibly Freud's emphasis on sex has contributed to the mistaken idea that the unconscious is somehow disreputable.

Apparently a collective unconscious is now concerned about the danger of AIDS and sex. Violent love plots in movies portray these fears, such as in *Fatal Attraction* (1987), *Internal Affairs* (1990), and *Single White Female* (1992). The rise of Neo-Puritanism—the heightened concern with sexual harassment, pornography, and the sexual affairs of politicians—may reflect the fear of AIDS in the entire populace.

Unconscious Obligatory Ethics

Karl Marx emphasized that the unconscious regulates our actions, saying that much depended on social and economic conditions actually impelling people unconsciously to do many things that they justified in some other way on a conscious level. Marx maintained that the exploitation by government and society of the means of livelihood is one of the main motivators of human action. Particular behavior patterns become an expected response to economic repression. He wrote, "It is not the consciousness of men that determines their being, but, on the contrary, their social being that determines their consciousness."

Chapter 7 mentioned the saying, "When you've got 'em by the neck, their hearts and minds will follow"—a classic example of the unconscious mind calling the shots. Knowing we are trapped in a bad situation, we repress the fact that we are helpless, consciously insisting that things are wonderful in our present condition. We are able to delude our conscious minds that we have freely chosen this of our own accord.

Definitions of, and opinions about, consciousness vary widely, from notions that dreaming is a higher form of consciousness, to the idea that bacteria are conscious. Also, choosing between pure conscious and unconscious mental activity is not so simple. Multiple altered states of consciousness will be discussed in chapter 14.

References

Barrett, William. *Irrational Man*. New York: Doubleday Anchor Books, 1962.

Corliss, William R. *The Unfathomed Mind: A Handbook of Unusual Mental Phenomena*. Glen Arm, Md.: The Sourcebook Project, 1982.

Crick, Francis. *The Astonishing Hypothesis: The Scientific Search for the Soul*. New York: Charles Scribner, 1994.

Crick, Francis, and Christof Koch. "The Problem of Consciousness." *Scientific American* (September 1992): 153–59.

Dennett, Daniel. *Consciousness Explained*. Boston: Little, Brown, 1991.

Dewart, Leslie. *Evolution and Consciousness*. Toronto: University of Toronto Press, 1989.

Duncan, Ronald, and Miranda Weston-Smith. *The Encyclopedia of Ignorance*. New York: Wallaby Book, Pocket Books, 1977.

Frankl, Viktor E. *The Unconscious Gold*. New York: Touchstone, Simon and Shuster, 1975.

Freud, Sigmund. *An Outline of Psycho-Analysis*, edited by James Strachey. New York: W. W. Norton, 1969.

Gallwey, W. Timothy. *The Inner Game of Tennis*. New York: Bantam, Random House, 1974.

Gilovich, Thomas. *How We Know What Isn't So*. New York: Free Press/Macmillan, 1991.

Humphrey, Nicholas. *A History of the Mind*. New York: Simon and Schuster, 1991.

Jaynes, Julian. *The Origin of Consciousness in the Breakdown of the Bicameral Mind*. Boston: Houghton Miffin, 1990.

Key, Wilson Bryan. *Subliminal Seduction*. New York: Signet, New American Library, Times Mirror, 1973.

Loehr, Jim, and Cindy Hahn. "How to Close Out a Match." *Tennis* (January 1992): 42–45.

Maltz, Maxwell. *Psycho-Cybernetics*. New York: Pocket Books, Simon and Schuster, 1966.

Miller, Jonathan. "Trouble in Mind." *Scientific American* (September 1992): 180.

Murphy, Joseph. *The Power of Your Subconscious Mind*. New York: Bantam Books, Prentice-Hall, 1982.

Ornstein Robert. *The Evolution of Consciousness*. New York: Touchstone, Simon and Schuster, 1991.

———. *Multimind: A New Way of Looking at Human Behavior*. New York: Anchor Books, Doubleday, Dell, 1989.

———. *The Psychology of Consciousness*. Orlando, Fla.: Harcourt Brace Jovanovich, 1977.

Penrose, Roger. *The Emperor's New Mind*. New York: Oxford University Press, 1989.

———. *Shadows of the Mind: A Search for the Missing Science of Consciousness*. New York: Oxford University Press, 1994.

Priest, Stephen. *Theories of the Mind*. Boston: Houghton Mifflin, 1992.

Restak, Richard. *The Brain Has a Mind of Its Own*. New York: Harmony Books, Crown, 1991.

Schacht, Richard, John Lachs, and Michael Hassell, eds. *The Giants of Philosophy: Friedrich Nietzsche*, audiotape. Audio Classics Series,narrated by Charlton Heston. Nashville, Tenn: Knowledge Products.

Stone, Mark, John Lachs, and Michael Hassell, eds. *The Giants of Philosophy: Arthur Schopenhauer*, audiotape. Audio Classics Series, narrated by Charlton Heston. Nashville, Tenn: Knowledge Products.

Smith, John E., ed. *The Giants of Philosophy: G. W. F. Hegel*, audiotape. Audio Classics Series, narrated by Charlton Heston. Nashville, Tenn: Knowledge Products.

Stukenborg, Phil. "Patterson Felt When to Quit." *Memphis Commercial Appeal* (May 2, 1992).

Westen, Drew. *Is Anyone Really Normal? Perspectives on Abnormal Psychology*, audiotape. Springfield, Va.: The Teaching Company.

13

Genetics and Sociobiology

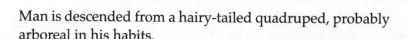

Man is descended from a hairy-tailed quadruped, probably arboreal in his habits.

Charles Darwin

If you'd read your Bible you'd find out that they ain't no man done come from no monkey.

Revival tent meeting, Memphis, Tennessee, 1948

Controversy—Opposition

Culture (all nongenetic transferred information) has become so pervasive in our lives that it is easy to forget that the foundational structure of our being is based on the biological imperatives of genetics and evolution. The old argument pitting heredity against environment, or nature against nurture, continues. Ancient kings did not worry much about this; they just assumed their royal blood would prevail in their progeny and determine the quality of the individual. Hippocrates recognized that baldness and blue eyes ran in families, and the Greeks actually encouraged eugenics, human improvement by genetic control, by urging successful young men to breed while discouraging misfits and criminals from doing so.

In the nineteenth century, however, Darwin delayed publication of his seminal work on evolution because he feared recrimination by religious authorities. Genetics also did not set well with the modernists at the first part of the twentieth century. It wasn't "nice" to say that we can't fully control our lives. The behaviorists, thinking that with enough time and effort anybody could be fixed, considered the idea of eugenics to be unmitigated evil. Democratic ideals demanded the assumption that all men are created equal and that there could be no inherent behavioral differences between individuals, families, genders, or races. The egalitarian feeling in Western democracy was that, with proper environment and education, everyone could be equally productive and joyful. Those modern psychologists, such as John Watson and B. F. Skinner, who emphasized behaviorism or conditioned responses, believed that the cultural conditions of praise and punishment predominantly governed our behavior.

William Shockley, Arthur Jensen, Richard Herrnstein, and Charles Murray were highly criticized for entertaining such ideas as behavioral racial differences. The eminent sociobiologist E. O. Wilson, author of *On Human Nature* (1978), has also come under fire for braving the opinion that much of our behavior, particularly that involved with ethics, aggression, romance, and religion, depends upon our genetic proclivity. Today most social scientists think that certainly both genetics and culture play a role in determining an individual's behavior; however, most authorities are now giving genetics more credit than it has been given in the first part of the twentieth century, and are now consigning genetics the larger role. The nurturists seem to be losing the longstanding war.

But many nonscientists today haven't gotten the word; they deny inherent gender or racial differences in behavior, tending to blame individual differences on cultural background alone. Wishing to be politically correct and not to hurt anyone's immediate feelings, they are similar to those who threatened Galileo because his ideas offended the church's concept of an earth-centered universe. Egalitarians enjoy the notion that all humans are equal, and that they should always be. Moreover, they insist that any differences in attainment are caused only by social injustice. Those who disagree they brand as "elitist." These well-meaning people don't realize that it is eventually harmful to treat unequals equally, whether it be individuals, families, genders, or races. Inherent talents and liabilities should be recognized as such. Because some even tend to equate modern geneticists with Nazi eugenics conducted under captive circumstances, the behavioral aspect of genetics remains politically unacceptable.

Some feminists bend over backwards to refute ideas that differences in the behavior of the sexes are based on biology. Unrecognized biological differences between the sexes have caused much frustration and false blame. Even the possibility that homosexuality could have genetic origins has become controversial.

To many, the entire concept of humans being different

genetic specimens is distasteful. Some are offended by medical research on blacks with sickle cell anemia, Jews with Tay-Sachs disease, and individuals of Mediterranean extraction with thalassemia (a form of anemia). But we have to face scientific facts honestly. Generally, African pygmies are shorter than Watusi warriors, and Japanese are generally shorter than Germans. Many Japanese and Native Americans have gray, dry earwax. It should not be totally unthinkable that when individuals' body and skin are different genetically there may be significant differences in brain structure and function as well. These differences are not necessarily bad, and may well reflect special skills and talents in both physical and mental attainments. The taboo against discussing differences in intelligence between races persists, despite the general quiet acceptance of these differences by behavioral geneticists. A continuing problem for scientists remains the indefinable nature of both *race* and *intelligence*. Today, considering the complexity of racial immigration and intermarriage, most cultural anthropologists doubt that the term *race* is useful. Is the child of a black and a Jew a dark-skinned Jew or a light-skinned black? I have a physician friend from India who makes a point of referring to himself as a black man. As you stroll the streets of Havana, Honolulu, or São Paulo, or observe subway riders in New York City, you become aware that race is largely a social construct.

For scientific studies, the effects of nurture (nutrition and education), on IQ can never be completely separated from those of nature. Because current researchers have declared that there is no such thing as general intelligence, recent interest has swung to the various *components* of intelligence, such as spatial, verbal, and arithmetical intelligence. We have not yet designed accurate tests to measure the vital real life "people skills," including empathy and the ability to integrate one's emotions into one's intellectual processes.

It must always be kept in mind that any difference between individuals within a particular racial group is greater than differences between groups, that is, group averages.

Some of the research in genetics has been thwarted by efforts to cancel research funds. The National Institutes of Health withdrew funds from an academic conference on the search for a genetic basis of criminal behavior. The thought that one may have a genetic predisposition for criminal behavior was offensive to some people. Apparently some individuals had the idea that there was a simplistic crime gene being promoted. Others saw the project as a racist plot.

No reputable scientist today believes in some simple biological determinism that mandates a genetic form of behavior manifesting itself in a pure fashion independent of culture. There could be no such thing as a "crime gene" because crime is a culturally defined word. Even courts have trouble deciding what constitutes a crime. However, personality traits such as aggressiveness and impulsivity may be inherited, as may a need for experiencing excitement.

All scientists recognize the complex, bidirectional causality between biology and culture, particularly with our genes and our social environment. Our genetically given temperament affects how our environment responds to us, and we to it. A highly intelligent, aggressive child is treated differently by parents, friends, and teachers than a shy, less assertive individual. An unusually ill-tempered child may be abused by parents. This interplay between infant and caretakers is extremely important for total personality development in the first two years of life, because the child's psychological posture toward life is essentially established in infancy and in early childhood. Biology includes genetics and pathophysiology (impaired bodily function) associated with disease. Defining behavior is problematic because there are no objective methods for measuring behavioral traits such as trustworthiness or shyness. To further complicate the situation, we know that many genetic diseases require some form of environmental factor or stress to make the illness manifest. For instance, diabetes has a basic genetic background but other illnesses, aging, and obesity definitely play their part in making diabetes an overt disease. Discriminate and complex human attitudes cannot be determined by a single gene. Even in simpler organisms like insects behavior is regulated by many genetic contributors, acting subtly together.

We also know that DNA, the genetic code, seems to be a rather complex feedback system that can and does change slightly within the course of a lifetime, so inheritance is not as rigid as previously thought. Some genes appear to "learn" or change in relation to environmental stress, and may change through generations as well.

Darwin, Mendel, Watson, Crick

Darwin's theory of evolution became well known after 1859, and the experiments of Gregor Mendel, an Austrian monk, served to back up Darwin's theory. Starting his work in 1865, Mendel catalogued the color and sizes of plants and derived the laws of heredity, but his work was not appreciated until 1900. In 1869, DNA was discovered, but its significance was not noted until 1953, when James Watson and Francis Crick determined the manner in which DNA is constructed.

Many altruistic forms of behavior among animals such as

sharing, grooming, social support, protection, and sacrifice of life are genetically determined and are known as kin selection. Altruism and cooperation in families is explained by the fact that they share genes—brothers and sisters have about one-half of their genes in common.

It is possible that fear between races and strangers has a genetic origin. We can assume that there was some survival value in one tribe being fearful of another, competitive tribe on the other side of the mountain. Humans who were naturally fearful of those who looked different from members of their own tribe, and didn't stray into enemy territory, survived to pass on their genes. We are genetically mandated to respond to harm from others accordingly, by tit-for-tat, because any organism that fails to protect itself soon becomes extinct. From an evolutionary standpoint, retribution is not irrational.

There are many similarities in the behavior and genetic makeup of humans and primates. Recent studies document the similarity of violent behavior of young male Rhesus monkeys and young human males. When young male monkeys leave the social stability of a troop, they often become hyper-aggressive. These cast-off monkeys show low levels of the chemical serotonin in their cerebral spinal fluid, similar to the levels found in certain violent humans.

Temperament

There are some hereditary strokes of character by which a family may be distinguished.

Junius, 1769

Psychologists are finding more and more evidence that genetics determines temperament and personality. This is obvious to dog breeders when they observe shy puppies grow to be shy adults and aggressive puppies become aggressive adults who breed true. Since antiquity, men have selectively bred animals for specific behavior; horses for racing, some dogs for hunting and others for protection. Beekeepers can choose to buy fertilized queens that produce gentle bees. Although this is accepted without question in animals, we are still hesitant to apply these same thoughts to our own higher animal species—humans.

We now know that people inherit different temperaments, such as tendencies to be happy or sad, outgoing or shy. Such knowledge relieves some of the guilt of parents of problem children but also obligates some humility when children do marvelous things. Dr. Nathan Fox at the University of Maryland relates that by analyzing the infant brain wave response to various stimuli we may be able to predict whether certain babies will be shy later in life.

Natural talents like musical ability and athletic ability unquestionably run in families, but both genetic and environmental factors are required for optimal attainment of any talent. Most of the significant genetic processes regarding behavior are due to the effect of multiple genes, each having only a small effect. Intelligence is thought to be transmitted by this polygenetic type of inheritance. Genetics primarily determines many skills in perceptual motor tasks, and also heavily influences sociability.

As we mentioned in the chapter on language, children apparently have an innate ability to learn the grammar of a language. Certain people have a familial defect in this language gene, however, and must learn language slowly, through other more indirect intellectual processes. We become aware that genetics is quite important after we raise children in the same environment and see that each child is unique and differs from the others considerably in overall temperament. Studies of twins, including identical and fraternal twins reared apart and reared together, reveal high correlations on personality tests with personality attributes such as introversion and extroversion. Studies of children and their adoptive parents as well as their biologic parents show that children are inclined to have the same personalities as their natural parents rather than their adoptive parents. Studies of identical (monozygotic) twins show that they tend to be uncannily similar in personality even if raised apart in different countries; however, fraternal (dizygotic) twins share attitudes and temperament less frequently than do identical twins. Fraternal twins share half rather than all of their genes, on average.

When comparing the smoking habits of identical twins with fraternal twins, the identical twins tend to exhibit more similar behavior. This gives some scientists support for the theory that heredity plays a role in why people start, stop, or continue smoking. More recent twin studies tend to confirm the impression that identical twins raised apart have amazingly similar attitudes, including tough-mindedness and political leanings. The divorce records of identical twins are more consistent than those of fraternal twins. Of course, cultural factors also govern the incidence of divorce.

Perhaps a genetic predilection controls our overall attitude toward life. Some individuals have a locus of control that is internal, making them feel that they are able to direct their own destiny, but others have an external locus of control and believe that they are helpless and knocked around by fate. Individuals with an internal locus are more methodical and disciplined in their lives, whereas the individuals with an external locus act as if there is no use in trying to regiment themselves and look to others or to institutions for guidance.

Evidence is also mounting for a genetic propensity to a specific threshold of stimulation of the sympathetic nervous system. Certain individuals react emotionally at a lower level of stress than others, and particular individuals manifest immunologic reactivity and neuroendocrine response in a characteristic manner that is genetically determined. This complexity goes beyond a simple gene-culture relationship and extends into the realm of physiology. Individuals inherit their own characteristics of brain chemistry concerning the physiological modulators of serotonin, dopamine, and other neurotransmitters.

Human Genome Project

The Human Genome Project is off and running. In ten or fifteen years it is hoped that this project will have mapped and interpreted all of the structures that constitute our genetic heritage, and that we will understand the role of each of the 100,000 human genes. It is presumed that the project will find genetic variations between racial groups, and even now some say that the Y chromosome in Japanese men is longer than it is in men in other populations. Everyone will be found to have some genetic variation, which may include rare talents. The Human Genome Project will probably enable us to detect susceptibility to extremely common diseases such as hypertension, atherosclerosis, and cancer. Controversy exists presently about whether employers should discriminate against people having a proven potential illness such as Alzheimer disease or Huntington disease, an incurable neurological degenerative process that has its onset in middle age. The recent identification of the cystic fibrosis gene on chromosome 7 represented a major advance. In the future we will have an improved ability to isolate and manipulate the genes involved in diseases. About four thousand human genetic diseases are now known to exist. New therapies can now be designed for them, including introduction of a normal gene to correct the defective gene.

Knowledge of genetics will certainly influence the lifestyle and behavior of individuals. People who know they harbor the gene for familial colon cancer would certainly get periodic diagnostic tests such as a barium enema and colonoscopy to check for early cancer, and those who harbor the gene for lung cancer surely would not smoke.

Complex medicolegal and ethical questions arise in having knowledge of your own genetic makeup and that of your progeny or of a possible future spouse. Even today people are faced with the agonizing decision of whether or not to be tested for Huntington's disease. An individual with a family history may realize that he or she has a fifty-fifty chance of eventually getting it. We can diagnose Huntington disease, which is on chromosome 4, by genetic analysis and also by radiological imaging methods utilizing positron emission tomography. The latter involves injecting into the blood an isotope which is taken up in abnormal locations within the brain in a pattern characteristic of this disease.

Forms of in-house eugenics are already being used, as many couples with a family history of severe inherited diseases are choosing not to have children. In the future, chromosome analysis will enable us to identify markers for many types of genetic illnesses. Would you want to marry someone who has a 40 percent chance of having a manic-depressive illness, or would you wish to adopt such a child? If you knew that an individual had a significantly greater chance of being manic-depressive, you might be solicitous of any unusual things in his or her comportment that would suggest a developing psychiatric illness. Such seeking could be self-fulfilling.

Diseases

A genetic background for diabetes, cystic fibrosis, and sickle cell anemia has been apparent for decades. More recently, specific genes have been identified for neurofibromatosis, which is a condition characterized by multiple small nerve tumors. Many common ailments such as particular forms of deafness, arthritis, and atherosclerosis are identified by specific genes. A group of genes on chromosome 9 are involved in malignant skin melanoma. Chromosome 3 is involved with kidney cancer. It has recently been discovered that certain genetic diseases, including forms of muscular dystrophy, become more severe with advancing generations, the disease worsening in the children and grandchildren of an individual with the disease.

Tourette syndrome is a neurological condition characterized by multiple eye ticks, head jerking, facial grimaces, and cursing. Previously, it was thought to be a psychiatric disorder, but it is now seen to be definitely genetic in origin, affecting three times as many males as females. There are on record entire families afflicted with the disorder, varying in severity between the individuals. Medication, however, has been proven beneficial.

A family predisposition to breast cancer is well known. A woman whose mother had breast cancer should be very conscientious about mammograms and frequent self-examinations. The gene for early onset familial breast cancer (about 5 percent of total cases) has been found to reside on chromosome 17. The knowledge of the existence of this gene influences our behavior today. Should a woman undergo a bilateral mastectomy, obtain more frequent mammograms, or abort a fetus with the gene?

Knowing your medical roots has a distinct benefit. Those with a prominent family history of early deaths by heart disease or strokes should maintain a proper diet, get plenty of exercise, and obtain frequent blood pressure checks to prevent atherosclerosis. Genetic counseling to predict the chance of a familial problem in your offspring would be of value, as well as prenatal diagnostic techniques such as amniocentesis.

Recent advances in molecular genetics have enabled people to have better family counseling regarding the decision to have children. For example, people from families with any occurrence of cystic fibrosis can now be given tests to see whether or not they are carriers. By utilizing DNA fragment analysis, carriers of Fragile-X syndrome, an inherited form of mental retardation and autism, can now be detected. A screening test now exists for Tay-Sachs disease, a metabolic abnormality found among East European Ashkenazi Jews and their descendants.

The definition of the learning difficulty known as dyslexia and its genetic transmission remains uncertain. Dyslexia generally is a heterogeneous disorder but some families show a striking dominant transmission from father to sons.

Most diseases have some degree of genetic inclination; ailments such as osteoporosis, color blindness, and peptic ulcer are examples. If a child has an abnormality of the ureter (ureteral reflux) associated with a urinary tract infection, it is known that approximately a third of the siblings will also have ureteral reflux. If one parent has allergies, approximately 40 percent of his or her children will have allergies. If both parents have allergies, up to 70 percent of their children will have them. Asthma is an example of a disease with an allergic component influenced by heredity, and also one in which several factors have to coincide in order for the full disease to be manifest. Emotional stress, viral infection, and exposure to cigarette smoke are environmental factors that influence the occurrence of asthma.

Alzheimer Disease

Alzheimer disease, the most common cause of elderly dementia, afflicts between 5 and 10 percent of people over sixty-five years old. Pathologically, it is characterized by the deposition of an abnormal protein within the brain, which destroys neurons (brain cells). The genetic transmission of Alzheimer disease, by chromosome 19 and 21, is particularly notable in the early onset type below age sixty. Other factors determine at what age the disease will become manifest, and perhaps several conditions have to be present before it presents itself; such as certain viral illnesses or exposure to unusual toxins. Exposure to aluminum has been of interest, and some think Alzheimer patients have inborn error of metabolism for the handling of certain trace metals. Researchers are now perfecting tests for early diagnosis of hereditary Alzheimer disease. If successful, early diagnosis would allow victims to plan for their future and make arrangements for their disease while they still have full control of their mental ability. Few people would wish to subject themselves to the test until methods are discovered to prevent the disease once they know the test is positive and will eventually strike.

Mental Disorders

Statistically, suicide has genetic links, probably because a large number of suicides are found in patients having manic-depression (bipolar) disorder, which has a strong genetic background. There is a 67 percent concordance rate for manic-depressive disorder in identical twins (in which both show it) and 20 percent concordance rate in fraternal twins. Schizophrenia likewise occurs in 76 percent of identical twins reared apart and in 91.5 percent of such twins reared together. We can therefore conclude that this is mainly a genetic disease but environment still plays a significant role.

Alcoholism

Twin and adoption studies have shown that alcoholism has a familial background, with particular types showing a father/son transmission. Identical twins have a high concordance rate—55 percent. Alcoholism is difficult to define specifically, and most people involved in alcoholism treatment do not consider it truly a genetic disease but a complex disorder of behavior with a hereditary component. Recent interest in a possible dopamine receptor gene for alcoholics has failed to provide proof that is exists. Abnormalities in dopamine flow in the brain have been implicated in a number of neurologic and psychiatric disorders, including schizophrenia, hyperactivity, Tourette syndrome, and drug addiction. Perhaps an inherited dopamine receptor abnormality represents a weakness for any addictive or compulsive behavior. A defect in the uptake of dopamine in the central nervous system tends to thwart pleasure; apparently affected individuals seek pleasure by pursuing an abnormal activity such as drug abuse, alcoholism, gambling, excessive sex, or love addiction.

Some individuals have inherited an abnormal alcohol metabolism and are unable to respond to and break down alcohol in their liver as do others. There is some evidence that alcohol metabolism may be different in Asians and Native Americans than in Caucasians.

Familial Traits of Physiology

Other familial genetic traits that you may not be aware of are the ability to curl your tongue, or the way you prefer to cross your arms, left over right or vice versa. Your handedness is genetic to some extent. If both parents are left-handed, 50 percent of their children also will be left-handed. There is a high incidence of concordant left-handedness in identical twins. Characteristics of human taste are inherited. A certain chemical can be tasted only by those who are genetically endowed to taste it. Some people inherit the tendency to eat artichokes and then taste water as sweet. Some so-called familial disorders are not necessarily genetic. An entire family may be exposed to an unusual toxin that causes all to manifest a certain behavior or disease. For example, a family could be exposed to lead and hence manifest symptoms of lead poisoning. Pellagra, which is manifest by neurological symptoms such as depression and hallucinations, was once thought to be a genetic problem but was later found to be caused by a deficiency of niacin, a form of vitamin B. Numerous families once thought to possess hereditary feeblemindedness were later found to have alcoholic mothers and multiple children with fetal alcohol syndrome.

Genetic Manifestations in the Elderly

The mistaken notion persists that genetic conditions are always manifest early in life. An individual who inherits the shyness gene tends to be shy as an infant and as an adult, but the shyness may be more noticeable in the adult. Certain genetic traits may be manifest only late in life, as only the very elderly can truly show the genetic tendency to live over a hundred years.

Gender Differences

Basically, the presence of a Y chromosome determines that someone is a male. In about one in twenty thousand people, however, this Y chromosome is defective and fails to supply the proper signal to produce male characteristics. Therefore these individuals will be female anatomically but male on a genetic level. This is the reason for the difficulty in ascertaining sex for Olympic competition. Besides these rare situations, in general males and females are chromosomally different. Current gene researchers are interested in evidence that hereditary factors might be a causative factor in male homosexuality, transmitted on chromosome X q 28. Normally, women have two X chromosomes while men have an X and short Y chromosome. Every cell in the two sexes is different, and more and more information is being accumulated to establish that men's and women's behavior differs markedly, independent of environment. The fetal brain is flooded with specific sex hormones. The testosterone elaborated by males may create more specialization of the two cerebral hemispheres. Functional magnetic resonance imaging studies show that girls tend to use both sides of their brain more symmetrically than do boys. Girl babies tend to focus their eyes on faces; boys look off in the distance. Small boys favor play with trucks, cars, and other boys, while girls naturally gravitate to dolls. The behavioral effects of the sex hormones, estrogen and androgen, cannot be denied because this has been experimentally shown in castrates (eunuchs) and in situations when these hormones are administered therapeutically. Female laboratory animals demonstrate sexual behavior characteristic of males after they are treated with testosterone. In aggressive female baboons that reach high social rank, enough stress exists to have an adverse effect on fertility, constraining the genetic trait of assertiveness in females. In humans as well as animals, males generally tend to be more adventuresome and mischievous than females. Boys raise their hands to answer in school more often than girls. In nearly all primitive human societies the men hunt and explore and the women gather food and care for children. Of course, the social-cultural environment is also paramount in establishing attitudinal differences between the sexes.

Men are more apt to be left handed than women. Men are better able to mentally rotate three-dimensional objects, therefore, generally, their spatial evaluation ability is greater than women's, as is their mathematics ability. Women are significantly better than men at reading and remembering the location of items found on a desktop. They also surpass men in discerning emotion from subtle facial expressions in others. Regarding taste preference, women generally crave high-fat sweets, like chocolate, and men prefer high-fat protein, like meat.

Of course, any differences in behavior tests between genders are only statistical and do not apply to any given individual. Obviously, some women are far better at spatial imagery and math than are some men, and many women are far more adventuresome. Individual differences in human behavior are greater than those associated with gender or race. Woman-woman and man-man differences are greater than differences between groups of women and men. Still, to deny biological differences often leads to frustration, as when frail women enter careers as firefighters or soldiers.

Many differences in the sexual behavior of the genders may well be biologic, for throughout the animal kingdom males are inclined to be larger, stronger, lead the social organization, and be more sexually promiscuous. Various gender attitudes are not based purely on learned social prejudices but have evolutionary survival value. The most successful mating strategies are carried in our genes. Consistently across history and all nationalities men have sought young, physically attractive women, while women have sought older, financially secure men. The woman is more selective and requires a longer time to accept a man. The younger woman is more reproductively fit, and the high-status older man is a more dependable provider for the women and her progeny. Children of such parents then survive to propagate the genetic bent to behave in a similar way. The caricature of the vixen gold digger on the arm of her sugar daddy has a greater biologic basis than we admit. Since a human is a vehicle for a gene to make another gene, genes that are best at improving reproduction tend to replace those that enhance only survival of the individual person. Behind the scenes of our romantic and ethical human nature lies a cold, genetic self-interest.

References

Boyce, W. Thomas, Ronald G. Barr, and Lonnie K. Zeltzer. "Temperament and the Psychobiology of Childhood Stress." *Pediatrics* (September 1992): 483–85.

Briley, Michael. "Arthritis: A Family Affair?" *Arthritis Today* (March–April 1992): 24–28.

Buss, David M. *The Evolution of Desire: Strategies of Human Mating.* New York: Basic Books, HarperCollins, 1994.

Carmelli, D., G. E. Swan, O. Robinette, and R. Fabitz. "Genetic Influence on Smoking: A Study of Male Twins." *New England Journal of Medicine* 327 (1992): 829.

Degler, Carl N. *In Search of Human Nature: The Decline and Revival of Darwinism in American Social Thought.* Oxford University Press, 1991.

Dozier, Rush W. *Codes of Evolution: The Synaptic Language Revealing the Secrets of Matter, Life, and Thought.* New York: Crown Publisher, 1992.

Fisher, Helen E. *Anatomy of Love: The Natural History of Monogamy, Adultery, and Divorce.* New York: W. W. Norton, 1992.

Fox, Robin. *The Challenge of Anthropology.* New Brunswick, N.J.: Transaction Publishers, 1993.

Fulginiti, Vincent A. "Genetics: The Quiet Revolution in Science and Medicine." Editorial, *American Journal of Diseases of Children* (November 1993): 1139–41.

Gazzaniga, Michael S. *Nature's Mind: The Biological Roots of Thinking, Emotion, Sexuality, Language, and Intelligence.* New York: Basic Books, HarperCollins, 1992.

Gorman, Christine. "Sizing up the Sexes." *Time* (January 20, 1992): 42–48.

Gray, John. *Men Are From Mars, Women Are From Venus.* New York: HarperCollins, 1992.

Green, Eric D., and Robert H. Waterston. "The Human Genome Project: Prospects and Implications for Clinical Medicine." *Journal of the American Medical Association* (October 9, 1991): 1966–74.

Greenspan, Ralph. "Understanding the Genetic Construction of Behavior." *Scientific American* (April 1995): 72–78.

Hall, J. A. *Non-Verbal Sex Differences: Communication Accuracy and Expressive Style.* Baltimore, Md.: Johns Hopkins University Press, 1984.

Herrnstein, Richard J., and Charles Murray. *The Bell Curve: Intelligence and Class Structure in American Life.* New York: Free Press, 1994.

Hicks, R. E., and R. M. Kinsbourne. "Human Handedness: A Partial Cross-Fostering Study." *Science* 192 (1976): 908.

Horgan, John. "Eugenics Revisited." *Scientific American* (June 1993): 123–31.

———. "Genes and Crime." *Scientific American* (February 1993): 24–29.

———. "Profile: Edward O. Wilson: Revisiting Old Battlefields." *Scientific American* (April 1994): 36–41.

Juengst, Eric T. "Priorities in Professional Ethics and Social Policy for Human Genetics." Editorial, *Journal of the American Medical Association* (October 2, 1991): 1835–36.

Kagan, Jerome. "Behavior, Biology, and the Meanings of Temperamental Constructs." *Pediatrics* (September 1992): 510–13.

Kagan, Jerome. *Unstable Ideas: Temperament, Cognition and Self.* Cambridge, Mass.: Harvard University Press, 1990.

Kalow, W., et al., eds. "Ethnic Differences in Reaction to Drugs and Xenobiotics." *Prog. in Clin. and Biol. Res.* 214 (1986):1–600.

Kendler, Kenneth S., Andrew C. Heath, Michael C. Neale, Ronald C. Kessler, and Lindon J. Eaves. "A Population-Based Twin Study of Alcoholism in Women." *Journal of the American Medical Association* (October 14, 1992): 1877.

King, Mary-Claire, Sarah Powell, and Susan M. Love. "Inherited Breast and Ovarian Cancer." *Journal of the American Medical Association* (April 21, 1993): 1975–80.

Konner, Melvin. *Why the Reckless Survive and Other Secrets of Human Nature.* New York: Penguin Books, 1991.

Lerner, Richard. *Final Solutions: Biology, Prejudice, and Genocide.* University Park: Pennsylvania State University Press, 1990.

Lewis, Michael. "Individual Differences in Response to Stress." *Pediatrics* (September 1992): 487–90.

Lueptow, Lloyd B., Lori Garovich, and Margaret B. Lueptow. "The Persistence of Gender Stereotypes in the Face of Changing Sex Roles: Evidence Contrary to the Sociocultural Model." *Ethology and Sociobiology* (November 1995): 509–30.

Neuhauer, Peter B., and Alexander Neubauer. *Nature's Thumbprint: The New Genetics of Personality.* Reading, Mass.: Addison-Wesley, 1990.

Overbye, Dennis. "Born to Raise Hell?" *Time* (February 21, 1994): 76.

Porges, Stephan W., Karen A. Matthews, and David L. Pauls. "The Biobehavioral Interface in Behavioral Pediatrics." *Pediatrics* (November 1992): 789–96.

Rennie, John. "DNA's New Twists—Jumping Genes." *Scientific American* (March 1993): 122–32.

Ridley, Matt. *The Red Queen: Sex and the Evolution of Human Nature.* New York: Macmillan, 1994.

Seligman, Daniel T. *A Question of Intelligence: The IQ Debate in America.* New York: Birch Lane Press, 1992.

Torrey, E. Fuller, Ann E. Bowler, Edward H. Taylor, and Irving I. Gottesman. *Schizophrenia and Manic-Depressive Disorder: The Biological Roots of Mental Illness as Revealed by the Landmark Study of Identical Twins.* New York: Basic Books, 1994.

Toufexis, Anastasia. "Seeking the Roots of Violence." *Time* (April 19, 1993): 52–53.

Walsh, Anthony. *The Science of Love*. Amherst, N.Y.: Prometheus Books, 1991.

Walsh, Anthony, and Grace J. Walsh. *Vive La Difference: A Celebration of the Sexes*. Amherst, N.Y.: Prometheus Books, 1993.

Weber, Barbara L., and Judy E. Gerber. "Family History and Breast Cancer." Editorial, *Journal of the American Medical Association* (October 6, 1993): 1602.

Wilson, Edward O. *On Human Nature*. Cambridge, Mass.: Harvard University Press, 1978.

Wright, Robert. *Three Scientists and Their Gods*. New York: Times Books, 1988.

———. *The Moral Animal: The New Science of Evolutionary Psychology*. New York: Pantheon Books, 1994.

14

Physiological and Medical Determinants of Behavior

He will be the slave of many masters who is his body's slave.

Seneca

You are your body, its anatomy, functions, and diseases. In your body lies a universe of complexity about which most people are relatively ignorant, compared with their knowledge of sports, movies, cars, and countless other subjects. In this chapter I will try to cover a small portion of the millions of physiological and medical influences on your brain, and hence your behavior. I have tried to emphasize those of which you might not be aware.

The Physical Environment

Many environmental factors influence our behavior. When we first go outside on a cold morning our teeth chatter and we are obviously affected in a conscious manner. But more often environmental conditions are of such low level that they never reach our conscious awareness. The overall temperature of our surroundings, the humidity, the barometric pressure, and the amount of ozone in the atmosphere all have effects on our comfort. Certain subtle combinations of these factors may be additive, when perhaps we wouldn't be affected by any one of them separately. Room color has an effect, with bright, pleasing colors, such as yellow, tending to elevate our mood and dark colors engendering depression. Red is exciting and green restful, but because pink will tend to allay excitement and may actually cause sedation, agitated criminals are sometimes put into a pink room to calm them down. Bright lighting, such as that used in a supermarket, is stimulating; however, prolonged stimulation in this glary environment eventually causes fatigue. Flickering light from candles or a fireplace usually evokes a warm, relaxed mood. Background noise, such as an air conditioner constantly humming in the background, can produce a low-grade edginess that we may not be aware of. High levels of noise create fatigue, and this is one of the reasons that we feel tired after a two-hour plane flight. Background music will affect mood and behavior; obviously, when out with our best date mood music enhances our emotions. Itchy clothing or an uncomfortable chair may create very subtle anxiety and irritability. Minor work setting inconveniences, such as a computer screen or X-ray viewing light box being too high, can tend to strain our neck muscles. All of these mild inconveniences become noticed more readily late in the day or at night, when our pain threshold is normally lowered. The need to go to the bathroom or to have sex are two of the many physiological behavior determinants of which we are often not consciously aware.

The Senses

We should savor all of our natural senses. The blind, deaf, and mute author Helen Keller said, "I who am blind can give one hint to those who see. Use your eyes as if tomorrow you will have been stricken blind. Hear the music of voices, the song of a bird, the mighty strains of an orchestra as if you would be stricken deaf tomorrow. Touch each object as if tomorrow your tactile sense would fail. Smell the perfume of flowers, taste with relish each morsel, as if tomorrow you could never taste or smell again. Make the most of every sense."

Smell is our most primitive sense, being located in the part of our nervous system that is most directly exposed to the outside world. Our olfactory organ in the roof of our nose is directly exposed to chemical stimuli. Our sense of smell heavily influences our sense of taste. Although we taste only four basic properties—salty, bitter, sweet, and sour—any further fine tuning depends on our sense of smell. Humans have lost some of their sense of smell through evolution because we now communicate mainly by language. Animals, of course, communicate by smells. Insects use pheromones and animals leave scents to designate territory. Primates' sexual and social activities are based on smell; they can detect small genetic differences and actually prefer to mate with those who have a different odor. Perhaps this is nature's way of preventing inbreeding. Like a fingerprint that is genetically determined, our bodies have a unique smell. Human mothers are able to identify their newborn babies by their singular odor. Human beings can be tracked by bloodhounds because an odor trail of microscopic particles in the air or in the grass remains for twenty-four hours. A gentle wind will shift the path of these particles, thereby making tracking more difficult.

The sense of smell may be altered by certain diseases, such as an allergy or the common cold. Most of us are unaware of the constant flow of mucous secretion that flows far back into our nasal passages and pharynx and is sniffed back and swallowed. This amounts to almost one quart per day. Head trauma may also adversely affect the olfactory apparatus. Patients with Alzheimer disease and Parkinson disease tend to lose their sense of smell, but all of us tend to lose our sense of smell with advancing age. Of those over eighty years old, almost half have almost completely lost this sense and are actually in danger because of the need to smell smoke and escaping fuel gas. Females, particularly in children, have a better sense of smell than males. Many women have a diminution of the sense of smell after menopause, but with estrogen treatment they can recover their full ability.

We now have many odors in our environment that overwhelm us, such as perfumes and hair conditioners. Enthusiastic commercial effort now goes into adding odors to products, from plastic Christmas trees to kitty litter. Certain odors alter our moods, some relaxing us and some actually agitating us. Starting with perfumes designed for aphrodisiac effect, aromas abound that inspire us even though we are not aware of it. Studies suggest that the fragrances of vanilla and peppermint are soothing and that chocolate improves scores on memory tests. Smells tend to evoke emotional response because the smell centers in the brain are connected to the limbic system, which controls emotion and sexual urges. When I was playing football in grade school we applied sticky pine tar to our fingers so we wouldn't fumble the ball; today the smell of pine tar carries me back to the excitement of those games.

Sometimes people have an unusual craving for certain tastes and foods. A compulsion to chew ice, paper, or dirt may be a basic response to anemia. This craving is known as pica. People with anemia and pica have a bizarre yearning for a substance like baking soda.

We all have a blind spot in each eye, due to the optic nerve coming into the retina in one small area. Locate your blind spot by covering your left eye with your left hand. Holding your right index finger approximately one foot in front of your face, cover up a distant small object with your index fingernail. Move your index finger slowly toward the right, continue to focus on the distant object, and you will see your fingernail disappear. As you continue to move it to the right it will reappear. The same thing can be done with the left eye by covering up the right eye. It is possible that your blind spot could interfere occasionally with sports such as baseball or tennis, particularly if you have sight in only one eye. You might lose a ball coming at just the right angle.

You can stare intently at a black object on a white background for thirty seconds and then look up at a dark wall to see that object moved to the wall but appearing white instead of black. This is caused by an afterimage, and it is due to the effect of stimulating a localized area on the retina. Bright objects appear larger than dark objects because strong light stimulates adjacent receptors in the retina as well as those struck directly.

Our sense of touch is predominantly mediated by the

largest organ of our body, the skin, which weighs from six to ten pounds. We shed about one and a half pounds of it each year, and much of it becomes the major component of house dust. Touch is a fundamental need of newborns, and they may perish without it. Touch deprivation, in babies and adults, is real indeed. In today's primitive hunter-gatherer societies, touching babies comes naturally, with skin-to-skin contact with the mother being the norm for most of the first year. Today, in our society, we go to great lengths to isolate our babies in their own crib.

Many professionals, from physicians and chiropractors to manicurists, fully appreciate the human need for touch. Massage therapists are familiar with the endorphin-releasing and sleep-inducing properties of bodily contact. A gentle touch on the arm or face by another is effective in rapport, and most of us would never guess that a subliminal touch by a salesperson or waitress is effective in increasing sales or a tip.

At times multiple senses can be involved in the generation of a particular sensation. Motion sickness may be caused by a mismatch of the senses. The vestibular system in the inner ear, which regulates balance, sends messages to the brain about body position and movement. In motion sickness, these messages are contrary to the information relayed by the eyes. On a boat, for instance, the inside of the cabin moves with the passenger, but the inner ear senses the undulating motion of the boat. This incongruity of the senses provokes the flood of stress-related hormones such as epinephrine and vasopressin, which creates the nausea. Some studies have shown that the susceptibility to motion sickness is genetic in origin and, in particular, the Chinese are especially at risk.

Handedness

Humans tend to be right handed in all cultures and races, but other animals show no preference in handedness. Theories abound regarding the origin of handedness, genetics apparently being an important factor. Some researchers have considered left handedness to represent an actual injury to the developing fetus, causing an abnormal endocrine response in utero. The exact percentage of left-handed people is debatable because it is difficult to classify many ambidextrous people. In general, lefties tend to be more ambidextrous than righties.

In about 95 percent of right-handed individuals language is controlled predominantly by the brain's left cerebral hemisphere, which controls the movements of the right hand. Left-handers also have the speech centers on the left side of the brain, but only about 70 percent of the time. Left-handers are also less consistent, some having the reversal of the normal specialization of the two hemispheres, and some having speech centers on each side.

In lefties the locus of language and motor function in the brain tends to be more generalized. Many star athletes and artists have been left-handers, who apparently utilize both sides of their brain more effectively than right-handers. Star tennis players Rod Laver, Martina Navratilova, and Jimmy Connors are lefties, as were Michelangelo and Leonardo da Vinci. Lefties are known to be at a greater risk for injuries in school athletics, but why this is is debatable.

Aging

Much of our behavior is altered by the bodily changes that
come with advancing age. This process occurs so gradually
we may not comprehend its effect on our ability and desire to
do things that we have long taken for granted. In contrast,
we easily recall when we went through puberty, and how our
desires and priorities changed in response to hormones.

Much of our longevity is genetically determined. Some
think that we have a set timetable predetermined within ourselves, since after cells in the body have divided approximately fifty times, they become defective, eventually inoper-
ative, and soon die. Superimposed upon this basic timetable
are environmental ravages from exposure to toxins, viruses,
and radiation, all of which cause the elaboration of free oxy-
gen radicals in our system, damaging and aging cells. The
idea of antioxidants to counteract the free radicals has
recently become popular. Vitamin C, vitamin E and beta-
carotene are some of the better-known antioxidants. Under-
nutrition (reducing caloric intake) has also been espoused as
a means of life extension, and has been shown to be quite
effective in animals. Regular exercise, both physical and
mental, seems to retard aging.

Surprisingly, there is some good news regarding the
physical aspects of aging. Older people have fewer colds, less
dental decay, a lessened tendency to motion sickness, and
require less sleep. Sexually, they are less impetuous, with
men being able to control and delay orgasm.

With advancing age we may notice that we have to get up
during the night to urinate. In older males this is partially
related to an enlarging prostate gland, but in both sexes it is

caused by a normal decrease in the amount of antidiuretic hormone produced by the pituitary. In younger people the antidiuretic hormone acts during sleep to decrease urine output by the kidneys; the diminution of this hormone in later life causes an increased volume of urine.

The normal aging process causes a decrease in sexual activity. In males the average number of orgasms decreases from 120 per year at age thirty to 35 per year at age sixty. Couples may not recognize that their sex life is affected by overall changes in their bodies and not only by willful behavior.

Older persons might feel the effects of an overdose of medication if they receive the same dose that they took thirty years before. Our metabolism slows as we age and drugs tend to accumulate in the body that would once have been excreted. Another variable when taking medication during aging is a decrease in the amount of stomach acid and unreliable absorption of certain medications, which may bring about a delayed and more sustained effect. An absolute decrease in body weight that some elderly persons acquire is also a factor to consider in the dosage of medication.

The sense organs are insidiously affected by the aging process. The lens of the eye becomes less elastic and also becomes yellower, which creates a need for reading glasses. Changes in the retina and pupil combine to create difficulty seeing at night. We may develop a dislike for night driving or dark restaurants in our later years and be unaware of the true reasons for this. The hardened lens makes us more sensitive to bright lights and the glare of the sun, but we might not realize that this is why we don't enjoy a walk at noon as much as we once did. Our depth perception also decreases, explaining why we might miss an easy putt on the golf course or overfill a coffee cup.

Sometimes people are not aware of other defects or actual strengths of their senses. Baseball slugger Ted Williams happened to be blessed with a rare visual acuity but during his playing days he didn't know this. The form of his swing got all the credit.

After age fifty we begin to lose hearing for the higher-pitched tones, which is caused by the aging of the auditory nerve and is called neurosensory hearing loss, in contrast to conduction hearing loss, which can be caused by accumulated ear wax or an ear infection. Many consonants are made with a high-frequency sound. Older people may lose hearing for "sh" because it is a high-pitched sound, making the word *shoe* sound like *oo*. The decrease in hearing with age tends to be somewhat more prominent in men than in women and may be related to exposure to loud noises in male work settings and during hunting and military service.

As you get older you generally lose your sense of taste, partly because of a decrease in the absolute number of taste buds on your tongue, and also because of decreasing ability to smell. A loss of smell (and consequently taste) can also be seen after diuretic therapy for generalized swelling or high blood pressure, when copious amounts of urine are passed, creating a zinc deficiency.

Aging and the Brain

With aging the brain weight decreases about 15 percent, at maximum. The loss of cerebral cortex mainly occurs in the frontal and temporal regions. Cortical loss in the motor region of the frontal lobes leads to reduced coordination of muscle movements and accounts for the tremor of the aged.

Blood flow to the brain and glucose utilization don't change much with age. Contrary to past teaching, the actual number of brain cells (neurons) in the brain lost with aging is not great. The large neurons actually shrink to a smaller size and lose many of their connections but are still able to send out new branches called dendrites. Neurons in the substantia nigra region (near the brain stem) are reduced in number significantly, which may cause abnormal movements such as those in Parkinson disease.

There has recently been considerable interest in substances called nerve growth factors and their ability to prevent the effects of aging on neurons. These many chemical nerve growth factors are produced by the brain but can be given therapeutically, preventing memory deficits that occur in some aging animals. Neurophysiologists are optimistic about reducing aging in the brain and recommend maintaining adequate blood glucose levels, keeping mentally active, and taking certain medications, such as the antioxidants, that may delay aging and even prevent illnesses such as the Alzheimer and Parkinson diseases.

With aging there occurs some decrease in performance IQ, as shown in studies with tests for short-term visual memory and speed of processing information. No such decrease occurs, however, in verbal IQ, such as with vocabulary. Our fund of information and general comprehension are maintained well into our eighties, and people who remain active, love life, and are challenged continue to have excellent brain function. This has been shown in experimental animals and also with obvious examples such as Konrad Adenauer, a leading political figure in postwar Germany while in his nineties, and with George Burns and Bob Hope. Older people do not lose judgment and their orientation to society, but they may be slower to respond in timed tests. By calling on their sizable store of knowledge and experience with problem solving and critical thinking, older individuals may succeed in fields of diplomacy and law in later years.

With constant, vigorous stimulation of your mind and body, and with active social involvement and mental exercise, you can actually increase the number of synaptic connections of the brain cells, which continue to form throughout most of life. Boredom and isolation, on the other hand, tend to decrease them. Depression and long-term, repressed anger all tend to have an adverse effect on the immune system, which shortens life. After retirement, if one does not remain alert and challenged, the immune system tends to rest and make one more vulnerable.

Brain Structure and Function

James Watson, the Nobel Prize–winning biologist, has called the brain the most complex thing we have yet discovered in our universe. Congress declared the 1990s the Decade of the Brain.

Studies on conscious patients undergoing electrical stimulation of certain parts of their brains has enabled scientists to make determinations about what parts of the brain specialize in certain functions. Diagnostic methods of determining brain anatomy and physiology have come a long way since the introduction of the electroencephalogram, which has been around for many decades. During my radiology residency in the 1960s much effort was spent working with pneumoencephalograms, a procedure whereby air injected into the spinal canal bubbled up into the ventricles of the brain, making it possible for us to see internal structures. Cerebral arteriograms (injecting liquid contrast material into the arteries supplying the brain) were also common procedures. In the 1970s computer assisted tomography (CAT scans) enabled us to see internal structures more clearly, without potentially harmful consequences. In the 1980s magnetic resonance imaging gave us better and more detailed evaluation of internal structures, then positron emission tomography (PET) came on the scene, proving useful in localizing physiologic activity, in particular, by the utilization of isotope-tagged glucose which is taken up from the blood by the most active parts of the brain. Currently research is progressing on magnetoencephalography, which analyzes the very weak magnetic fields that result from neural activity. This newest diagnostic approach is in the experimental stage and is useful in localizing the site of epileptic seizures. Newer techniques of magnetic resonance imaging provide correlation with specific thoughts and specific anatomical sites in the brain, verging on a radiological "mapping of the mind."

Today, there are many hard-nosed determinists who feel that a separate "mind" or "soul" does not exist. In actuality, such conscious thoughts are only neurochemical processes in the brain. Furthermore, the brain is merely a mechanism for producing more gonads to propagate the spread of DNA.

Our brain weighs about three pounds and has about 100 billion nerve cells (neurons). The nerve endings (synapses) are constantly changing and making new connections. The estimated 100 trillion synaptic connections are stimulated and strengthened by repeated use. In the fashion of Darwinian natural selection, the surviving connections are those that prove most useful in coping with the outside world. Therefore, there is a greater number and complexity of connections in the area of the cerebral cortex controlling the hands of a skilled workman. Nerve impulses are transmitted across these synapses by chemicals called neurotransmitters. Child and adult brain structures are partly determined by their experience and intentions in particular areas of activity: individuals select and develop certain circuits. However, there are genetic limitations on the circuits available for selection.

The brain consists of two large cerebral hemispheres, left and right, connected by a relatively small midline bundle called the corpus callosum. Below these hemispheres, toward the back, resides the cerebellum, with the brain stem (medulla) below it. We know that the highest mental functions generally reside in the cortex (surface layer) of the cerebral hemispheres, particularly in the frontal regions. The cerebellum not only controls balance but also collects the memory of unconscious movements, such as walking, serving a tennis ball, or typing. The brain stem controls automatic functions, such as breathing. The hippocampus, deep within the temporal lobes of the cerebral hemispheres, coordinates memory, and the nearby amygdala controls emotions. Researchers have found that the brain works like many specialists operating together, with ample communication between them. Surprisingly, the brain hears loud sounds in a totally different place than it hears quieter sounds. The area concerned with recognition of a face is in a location different than that recalling man-made objects. Certain tasks proceed in unexpected parts of the brain. Completing a word fragment is done in the visual processing area toward the back of the cerebral hemispheres. Some complex functions involve (light up on PET scans) many parts of the brain simultaneously. Highly intelligent people are shown to use less mental energy than the less intelligent, which may reflect a more efficient neurophysiology in the more intelligent.

All of the areas of the brain work together, but, in general, the left hemisphere is more concerned with moving the right-side extremities and with language processing, while the right hemisphere is more concerned with moving the left-side extremities, spatial handling, imagination, and artistic ability. The left hemisphere tends to be more analytic and concerned with proper sequencing of time and space, while the right brain tends to be holistic and intuitive. Determining an over-all pattern such as reading is a predominantly right-brain function, as is geometrical thinking and music perception.

There is some evidence that females have a larger midline corpus callosum that connects the two hemispheres and allows greater cross-communication by nerve fibers, leading to speculation that females are then able to use both sides of their brain somewhat more than males.

There is communication between the hemispheres not only by way of the corpus callosum but also by lower structures in the midbrain. After operations for epilepsy where the corpus callosum is surgically divided, results have been variable. The overall behavior of such patients has not been dramatically altered, but careful testing of these individuals has revealed important changes. Usually only the left side of the brain can write, speak, or do arithmetic. If the conscious state is determined primarily by the ability to perceive and transmit language, then it is the left hemisphere that mediates consciousness. But in some reported cases, a few months after their corpus callosums were divided, patients became able to speak with their right as well as their left hemispheres. There existed two separate conscious states that were not necessarily in agreement with one another and had different personalities. This adds an interesting dimension to the question raised in a previous chapter: "What is a self?"

Sleep and Circadian Rhythm

Rhythmic activity, found throughout nature, is genetically determined. Certain plants open their leaves every twelve hours, regardless of sunshine, and particular algae produce a glow every twenty-four hours. Our bodies undergo rhythmic physiology throughout the day, month, and year. Blood clots more easily in the morning and we are mentally more alert and optimistic around noon, but our physiology reaches a peak in the midafternoon, when our temperature, pulse, and blood pressure are all highest. Humans obviously have a biological clock that determines the cycles of reproduction in the female.

Most researchers think the pineal body at the base of the brain regulates the circadian rhythms. Pineal activity is related to the amount and timing of light perception. In the fall, as the days become shorter, some people become melancholy. This condition, called seasonal affective disorder (SAD), can be quite bothersome to those who become significantly depressed in midwinter. Alleviation is obtained with exposure to bright light for two hours in the early morning.

At the present time about one out of four American workers are involved with some form of night shift work that interrupts the circadian-rhythm sleep/awake cycle and causes a number of physiological disturbances. Ordinarily, body temperature reaches the lowest point around 4:00 A.M. during sound sleep. Although we change shifts to work at night, our body temperature continues to decrease at this time. Other cycles are involved, including overall physical activity, meals, and contact with light or darkness. An alteration occurs in the physiology of the stomach related to the production of gastrin and pepsin. Those working night shifts tend to eat at irregular intervals, which alters the acidity of the stomach and creates digestive disturbances and even peptic ulcer. These workers are more prone to heart disease, possibly because less exposure to daylight elevates blood cholesterol.

People on late-shift work tend to have an increased number of accidents and may excessively use alcohol or drugs (particularly caffeine in coffee) to compensate for the changes in their disturbed physiology. Affected workers may show behavior disturbances: mental lapses, confusion, and irritability. Being out of sync with the activity of others, they have social disharmony at home and at work. Often, these workers do not suspect that their irascible conduct is related to their odd working schedule. Late-shift work often brings problems to those who require peak thought processes, such as policemen and physicians.

Many Americans often have self-induced sleep deprivation. In our hectic lives, when we try to include too much activity into a day and in the end flop in front of the television set to see the late show, we fool ourselves into thinking that we can do just as well with five or six hours of sleep as we can with eight. You don't do as well at school, and you may go to sleep at the wheel. Sleepy people tend to be sullen and are inferior at interpersonal relations. Teenagers are the least apt to know that their physiology requires at least eight hours of sleep, which is even more than older children require.

On the weekends we usually stay up later on Friday and Saturday night, then sleep later the following mornings. This alteration of the normal rhythms is said to account for the melancholy period that occurs about 3:00 P.M. on Sunday. Other causative factors include awareness that the weekend is drawing to a close and that Sunday afternoon is relatively unstructured and empty. This Sunday afternoon mood low is the payback for the "Thank God It's Friday" high.

Sleep apnea is a very common and often unrecognized disorder, usually occurring in overweight people. It involves cyclical stoppage of breathing, buildup of carbon dioxide, and snoring, which repeatedly interrupts sleep. Sleep apneics wonder why they are tired during the day, even though the previous night's sleep was so erratic.

Altered Mental States

Superimposed upon the types of unconscious and conscious activity, various altered states affect our total brain activity. We have an excessively stimulated state when we are *emotionally stressed*, resulting in a decrease in optimal functioning and an actual lowering of our IQ. We can also be *somnolent* and often enjoy periods of *hypnogogic reverie* (daydreaming). We go through different stages of *sleep*, with our deepest sleep occurring approximately 1.5 hours after we retire. We may undergo induced forms of *hypnosis* with gradations of depth. *Drugs* and *anesthesia* create altered states, and there are described stages of anesthesia. In the *persistent vegetative state*, we are not aware of our surroundings, but we respond to painful stimuli and may have sleep/awake cycles because these are generated in the more primitive areas of the brain. In *deep coma*, we have no wake or sleep cycles and no response to pain. *Transcendental meditation* can alter brain waves, indicating an alert wakefulness and quiescence of the fight-or-flight activity of the sympathetic nervous system. Our intellectual status varies with *age*, with overall *mood*, and with the days of the week and the time of day. I tend to think more clearly on the weekend, after ample recreation and a full night's sleep.

Sensory deprivation, such as solitary confinement in a dark room, can affect one's conscious state, as can being alone at sea or in the desert. One can experience a bizarre alteration of consciousness by being immersed in a saltwater tank without sound or sight. Long immobilization in a body cast can also render similar effects, as can prolonged observation of a radar screen. The monotony of long-distance highway driving (especially through a desert) creates "highway hypnosis." During states of sensory deprivation, people become disoriented and are highly susceptible to hypnosis.

Subtle combinations of these effects, such as being slightly angry and slightly inebriated in a humid bar where loud music is blaring, might lead to homicide. None of these factors alone would be recognized as having a significant impact on one's emotions.

Psychoneuroimmunology

Scientific evidence is mounting that psychological factors influence the maintenance of health and the development of disease. Stress, grief, and mental illness all adversely alter the immune system. The brain regulates the sympathetic nervous system along the spine, which in turn modulates immunity by way of the nerve supply to blood-forming organs— the bone marrow, lymph nodes, spleen, and thymus gland, which are important components of the human immune system. In a matter of seconds after a painful cut, healing white blood cells leave your bone marrow to travel to the site of injury. The brain also produces various neuropeptides that support the working cells of the immune system. Confident, optimistic activity bolsters the psychoneuroimmunologic system; passivity and pessimism weaken it. Students under overwhelming academic pressures are more likely to have viral illnesses such as infectious mononucleosis. Women whose husbands had recently died were shown to have a decreased activity of NK (natural killer) cells, which destroy tumor cells and virus-infected cells. Medical students immediately before examinations were shown to have reduced NK cell activity due to stress. However, some of these medical students, termed "good copers," felt as if they were not under unusual stress and their NK cell activity was not depressed. Higher-brain function is also involved in the hormones secreted by endocrine glands, such as the pituitary, adrenal, and thyroid.

Activation of the stress system promotes behavioral changes that enhance the adjustment of the entire body toward the stressful agent. With proper coping, brief and limited stress (eustress) provides just enough challenge to our bodies to provide a pleasant excitement that benefits our emotional, and hence physiological, well-being. Eustress and its positive compensatory mechanisms of hormonal activation cause arousal, focused attention, decreased appetite, and decreased sex drive. One's ability to cope with stress in the optimal physiological way may well be genetically determined.

A positive mental attitude about disease or misfortune can certainly augment our physiology. Patients with malignancy who have the attitude that they can't die, their lives are too important, and that they have pressing obligations to their dependents, are more likely to have their cancer undergo remission. Various relaxation techniques utilizing meditation and self-hypnosis are also often effective, again demonstrating a definite mind-body link. Don't underestimate the ability of the mind to maintain health, heal disease, and even increase life expectancy.

Our complicated psychoneuroimmune system generates some strange mind-over-body reactions, such as older spouses dying soon after their mates (sympathetic death). For those cultures in which voodoo plays a significant part witch doctors have been known to cause death by the suggestion of their curse. Warts have sometimes been cured with hypnosis, which demonstrates control of the nerve and blood supply to the skin by direction from the higher conscious and unconscious centers of the brain. Death rates for certain ethnic groups are higher after anticipated holidays. Examples include Chinese-Americans, who have a lower death rate before the Harvest Moon Festival, and Jews before the Passover. The dates of these holidays change from year to year, so this association is not related to season.

The Placebo Effect

All practitioners of the healing arts have had a secret gimmick going for them that is not generally known by their patients. Among those who benefited through the ages were Hippocrates, the Hopi Indian medicine men, modern physicians, faith healers, acupuncturists, and their patients. It has been shown in many controlled studies that 30 to 40 percent of patients show some benefit from a placebo, such as a sugar pill, given by a caring, enthusiastic health provider. Belief in the effectiveness of a medication or other therapy has its own, self-fulfilling, biochemical effect. Multiple and larger capsules have a more powerful placebo effect than one small capsule, and injections have even more. After all, for centuries doctors have helped patients without accurate diagnostic methods or effective medication such as antibiotics or steroids. I can remember relief from sore throat caused by having it "painted" with some worthless concoction.

In the doctor's office all of the mental background prevails to aid the power of suggestion and expectation. The patient's ego is on the line, he or she having decided to go to a particular practitioner. The person's money is on the line, because of the fee. The natural inclination is to want to please a person in a position of authority, and if the medical figure is personable and shows concern for the patient, psychologically these factors are seductive. Most illness is mild and limited, and patients will usually improve with time alone. Patients also tend to go to the doctor when the symptoms of a self-limiting disease, such as a cold, are peaking. The expectation of improvement reduces the anxiety present with any illness. The doctor's treatment is given credit, however, because the improvement followed it. Thus occurs another undeserved triumph of *post hoc ergo propter hoc*—after that, therefore because of that.

Another factor explaining the benefit of a placebo is the elaboration of endogenous endorphins by the brain, spinal cord, and peripheral nerves. These endogenous morphines are chemicals that function as modulators of brain chemical neurotransmitters. They have complex functions including regulation of appetite, gastrointestinal function, stress, and pain, and also influence heat regulation and endocrine function (they stimulate natural killer cell activity). Endorphins are elevated by happy thoughts and activity such as exercise, laughter, eating good food, and smelling pleasant odors. They are natural stress reducers and pain suppressors, producing tranquillity, euphoria, and muscle relaxation. Recall that if you go on a "laughing jag" you will soon become weak all over. Crying also releases endorphins, which explains why you usually, but temporarily, feel euphoric after crying.

Under hypnosis people can be relieved of pain because of the placebo effect and the secretion of endorphins. Even burn dressings can be changed with less pain when patients are under hypnosis. Faith healers take advantage of the placebo effect in people with chronic pain because, during the temporary emotional response, pain from arthritis is actually decreased after the excitement of public "laying on of hands." Acupuncture is often effective in pain relief due to the placebo effect and endorphin secretion at the needle sites. Music, providing relaxing pleasure and distraction, has been shown to ameliorate a mildly painful procedure. Any type of therapy, even surgery, depends somewhat on the placebo effect. Various unconventional healing methods, such as the use of New Age crystals and bioenergetics (exchange of energy between patient and therapist), largely depend on these factors, as do the more conventional chiropractic manipulations and massage therapy.

Pharmacological Behavior Alterations

When I was in high school, one night when waiting at a traffic light a huge truck smashed into the back of my car, knocking it out into the intersection. Luckily, no one was hurt, but my car was damaged significantly. The driver of the truck muttered something about being on some pills that made him sleepy. His company paid for the damages. When I was a young military physician I rather liberally prescribed tranquilizers without thinking much about the consequences. One day one of my patients returned and said that the tran- quilizers were helpful, but recently while driving she was so sleepy she struck and injured a pedestrian.

The effects of medication, including abnormal medication reactions, are underestimated as influences on our behavior. In general, too many pills are prescribed and taken, partly because patients demand them from doctors and often will go elsewhere if the doctor does not accommodate them. A sur- prisingly large percentage of vehicle accidents are related to tranquilizers, mood elevators, and allergy medications (anti- histamines), the effects of which are often enhanced by alco- hol intake. Various analgesics like Darvon and codeine will have effects on our actions, such as impairing motor coordi- nation and short-term memory. Many people may not know that their unusual mental symptoms are related to their med- ication. A large percentage of all medications tend to cause some drowsiness and dizziness, and many drugs cause anxi- ety and/or depression. Cortisone preparations (corticosteroid hormones) can cause psychosis in rare instances.

Drugs in combination often result in unexpected effects. Anticoagulants, when combined with aspirin and certain corticosteroids, can create bleeding problems. With all the complicated medications being given today, pharmacists and physicians may have to use a computer to determine if there are antagonistic or potentiating effects of a particular combi- nation.

These adverse effects are more common in older individ- uals who absorb and excrete the medications in a slower and less reliable way. The aged also tend to take many different inappropriately prescribed medications and often confuse them, taking incorrect doses. It has been estimated that one-fourth of those individuals over age sixty-five are experiencing some form of untoward drug effect, for example, appearing to be delusional.

Physical Addiction

True physical addiction can be defined as the condition in which the brain is biochemically changed due to chronic use of certain substances such as alcohol, cocaine, or nicotine, and in which abrupt cessation of use causes physical symptoms of withdrawal. The pleasure centers in our brain are located deep within the limbic system, with the nucleus accumbens appearing to be the particular reward center for cocaine and amphetamines. Cocaine produces an accumulation of the neurotransmitter dopamine, which creates the pleasure. Similar physiology is involved with alcohol intake and sexual excitation. Certain cues and habits serve to start this flow of dopamine even before the drug is used or the sex act consummated.

Many addictions are now called diseases in an attempt to excuse the addicted individual of personal responsibility, but many maintain that people tend to abuse drugs and alcohol, not because they are helpless, but because they wish to have the temporarily pleasurable sensation. Addicts still have some control over their "disease" because many have stopped their nicotine or alcohol addiction with their own will power.

There is a definite genetic tendency for all addictions. Many people have a generalized predisposition to addictive behavior and are addicted to alcohol, nicotine, other drugs, and often tend to express some compulsive form of sexual behavior. Many of us have a higher incidence of addiction to either gambling, work, food, or caffeine—anything that stimulates the pleasure centers. We are now referring to the majority of the population.

Drugs are readily available and used widely in the society. In men between twenty-five and thirty-four years of age, 83 percent use alcohol, 46 percent use tobacco, 22 percent use marijuana, and 10 percent use cocaine.

It has recently been discovered that the combination of cocaine and alcohol in the body forms a new substance called cocaethylene, which creates the same sense of euphoria as cocaine but is more intense and lasts longer. Between 60 and 80 percent of cocaine users also use alcohol.

The harmful effects of alcohol on our society are masked by the persistent image of drinking as being socially acceptable, glamorous, and somewhat amusing. Death on the highway caused by drunk drivers has been the most publicized tragic effect of drinking, but less well known are the facts that alcohol use is associated with 69 percent of deaths in boating accidents, 49 percent of episodes of interpersonal violence such as murder or attempted murder, and 50 percent of reported rapes.

Of tremendous importance are the effects of alcohol, nicotine, and other drugs such as cocaine on the developing fetus. Chronic cocaine use impairs the immune response of both mother and child. The obviously retarded infants with fetal alcohol syndrome may represent only the minority of affected cases. You do not have to be a confirmed alcoholic mother to harm your child because it is now known that even moderate social drinking can, at times, have a significant adverse effect on the developing fetus. Perhaps many people today are not recognized as having a slightly reduced intelligence because their mothers took a few too many social drinks while pregnant.

Fetal alcohol syndrome represents just one example of many possible dangers of the intrauterine environment. Placental abnormalities, nicotine, and various infections can also harm the fetal brain. Eventual vagaries of behavior in the adult can result from this intrauterine influence which is separate from the influence of genetics and the extrauterine environment.

We have discussed the illogical expectations of the search for a continuous, ecstatic "high" of "love" in chapter 7. Romantic love itself can be considered a form of addiction when it is new and full blown. Romantic love and sex, as we currently know them, stimulate the activity of the limbic system of the brain, which causes an increased production of excitatory neurotransmitters such as norepinephrine and dopamine, generating responses similar to those caused by amphetamines and cocaine. The resulting chronic, low-grade, physiological "high" cannot be continued for more than a few months. It has to come down to more normal physiological levels. When a heightened threshold for experiencing excitement naturally develops, the romantic relationship seems flat compared to its previous high. Initially, any imperfection in a love partner is ignored due to the altered brain chemistry, but after the decrease in the excitation occurs, these imperfections become noticeable. This should be expected in any romance or marriage. More practical concerns then hold marriage together, such as family interests and emotional support. Love then has to shift to another level, emphasizing companionship, security, and personal warmth, and this latter relaxation phase actually has its own neurochemical rewards: increased endorphins.

Mental Illness

Defining mental illness is problematic because the difference between organic, anatomic mental illness and neurosis is not clearcut. An individual can have a completely normal mental state but various brain scans can show obviously damaged brain structure. In contrast, one can have severe catatonic schizophrenia and yet show a completely normal brain structure as seen in these same sophisticated imaging procedures. Regardless of whether mental illness is caused primarily by structural disease or by subtle unconscious processes, there remains always the effect of one upon the other. The body and mind are interdependent, so the relationship of health and behavior is bidirectional.

Many of our dissertations on mind-brain relationships are probably no better than Aristotle's efforts to figure out these same things. Just as he had no knowledge of brain neurophysiology, the circulation of blood, the existence of atoms, genetics, and quantum mechanics, we are certainly limited by lack of knowledge. One hundred years from now we will laugh at our current ideas on the mind-brain relation.

An example of our lack of understanding is the entire conundrum of mental illness. Are people with injuries to their brain, such as those with intracranial hemorrhage in the premature newborn, responsible for their actions in later life? Is an Alzheimer disease patient responsible for carelessly setting a fire that kills many people? What about the mass murderer found at autopsy to have a brain tumor? Certain brain tumors in the limbic system (a deep cerebral complex consisting of the amygdala, the hippocampus, and the hypothalamus) can sometimes lead to violent outbursts. Heavy philosophical decisions regarding responsibility will always be changing, and will help to shape legal decisions.

Occasionally, specific types of encephalitis destroy areas of a person's hippocampus and the temporal lobes of the brain. Left with no memory, the unfortunate victims must live only in the present, with moment-to-moment consciousness. A similar syndrome is sometimes seen with long-term alcoholics.

Schizophrenia is a true physical illness with genetic propensity. Abnormal brain chemistry involves excess amounts of dopamine and serotonin, but treatment by medication blocks an excessive flow of these neurotransmitters.

The term *depression* has been distorted and inflated such that it now overlaps with the terms *disappointment* and *anxiety*. True manic-depressive illness is definitely genetic in origin. Some forms of depression are associated with a diminished amount of dopamine and are treated by medication that blocks the breakdown of dopamine. Depression can involve the normal letdown from a brain chemistry high; this is shown by the increased suicide rate after winter holidays. We often experience mild depression after graduation from high school or college, after our near-term goal has been met. Both postpartum depression and post-wedding depression are well known.

Some mental illnesses are not associated with structural or chemical abnormalities of the brain. Multiple personality disorder is understandably controversial but is valid in many cases. It is more common in women, and childhood physical or sexual abuse before age five years is a frequently uncovered background. Psychologically these individuals tend to escape the pain of the abuse memories by displacing the problems to another character and entering a fugue state by dissociating themselves. To handle the conflicting emotions they assign their different selves to multiple personalities manifesting varying body language and voice. Almost all of these patients have a child alter ego as one of their personae. Most cases of mild multiple personality disorder are never diagnosed, because they are not as straightforward as those portrayed in the movies. Wisdom can be taxed in criminal cases involving these hapless individuals.

Obsessive-compulsive disorder (OCD) is sometimes associated with certain neurological disorders such as tics and epilepsy, and usually involves people thought to be unusually well organized and tidy. OCD is genetically transmitted, although it is laborious to sort out the nurture/nature overlap in families that tend to be compulsive. Certain parts of the brain, such as portions of the frontal cerebral cortex and the deep basal ganglia, show abnormal glucose metabolism on positron emission tomography. Those suffering with fully manifest OCD lead miserable lives impeded by rituals such as repeated hand washing. Minor compulsions are normal in daily life. We like to have our desks clean when we leave the office in the afternoon, or have all the dirty dishes washed and put away at night. But when those with OCD walk down the street they may be compelled to step on each line of the sidewalk. They may get carried away with cleanliness, develop a morbid fear of germs, or become overly religious.

Captain Ahab was obsessed with Moby Dick and Inspector Javert in *Les Misérables* hunted down Jean Valjean for thirty years. Obsessive love is far more common than has been thought and is only now getting the publicity it deserves. Harassment and stalking after the end of a romantic relationship is surprisingly common. "I just can't get you out of my mind" is the song that these people play over and over in their minds. Some cases involve an element of physical addiction and withdrawal from the cerebral neurochemical dependence of new romantic love.

Hypochondriasis is a variably disabling condition that controls far more people than we realize. Everyone is at times prone to manifest mental stress through bodily symptoms, but some lives are totally ruled by imaginary illness. Hypochondriacs have little insight into their problem, and may not be aware they are narcissists who hurt others. They go from doctor to doctor, experiencing a certain amount of pleasure from the thrill of new tests and medication. Munchausen syndrome patients are hypochondriacs or malingerers who go from hospital to hospital and even country to country in search of the excitement that their compulsion directs.

Some hypochondriacs are known as medical hobbyists and are characterized by an intense interest in medicine and their own health. Often they are bored and therefore they direct all their efforts inward, to themselves. Their hobby is going to the doctor and hospitals but, unlike others' hobbies, theirs is usually subsidized by third-party health care payments. These individuals can never be satisfied, and often take pride in saying that they are unique souls who have peculiar medical symptoms and are rare in that they have unusual reactions to medications. With the threat of overhanging malpractice liability, physicians cannot take a chance, and their new hypochondriac patient is apt to get an expensive diagnostic workup. Medical hobbyists will not tell a new doctor that they have had thousands of dollars worth of tests that have shown nothing abnormal. The more attention and sympathy they receive, the worse their hypochondriasis becomes, because the more health care they experience, the more expert and involved in it they become.

Miscellaneous Physical and Medical Factors

An infinite number of physiological and medical factors govern one's behavior. Dietary indiscretion, of course, can put one on edge. Certain people may be unaware that they have lactose intolerance and are unable to digest milk products properly, which can create indigestion. Carbohydrates tend to elevate brain serotonin soon after eating, which creates a calming effect. Foods with high sugar content tend to be absorbed rapidly because the pancreas is stimulated to secrete insulin to help absorb the sugar. This leads to an overcompensation and lowering of blood sugar about 1.5 hours after the high-sugar meal. This low blood sugar (hypoglycemia) can create a jittery, headachy feeling.

We continue to be exposed to toxins such as lead. Children living in poverty in the United States tend to be significantly exposed to lead. It is estimated that 16 percent of all these children have blood lead levels in the neurotoxic range, which can cause many types of unusual mental handicaps. The various other toxic wastes that have contaminated our air, water, and soil for decades undoubtedly affect our brains and our behavior in unrecognizable ways.

Hypothyroidism (an underactive thyroid) lowers your rate of metabolism and may be responsible for lethargy and an overall cold sensation. Hyperthyroidism (overactive) can bring about seemingly abundant nervous energy, but easy tiring.

Some days we just don't feel good and may have some indigestion and sleepiness. These could be symptoms of our bodies fighting a virus. We now know that we actually thwart many viral infections during a year, manifesting full-blown illness with only the minority of infections.

Sometimes low-grade inflammatory reactions make us

feel under the weather. A slightly inflamed ingrown toenail, a blister on our foot, or a mild sunburn can produce irritability of which we may not be mindful. I can recall being quite quarrelsome with friends during Florida vacations after we had had too much sun. At that time we didn't appreciate the cause of our quarrels.

The big breakthrough in medicine during the past fifteen years involves the paradigm shift realization that our behavior is reciprocally responsible for most of our health. Lifestyle and body are inextricably connected. How we handle diet, sleep, exercise, drugs (including nicotine and alcohol), automobile driving (including use of seat belts), and sex largely determines our health. Medical care plays a relatively minor role. To complicate things, however, we are not completely responsible for our behavior and lifestyle. This is one of the main themes of this book. Genes have a major influence, and we do not freely choose our cultural, economic, political, and physical environment.

Nobel laureate Paul Berg has said, "I start with the premise that all human disease is genetic." Yet former Surgeon General C. Everett Koop is of the opinion that 85 percent of all disease in those under age 65 is related to lifestyle. Strangely, these statements are not mutually exclusive. In accord with the emphasis in this book of the overlapping, indirect effects of nature and nurture, both statements are correct.

References

Ackerman, Diane. *A Natural History of the Senses*. New York: Vintage Books, Random House, 1990.

Ader, Robert, David L. Felten, and Nicholas Cohen. *Psychoneu-roimmunology*. San Diego, Calif.: Academic Press, 1991.

Allman, William. "The Mating Game." *U.S. News and World Report* (July 1, 1993): 57.

Batten, Mary. *Sexual Strategies: How Females Choose Their Mates.* New York: Jeremy P. Tarcher, G. P. Putnam's and Sons, 1992.

Begley, Sharon, Linda Wright, Vernon Church, and Mary Hager. "Mapping the Brain." *Newsweek* (April 20, 1992): 66.

Chrousor, George P., and Phillip W. Gold. "The Concepts of Stress and Stress Symptoms Disorders." *Journal of the American Medical Association* (March 4, 1992): 1244.

Courchesne, Eric, Gary A. Press, and Rachel Yeung-Courchesne. "Parietal Lobe Abnormalities Detected with MR in Patients with Infantile Autism." *American Journal of Roentgenology* (February 1993): 387.

Dement, William C., and Mervill M. Mitler. "It's time to Wake Up to the Importance of Sleep Disorders." *Journal of the American Medical Association* (March 24, 1993): 1548.

Eaton, S. Boyd, Marjorie Shostak, and Melvin Konner. *The Paleolithic Prescription*. New York: Harper and Row, 1988.

Edelman, Gerald M. *Bright Air, Brilliant Fire: On the Matter of the Mind*. New York: Basic Books, 1992.

Fischbach, Gerald D. "Mind and Brain." *Scientific American* (September 1992): 48.

Fisher, Helen E. *Anatomy of Love: The Natural History of Monogamy, Adultery, and Divorce*. New York: W. W. Norton, 1992.

Foulks, Edward, and Thomas McLellen. "Psychologic Sequelae of Chronic Toxic Waste Exposure." *Southern Medical Journal* (February 1992): 122.

Frank, Jerome D., and Julia B. Frank. *Persuasion and Healing: A Comparative Study of Psychotherapy*. Baltimore, Md.: Johns Hopkins University Press, 1991.

Fugh-Berman, Adriane. "Why You Should Touch Your Patients." *Medical Economics* (December 13, 1993): 91.

Gershon, Elliott S., and Ronald O. Rieder. "Major Disorders of Mind and Brain." *Scientific American* (September 1992): 127.

Graham, Charles J., Rhonda Dick, Vaughn I. Rickert, and Robert Glenn. "Left Handedness as a Risk Factor for Unintentional Injury in Children." *Pediatrics* (December 1993): 823.

Kalin, Ned H. "The Neurobiology of Fear." *Scientific American* (May 1993): 94.

Le Geurer, Annik. *Scent: The Mysterious and Essential Power of Smell.* New York: Turtle Bay Books, 1992.

Moore-Ede, Martin. *The Twenty-Four Hour Society: Understanding Human Limits in a World That Never Sleeps.* Reading, Mass.: Addison-Wesley, 1993.

Pesman, Curtis. *How a Man Ages.* New York: Ballentine/Esquire Press Book, 1984.

Ramachandran, Vilayanur S. "Blind Spots." *Scientific American* (May 1992): 86.

Rosenthal, Norman E. "Diagnosis and Treatment of Seasonal Affective Disorder." *Journal of the American Medical Association* (December 8, 1993): 2717.

Restak, Richard. *The Mind.* Bantam Books, 1988.

Ruberman, W. "Psychosocial Influence on Mortality of Patients with Coronary Artery Disease." *Journal of the American Medical Association* (1992): 559.

Rubin, Rita. "Placebos' Healing Power." *U.S. News and World Report* (November 22, 1993): 76.

Rusting, Ricki L. "Why Do We Age?" *Scientific American* (December 1992): 131.

Selkoe, Dennis J. "Aging Brain, Aging Mind." *Scientific American* (September 1992): 135.

Shorter, Edward. *From Paralysis to Fatigue: A History of Psychosomatic Illness in the Modern Era.* New York: Free Press, 1992.

Spiro, Howard. *Doctors, Patients and Placebos.* New Haven, Conn.: Yale University Press, 1986.

Toufexis, Anastasia. "Drowsy America." *Time* (December 17, 1990): 78.

Turner, Judith A., et al. "The Importance of Placebo Effects in Pain Treatment and Research." *Journal of the American Medical Association* (May 25, 1994): 1609.

Ubell, Earl. "Could You Use More Sleep?" *Parade* (January 10, 1993): 16.

Waldman, Alan J. "Neuroanatomic/Neuropathologic Correlates in Schizophrenia." *Southern Medical Journal* (September 1992): 907.

Walsh, Anthony. *The Science of Love: Understanding Love and Its Effects on Mind and Body*. Amherst, N.Y.: Prometheus Books, 1991.

Webb, William. "Hypochondriasis: Difficulties in Diagnosis and Management." *Southern Medical Journal* (January 1979): 37.

Weil, Andrew. *Natural Health, Natural Medicine*. Boston: Houghton Mifflin, 1990.

Weinberger, Daniel R., et al. "Memory Circuit and Schizophrenia." *American Journal of Psychiatry* (1992): 890.

Willcox, Sharon M., David V. Himmelstein, Steffie Woolhandler. "Inappropriate Drug Prescribing for the Community-Dwelling Elderly." *Journal of the American Medical Association* (July 27, 1994): 292.

15

Mathematics, Probabilities, and Choices

You are your actions, and, perhaps surprisingly, these are based on choices that depend on quantitative knowledge of mathematics and statistics.

It is obvious that a knowledge of probabilities is essential to bet effectively at Las Vegas. Less apparent is the fact that many of our day-to-day actions involve quick, unconscious decisions based on statistics. Some of our actions, like deciding to invest money, depend upon consideration of the likelihood that we will be alive in five years. We are constantly considering alternatives, weighing options, and making cost/benefit analyses—and all of these are based on mathematics. We judge whether to try to make it through a yellow light based on the probability of having time to do so. We decide whether to carry an umbrella based on our estimate of the risk of rain. We choose to hit the tennis ball to our opponent's backhand based on the statistical fact that it is his or her weaker side. Any sudden act of bravery involves a rapid appraisal of the chance of personal harm.

The selection of a marriage partner involves not only romance and sexual attraction but the more rational quantitative considerations of age differential, financial stability, and likelihood of the physical ability to have and provide for children.

Broader than arithmetic, mathematics includes all the mental processes of quantification, measuring, and logic. Games from gin rummy to chess depend on mathematics. Computer scientist John von Neumann, using complex mathematical formulas, computers, and logic to deal with systems involving reactions and counterreactions, invented game theory, a strategy to calculate choices in any competitive situation. Game theory (decisional analysis) is now employed in handling many dynamic interactive systems such as military strategy, evolutionary economics, and evolutionary biology. Interactions between persons, corporations, and nations can be analyzed by computers. Permutations of the game known as Prisoner's Dilemma, where two fellow prisoners can choose whether to cooperate with or to risk betraying each other, have been programmed. Game theorist Robert Axelrod wrote in *The Evolution of Cooperation* (1984) that the pursuit of self-interest by mutual defection usually leads to a poor outcome for both parties, whereas mutual cooperation usually benefits both parties. It is generally best to cooperate with someone who will reciprocate that behavior in the future.

In the unthinking biological world, reciprocating cooperation also wins out, from symbiotic systems involving birds and bacteria to wolf packs. Any organism achieving a beneficial response from another is more likely to have surviving offspring that will continue cooperative behavior. In our daily choices of whether to cooperate with a group or to defect for personal gain, we do, surprisingly, use mathematical principles.

Ludwig Wittgenstein's philosophic analysis clarified that the logical grammatical structure of language is ultimately mathlike.

In *Mathematics and Humor* (1980), author and mathematician John Allen Paulos reveals that the logical structure of humor, including puns, paradoxes, riddles, and non sequiturs, is based on a sudden incongruity of logic—a surprising derailment of thought. Humor uses inverted logic and distorted patterns. We must have an understanding of logic to catch a joke based on reductio ad absurdum or spoonerism ("time wounds all heels").

Probabilities in Practicing Medicine

The practice of medicine is based upon sophisticated statistical determinations. In the opinion of Sir William Osler, Canadian professor of medicine, "Medicine is a science of uncertainty and the art of probability." A radiologist seeing a mass in the lung on a chest X-ray of a sixty-year-old smoking male would consider it a 90 percent probability of malignancy. Such a finding in a fifty-year-old nonsmoking female would have perhaps a 40 percent chance of malignancy, and in a five-year-old child, about 0.5 percent. We know that in a child the mass probably represents an early focus of pneumonia. We don't alarm the parents by telling them that there is a tiny chance of malignancy. Radiologists recommend treating the child for pneumonia and usually repeating the chest X-ray in ten days to see if it has cleared.

In reading mammograms radiologists must consider the consequences of false normal versus false abnormal readings. We weigh many things—past knowledge of disease, and the probabilities based on thousands of cases in the literature—and compare the specific findings on the individual patient with the statistical background. Statistics never apply to the individual; they can only be used to measure differences and identify trends in large populations.

Luck

Sheer luck of the draw is more important than we give it credit for in the events of our life. For starters, only one sperm out of millions gets through to contribute to our unique genetic makeup. We give ourselves credit and blame for occurrences that are merely the effect of random happening. We don't give pure chance enough credit for certain streaks. If we make five consecutive investments that turn out well in the stock market, we think we are very insightful, but we should remember that the probability of flipping five straight heads is one in thirty-two. If you assume there are one hundred stock market gurus predicting whether the stock market will rise or fall, at a given time, out of these, there will be about three that will have five consecutive correct predictions purely by random chance alone. These people crow about their success and are considered to be the real experts. After all, a broken (stopped) clock is correct twice each twenty-four hours.

What does it take to become a U.S. president? Out of 260

million people, there's only room for one in the Oval Office. Out of the thousands of qualified people, and hundreds of intelligent and energetic ones that really try to be president, only one "lucky" person makes it, having blissfully enjoyed many tiny breaks along the way, winning close local and state elections, and saying just the right thing at the right time.

Misunderstandings About Statistics

Since our behavior is influenced by our knowledge of mathematics and probabilities, it follows that many of our bad decisions and erroneous behavior patterns are due to a faulty knowledge of math. One of many misconceptions about statistics involves the lie of averages—the fact that an average is often meaningless. The man with his head in a hot oven and his feet in a bucket of ice water believes that, on average, he is pretty comfortable. An average human being would be a person with one developed breast and one testicle. Statistics derived from averages of many people are often meaningless when applied to specific people or events. Homicide is not a common cause of death for the average American, but this statement does not apply to twenty-year-old male gang members in Los Angeles. The average American woman has a one-in-nine chance of developing a breast malignancy during her lifetime, but most of these malignancies occur in the very old; the chance of having a malignancy before age fifty is one in fifty.

Another common misperception is that events tend to average out in the long run. Therefore, if a flipped coin lands heads five straight times, some think that the tendency toward producing an average would create greater pressure on the coin to come up tails on the next flip. The coin, however, is not at all concerned about catching up with the law of averages. Only erroneous humans are.

We should have large numbers in order to talk meaningfully about averages and percentages. Small numbers can be misleading. We hear of the experiment that showed 66.6 percent of subject mice were improved with a particular therapy. The experiment could possibly have shown 100 percent improvement if it were not for the one mouse escaping so that it couldn't be evaluated. A physician in a small practice may fudge on the statistics when reporting his work. One patient with a particular disease is alluded to with, "In my experience . . ." Two patients are, "In my series . . ." Three patients become, "In case after case after case . . ."

Sometimes an overplayed specific figure is applied to nebulous entities, which creates a false degree of precision. One could say that 36.3 percent of people in the world are ruled by democratic governments; however, it is impossible to define "democratic government" precisely. I could claim that I know that a certain geologic level near the bottom of the Grand Canyon is exactly one billion and four years old because a sign at the site when I visited there four years ago said that it was one billion years old. In 1993, members of the Southern Baptist Convention presented a study claiming 46.1 percent of people in Alabama were unsaved and risked hellfire. We can imagine a weather predictor, after being criticized for being too vague in his predictions, coming out with, "One hundred percent chance of possible rain."

In tennis, any ball that hits the line is good, even though it barely touches the outside edge. In calling their opponent's good shot, sometimes players, instead of saying, "Barely good," say with a smile, "99.7 percent out."

Because we have an innate desire for order, we try to establish structure and meaning for happenings in our life, sometimes imposing orderly patterns where none exist. We prefer the idea that we can somehow control our actions rather than the fact that often we must depend on discomforting blind luck and chaos. Athletes, after making five straight basketball field goals or hitting in twenty consecutive baseball games, would naturally be considered hot. However, in a series of twenty coin flips there is a 10 percent chance of having a streak of six straight heads or tails somewhere along the way. An average basketball player makes about 50 percent of his shots; therefore, if he takes twenty shots in a game, the chances are fairly good that he will have a streak of five or six hits or misses. Whether someone makes the shot one time has nothing to do with whether he makes it on the next shot. On the average, basketball players make 75 percent of their second free throws regardless of whether they make or miss the first one.

Fluctuations in the stock market are seen by many as having meaningful patterns and streaks, whereas most represent no more than random clustering tossed out by Lady Luck.

The misinterpretation of random sequences can lead to irrational ideas of bad luck or superstition, such as belief that a full moon is associated with larger numbers of murders and childbirth. Only the unusual events associated with the full moon are noticed, while the many prosaic events are ignored. The personnel of the emergency department night shift always mention the swarm of emergencies when there is a full moon. Others say that it is either feast or famine during the full moon, but just can't bring themselves to say there is no correlation with the moon and emergency department activity because they just don't want to be a killjoy.

If a large crowd at a football game flips coins during half-time, it would be unusual for no one to flip ten straight heads. In just two thousand coin tosses there should be, on average, at least one series of ten consecutive heads or tails. Many would be convinced that an individual who achieved this feat was skillful or could concentrate well on the coin toss. That person might also be accused of having extrasensory perception (ESP) or some supernatural power, but he might simply begin to think of himself as a skillful coin flipper and describe how he holds his wrist and positions his thumb for accurate flipping.

An individual should be able to recognize a streak of bad or good luck. Because one who has a good streak of investments may delude himself into thinking that he is so skillful that he is infallible, he might take an injudicious risk and lose all that he has gained. On the other hand, someone who has a streak of bad fortune may forever wrongly think of himself as incompetent and be afraid to take any reasonable risk. It is easy to get an unrealistic idea of being jinxed when playing tennis if you hit five consecutive balls that land barely out.

Do five consecutive winters that are warmer than average represent evidence of global warming? It is normal to have statistical groupings. Out of any twenty-year period, the chance of a run of five straight winters being warmer than average is 25 percent, hardly convincing evidence of a long-term warming trend.

We often think that statistics should come out fifty-fifty, but this is not usually the case. For instance, the chances of getting five heads out of ten coin flips is only 25 percent. The chances of getting fifty heads on one hundred flips is only 7.96 percent.

Our behavior continues to be adversely influenced by

incorrect and illogical concepts of mathematics. We establish our judgment of reality and probabilities by our own personal experiences and also by availing ourselves of reading material, listening to others, and the media depiction of the incidence of events. All of these methods of determining reality can cause distortions. Anyone unfortunate enough to be struck by lightning twice thinks from his own personal experience that lightning is extremely dangerous and wonders why people ever go outdoors to expose themselves to this danger. The general media tend to overemphasize violent crimes. Fortunately, in my own personal life I have not had a close friend or relative be murdered or die of AIDS. I have, however, had friends and relatives whose lives were adversely affected by alcohol abuse, so I personally think this danger is underrated in our world. Universal media coverage of sports distorts the incidence of success in professional athletes, misleading some naive youngsters to neglect or leave school in search of easy fame and fortune.

Another illogical belief concerns the lack of appreciation that the probability of two things happening simultaneously is less likely than one thing happening alone. If you ask people, "Which is larger, the percentage of *all* New Yorkers mugged in a year's time, or the percentage of *all* New Yorkers mugged while walking in Central Park in a year?" Many people will incorrectly say the latter. The existence of a combination of two factors is always less common than when only one factor is involved.

The mathematically naive can be fooled by statistics and mathematical trickery. Sometimes it pays for merchants to consider their customers inept at math. It was reported that a poor selling item was priced at $0.14, but when changed to two for $0.29 the sales promptly increased because many thought this represented a bargain. An unemployment rate of 8 percent does not mean that 8 percent of people are unable to find work. This 8 percent represents a pool of people who are temporarily unemployed at a given time. Some are changing jobs and may be unemployed only for one month, but nevertheless are placed in the unemployment pool statistics. We might consider an investment to be too risky if it has a 30 percent chance of failure but believe that it is reasonable if it has a 70 percent chance of success.

Because of the well-known large percentage of African Americans who live in poverty, we might think that poverty in America is predominantly a black problem. However, since blacks constitute only about 12 percent of the total population, in absolute numbers there are far more poor white people.

Cause Versus Coincidence

We may hear of a certain traumatic childhood experience causing mental problems in later life. In this situation we have to question whether this is a causal relationship or a coincidental relationship. We need to ask how many children with a similar traumatic experience are not neurotic and also ask how many neurotic people did not have this particular childhood trauma. Two things may be associated with one another, but one doesn't necessarily cause the other. A century ago, when an awareness of heredity was not widespread, many thought that baldness was caused by wearing tight hats, which were more often worn by men, in whom baldness predominates. Others thought this theory improbable and believed that baldness was a result of men wearing their hair shorter than women. Similarly when a police force is increased and the crime rate suddenly goes up, this doesn't mean that putting more officers on the street made the crime rate increase. It is more likely the case that the increased numbers of police permitted more thorough reporting of the crime that already exists.

Coincidences are erroneously cited as evidence to support occult phenomena, alleged paranormal events, or claims of clairvoyance by those who believe they possess or have witnessed supernatural power. Meeting someone from your own city while traveling in Europe or having someone phone you just as you were thinking of them is meaningless as a statistical event and doesn't represent anything mysterious. Even the more peculiar situations of alleged poltergeists, ghosts, spirits, and the like have been shown to be explicable in normal scientific terms. Once this occurs, the mystery evaporates.

Cause and effect are vastly complicated. Coronary artery disease has multiple causes, including genetic background, a sedentary lifestyle, a high-fat diet, and smoking. There are actually numerous more indirect causes of coronary artery disease, such as diabetes and stress.

Distortions of Reality

By disproportionate reporting, the media exaggerate the incidence of exciting and violent events in our world. We might think that accidents are more likely to cause death than disease, but in actuality all of us are fifteen times more likely to die from disease. Many think, incorrectly, that homicide in the general population is more common than suicide, and that more policemen are killed on duty than commit suicide. We worry about dying in tornadoes, being murdered, getting bombed in an airport while traveling, or being mugged on a New York subway, all of which are much less common than we think. The chances are one in millions of dying at the hands of a terrorist while on a trip abroad, but I have known people to cancel a trip to Europe based on this fear, yet not bother to wear seat belts while driving. Diseases caused by lifestyle (high-fat diet, smoking, lack of exercise, and lack of fiber in the diet) are much more prevalent than most people believe. Smoking kills 400,000 Americans annually, which is seven times as many as were killed during the long Vietnam War. Alcohol kills a 100,000 annually. In 1990, AIDS claimed 25,000 lives. When viewed in these absolute numbers, AIDS deaths seem greater than when mentioned along with cardiovascular disease, which killed more than 930,000. The chances of contracting AIDS from a sexual partner who is not in a known risk group and who uses a condom is one in fifty million. The public is afraid of radiation exposure from diagnostic X-rays, but the chances for harm are minuscule compared to the proven immediate benefit of the diagnosis of disease. There is a much greater chance of personal harm from driving in your car to the doctor.

As our society becomes more adept at understanding technical and quantitative concepts, we will be better able to utilize probabilities and statistical analysis. People want absolutes for rain prediction, but they will have to settle for a more realistic judgment, probabilities in which meteorologists assess weather conditions. Medical diagnosis employs probabilities also, and information about many diseases is being reported in ways that will encourage people to think more quantitatively. X-ray findings no longer have to be reported in absolutes of positive or negative but can be expressed in different levels of diagnostic certainty, such as 30 percent chance of malignancy.

Bias

We tend to interpret statistics in light of our own personal philosophy, or to fit our own perceptions of the world. Unconscious moral or political motives may determine our interpretation of data. On many complicated issues such as abortion, religion, feminism, and racial problems, statistics are often interpreted under the sway of our preconceived ethical and emotional background. Liberals accuse the media of being conservative, and conservatives accuse the media of being liberal. We accept flattering opinions about political candidates who agree with our own philosophy. We believe they win their television debates. We tend to attribute our successes to skills but our failures to bad luck. It is obvious to us that our team lost because of too many penalties called by biased officials; then we are surprised to read in the paper the next day that the winning team endured twice as many penalties.

We need to be leery of statistics regarding our health. Medical advice based on a large series, sophisticated research techniques, and expert statistical analysis should be taken seriously. Everyone has some personal anecdote in our personal life history to counteract current health admonitions: Examples include having an aunt who never exercised, ate huge amounts of ice cream, and lived to be quite old, or a relative who enjoyed smoking even to the age of ninety, or acquaintances who drank heavily and performed brilliantly.

Applying these exceptional instances to your own lifestyle could be a fatal mistake. If these are accurate accounts, they are extraordinary exceptions to scientifically established data showing the incidence of behavior patterns affecting overall health.

On the other hand, we shouldn't totally ignore something just because we read that it is statistically rare. A disease is not rare for someone who has it. We all have unusual things happen to us. We still have to watch out for lightning and snakes.

Gambling

Gambling provides the most obvious example of the use of mathematics and statistics in our behavior.

Blaise Pascal (1623–1662), a gambler as well as a mathematician and theologian, is said to have invented the computer as well as the roulette wheel. The European version of roulette has one slot designated for the house, making the house take one-thirty-seventh, or 2.7 percent. Owners of American gaming houses, however, figure that if one house slot is good, two house slots would be twice as good. Therefore, American roulette wheels have a house take of over 5 percent, which is just about as good a deal as we have in gambling.

Slot machines return to the player only $90 to $95 for every $100 put into them. They are not programmed to pay out after any specific given number of pulls. Instead, an electronic microswitch is triggered by random timing differences measured in milliseconds when you pull the handle of the machine. There is no way to use skill to beat a slot machine.

The horse or dog racetracks provide the least chance of winning, by setting up their own 15 percent take for profit and taxes. In addition, the track doesn't want to deal in small change; therefore the payout is rounded off in favor of the track, which brings its overall take to more than 17 percent. Race tracks are frequented by experts who appear to be very suave and tell you with half closed eyes and elevated chins about their "system." These individuals are never wealthy, however. Imagine trying to overcome a 17 percent disadvantage by so-called "skill." Other types of sports betting are no better. The bookies manage a take of up to 33 percent.

Despite the overwhelming odds, suckers still believe if they have lost five straight bets, the law of averages will prevail and their winning will "come due." The dice, the greyhounds, and the roulette ball could not care less about whether they are "due." Many still believe that they can establish some order in a random system, attesting to the human psychological need to see structure in the chaos of our life.

In general, the more complex the game, the greater the house take, and likewise for games offering larger odds. One of the attractions of lotteries or bingo is that there are many complicated ways of winning, creating the illusion that you have a greater chance. With the lottery it seems like you certainly should win because several different numbers are winning numbers and several different drawings are made.

Las Vegas also sports the added psychological snare of having highly visible throngs of people in a festive and social atmosphere. Many think, "All these people can't be wrong. They must win money or they wouldn't be here in Las Vegas enjoying themselves." Some get drawn into the details and complexities of gambling and even take courses on the various complicated games. They then become truly interested in the trivia of the process, which creates further self-delusion and further obscures the big picture. The casinos encourage a disorienting milieu, using alcohol, bright flashing colors, the pervasive racket of slot machines, and the absence of windows or clocks. You also bet chips instead of money. The addiction factor is also important, because a certain mild alteration of brain chemistry takes place as people excitedly place their bets. There is another psychological lure: an appeal to our slightly criminal tendency to get something for nothing.

Many think that they have a better chance if they are gambling against a country bumpkin rather than a more dapper individual, so more money is actually bet (and lost) with a yokel as the croupier or dealer.

Math Aversion and Ignorance

Many people have an illogical popular aversion toward mathematics. For some it represents a view of the world that is impersonal and coldly rational—antinarcissistic. Ignorance of mathematics makes many Americans prey to scams of pseudoscience. Quack medicine remedies flourish, since many have no concept of controlled double-blind scientific studies to prove the validity of any form of therapy. Many believe that just because they take an over-the-counter pill and feel better the next day, people often conclude with undue certainty that the pill definitely helped them get better. They are unable to compare their finding with that of another person with the same illness who *didn't* take the pill. If they felt worse the day after taking the pill, would they have blamed the pill? Beliefs in numerology, astrology, ESP, and premonitions are all based on erroneous popular misconceptions. Supernatural beliefs, magic, and myths are accepted not because they offer well-grounded evidence but because they make the world more intriguing.

Mathematics and probabilities control our behavior and the world around us far more than we think. Many important human activities such as business decisions center around quantitative concepts. *Time* magazine editor Henry R. Luce said, "Business, more than any other occupation, is a continual dealing with the future; it is a continual calculation, an instinctive exercise in foresight."

For these reasons, it is critical to develop positive and correct perceptions about statistics and probabilities at an early age. A negative attitude about mathematics in grade school may determine the direction of your future career. If you don't know anything about the physical or mathematical sciences, you really lack vital knowledge about the world in which you live.

We ourselves are made up of probabilistic entities. The subatomic world, regulated by quantum mechanic physics, is controlled by probabilities rather than tangibles as we know them in everyday life.

But, alas, as will become clear in the next chapter, mathematics itself is not as absolutely pure as we may like to believe.

References

Axelrod, Robert. *The Evolution of Cooperation*. New York: Basic Books, 1984.

Barrow, John D. *Pi in the Sky: Counting, Thinking and Being*. Oxford University Press, 1992.

Crevelt, Dwight. *Slot Machine Mania*. Grand Rapids, Mich.: Gollehon Press, 1991.

Gerrig, Richard. *The Life of the Mind: An Introduction to Psychology*, audiotape. Springfield, Va.: The Teaching Company, 1991.

Gilovich, Thomas. *How We Know What Isn't So: The Fallibility of Human Reason in Everyday Life*. New York: Free Press, Macmillan, 1991.

Glance, Natalie S., and Bernardo A. Hüberman. "The Dynamics of Social Dilemmas." *Scientific American* (March 1994): 76.

Goldberg, Steven. *When Wish Replaces Thought: Why So Much of What You Believe is False*. Amherst, N.Y.: Prometheus Books, 1991.

Huber, Peter. "The Lie of Averages." *Forbes* (December 20, 1993): 252.

McGervey, John D. *Probabilities in Everyday Life*. New York: Ivy Books, Ballantine Books, 1986.

McGinnis, J. Michael, and William H. Foege. "Actual Causes of Death in the United States." *Journal of the American Medical Association* (November 10, 1993): 2207.

Morgan, M. Granger. "Risk Analysis and Management." *Scientific American* (July 1993): 32.

Paulos, John Allen. *Innumeracy: Mathematical Illiteracy and Its Consequences*. New York: Hill and Wang, 1988.

Paulos, John Allen. *Mathematics and Humor*. Chicago: University of Chicago Press, 1980.

Plous, Scott. *The Psychology of Judgment and Decision Making*. Philadelphia: Temple University Press, 1993.

Rothman, Milton A. *The Science Gap: Dispelling the Myths and Understanding the Reality of Science*. Amherst, N.Y.: Prometheus Books, 1992.

Russell, Peter. *The Global Brain*. Boston: J. P. Tarcher, Houghton Mifflin, 1983.

16

Philosophy

Philosophy is like the mother who gave birth to and endowed all other sciences.

Albert Einstein

Throughout this book I have tried to impugn smug, simplistic ideas of human behavior. There is no better way to do this—and engender humility and tolerance—than to consider broad philosophical concepts such as *reality, truth,* and *free will.* Ultimately, who you are depends on the particular philosophy you develop in life. It affects how you view the world and it underlies the actions you take. Your ethics, goals, and sense of self hang on the answer to the question "What's it all for?" We dig deep inside to answer this question when we write our wills, choose whether to go into business or law, or decide to volunteer for military service. Your position on the liberal-conservative spectrum and your opinion on social issues such as capital punishment should be determined by a conscious awareness of your basic philosophy of life rather than dictated to you by relatives or the immediate cultural milieu.

I saved this chapter for last because all previous chapters are secondary to it. If I had discussed the "big picture" first, all other issues would have seemed trivial. What difference does it make that some advertisement is fraudulent if we can't be sure what truth is?

Philosophy will not tell you the meaning of life, but it instills valuable skills of critical thinking and a liberating curiosity. Those who are ignorant of it see the world as finite and absolute, their minds bound by dogmatism. Philosophy frolics in free thought, the most precious thing humans have. Yet many people ignore or ridicule philosophy, preferring to perform a psychological prefrontal lobotomy on themselves. Even today, in our sophisticated global environment of high technology, many college graduates have not taken a philosophy course. Worse still, they see philosophy as the irrelevant views of a few renowned Greeks.

Reality

We don't see things as they are, we see things as we are.

Anaïs Nin

Five centuries before Jesus, when Buddha was teaching that human experience was an illusion, the Sophists in Greece were also creating doubt about reality. Believing that reality was only what the mind of man made of it, the Sophists maintained, "Man is the measure of all things."

Later, Plato used the allegory of the cave to remind us that reality is indeed constructed by our minds. He described fictitious individuals who had spent their entire lives in a cave, their only experience with the outside world provided by shadows cast on a wall that they could see through a hole in the cave. People passing by were represented as shadows, and that alone created the cave dwellers' sense of reality. One of the cave dwellers eventually found a way out and experienced the bright sun of the "real" world. Later, he returned to the cave with his good news only to be met with disbelief and even threatened when he related his experience. Those in the cave saw his revelations as undermining their world and they were frightened to the core.

Most of us live our lives with the unquestioned idea that there are specific, real things "out there" to be seen correctly by us. But the history of philosophy offers many examples of thinkers who weren't sure that what we thought was real could actually be substantiated.

In the seventeenth century, Baruch Spinoza wrote that our senses perceive things in a faulty manner (for example, due to failing eyesight). The senses can play tricks on us at times (e.g., optical illusions). We also interpret our fallible sensory perception in variable ways. If we had been taught that the sun is only about two hundred feet above us and that it rotates about the earth, we could readily believe that this is reality. All we have to do is look up in the sky and see the sun apparently doing just that. Without additional knowledge about astronomy and mathematics we would have no way to dispute the descriptions offered to us.

Eighteenth-century thinkers such as David Hume and Immanuel Kant continued to express the idea that our minds stand between us and the world. Kant emphasized the difference between our sense experience and reality, using the example of how a stick protruding from the surface of water appears bent. He said that we cannot experience the world as it is before our mind influences it; we can only view life through our own perspective. Reality lies only in the mind of the beholder. We create the reality of a black, smooth, heavy, cold boulder only when we see it and try to pick it up.

Philosophers then realized that we had to understand the human mind in order to understand the external world. This concept of creating one's own reality has been called "constructivism" or "subjectivism." It maintains that personal versions of the world are all that exist. A sad man lives in a sad world.

In the nineteenth century, the German philosopher Friedrich Nietzsche said, "There are still harmless self-observers who believe that there are immediate certainties—certainties as though knowledge here got hold of its object purely and nakedly as the thing in itself, without any falsification on the part of either the subject or the object."

Arthur Schopenhauer (1788–1860) taught that the world was not totally created by the mind of man; there must be some sort of a real world out there or the mind would have nothing to act upon and distort. He mentioned, however, that the only way we can distinguish the dreaming from the nondreaming state is by waking up. In addition, humans are able to do some very precise things with what they have despite individual distortions—like repairing orbiting space telescopes and swishing thirty-five-foot jump shots.

We can imagine how it was as a newborn when we were

brought home from the hospital and looked upon the world for the first time. Thousands of different stimuli bombarded our eyes, ears, nose, and skin. This sensory chaos was received by us at first without any form, but slowly things began to make sense, and we were later able to relate one thing to another, to construct meaningful patterns, and eventually to name things. Our culture began to form our reality, but it was only *our* reality, not everyone's.

Our brains are constantly perceiving information from our sense organs and comparing it with other experiences. We then name this information and relate it to our particular goals at the present. This is how we construct our constantly changing view of reality—according to context. A clear liquid, when we see it in a mountain stream, is considered water, but in a bar it could be gin, vodka, or other things we can identify by taste. In a chemistry lab, clear liquid in a bottle should not be tasted.

Much of our assumed reality is illusory because of its erroneously assumed context. Consider this story: a father and son are hunting and a bear attacks the boy, mangling his leg. In attempting to save his son, the father is killed, but the boy escapes and limps, bleeding, into a rural hospital emergency room. The hospital surgeon takes one look at the boy and gasps, "I can't operate on this boy; he's my own son."

If your brain unconsciously organizes the above paragraph into expected patterns, you are probably puzzled. You may have assumed, incorrectly, that all surgeons are men. The surgeon, of course, is the boy's mother.

If you were raised on a remote island where, for thousands of years, no one doubted that thunderstorms were signs that the gods were angry, such a storm would be perceived and interpreted in an entirely different manner than today, when we can look at the weather cable channel and see the radar screen demonstrating this mindless natural occurrence.

Take four totally different individuals: a nuclear physicist, an eighty-year-old rural preacher, a stripper, and an eighteen-year-old ghetto gang member. Give each a separate free trip to Sophia, Bulgaria, for a weekend and then have them independently write a report describing the city. The difference in their realities of Sophia would amaze. As in radiology, we see mainly what we look for, and we recognize only what we know. Policemen are routinely frustrated by the differing interpretations of eyewitnesses to a robbery; often these people disagree completely about the height and appearance of the thief. A botanist looking at a forest or a radiologist looking at a chest X-ray sees a totally different universe from what a nonprofessional companion sees.

Indeed, our separate realities are only private shows taking place between the ears of each individual. Science, truth, and a sense of self are developed by the mind, not found, and can be described only by our flawed language system.

Remember the old philosophical question about whether there would be a sound if a dead limb fell in the forest and there was nobody there to hear it? You could go further and ask whether there would be a universe without a conscious inhabitant present to contemplate it. Did a Big Bang actually occur without someone, perhaps suspended in a hot air balloon, observing it?

So much of the reality we take for granted is only a cultural construct in our mind. We assume that Canada is north of California, but countries, states or directions do not exist in the "natural, real" world. An ancient mapmaker, Ptolemy, decided arbitrarily to put north on top of south, but could just as easily have done it the opposite way. The International Date Line, Wednesday, and 1996 can't be photographed because they are purely mental constructs. Incidentally, the most southern part of Canada, near Detroit, is farther south than the most northern tip of California.

Much of our sense of reality is tied up in language. We still consider words "things." We treat such abstract thoughts as hate or happiness as if they were real. Many terms are complementary and mutually define each other. We can't conceive of goodness without badness. There would be no light without dark, no up without down. This is the nature of how we define our world: the conceptual limits we place on it and their capacity to include and exclude information gained from experience.

Illusion

The term *illusion* is challenging to define because all interpretations of reality are illusory to some extent. I will divide illusion into three arguable, overlapping categories: first, those related to unusual physical phenomena of our external world before they are sensed by us; second, interpretations based on the physiology and pathology of our sense receptors; and third, interpretations dependent upon our final mental construction.

EXTERNAL PHYSICAL PHENOMENA

Due to the speed of light, distant objects are not seen in real time. We are only now seeing light from the star Betelgeuse that left its surface at about the time of Columbus. Other galaxies are millions of light years away, so that visible stars may now no longer exist. Because sound travels more slowly than light, we often hear thunder several seconds after we see lightning. An observer on a fast-moving star would see you at a different time than another observer moving more slowly, according to Einstein's theory of relativity.

A mirage is caused by atmospheric conditions reflecting light waves in an unusual manner. When hot air is layered near the ground and overlaid with cooler air, light will be bent so that distant objects will be visible. This explains trees and water appearing in the desert and may also explain some sightings of flying saucers (actually car headlights being reflected by mirage).

Holography is a complex, scientific marvel that produces three-dimensional visual images. At a museum of holography, I reached out for a bright red apple on a pedestal, only to grasp air.

SENSE-PERCEPTOR ABNORMALITIES

These can be due to alterations of sense-organ physiology or actual disease. Color blindness, caused by a hereditary difference in retinal receptors, occurs to some extent in up to 8 percent of males. Whose reality of color perception is then correct? We can speak only in terms of the reality of color perception of the majority.

Our "blind spot" is a normal, localized defect in our retina where the optic nerve enters, causing a small area of blindness in the periphery of our visual field. Our taste is affected by illnesses such as respiratory infections that interfere with smell. Even when we are recovering, things taste bitter. Referred pain phenomenon is experienced when pain occurs in places other than the location of the causative disease. Inflammatory processes in the upper abdomen, such as infected gall bladder, often refer pain to the shoulders because of the anatomic distribution of the nerves supplying the diaphragm. Phantom limb phenomenon sometimes occurs after amputations. Due to severed nerves, amputees feel that they still have their limbs, and the feeling is often painful. Neurological diseases can create many distortions of perception. People with brain tumors often experience bizarre visual or auditory perceptions. Medication or substance abuse are obvious causes of an altered sense of reality.

UNUSUAL MENTAL CONSTRUCTIONS

In an optical illusion, our eyes function well, but the final perception in our conscious mind is faulty. The reality is contrary to our expectations. The moon seems larger when it first comes up because we are comparing it to the small trees and houses on the horizon, but it is actually the same size as when it is overhead.

A tactile illusion occurs when we cross our index and middle finger and put a pencil between them. It seems that we then feel two pencils rather than one, because it is contrary to our previous tactile experience. A big, empty suitcase seems to weigh less than an equal-weight golf ball made of lead, because we expect a big object to weigh more, and we brace our muscles in preparation for lifting it. We're surprised that the golf ball weighs so much; therefore we overestimate its weight. A motion illusion occurs when we finally stop at a red light after driving on the expressway for an hour. We seem to be moving backward.

Temperature estimation, as judged with the skin, is relative. Put one hand in a pan of cold water and the other in hot water for three minutes, then put both hands in tepid water. The hand that had been in the hot water feels cool and the hand that had been in the cold water feels warm. A seventy-degree day breaking a long August heat wave feels cool. This same day, coming as a surprise in February, seems warm.

Hearing is also relative. I had the experience of having wax that had been accumulating for months removed from my ears. Upon leaving the doctor's office, I noticed that the birds were chirping unusually loudly, and when I arrived home, I noticed the floor squeaking. The first time I flushed the toilet it sounded like Niagara Falls. The reality of sound in my world had changed.

The magician's sleight of hand creates an anticipated illusion. Innumerable gullible pedestrians are relieved of their money by skillful sidewalk artists playing with those who think they can tell the whereabouts of a pea under three shells. The scamsters remove the pea when they slide the shell back and forth. A confederate is usually around to pretend winning this sucker's game.

In the chapter on the unconscious mind, I described the subliminal perception of rapidly flashed words. I mention this to remind us that reality for our unconscious mind is not the same as for our conscious mind. Hypnotic suggestion can also present a problematic complexity in our appreciation of reality and illusion.

Other Aspects of Reality

To modern subatomic science, there is no solid matter, only dancing particles of energy, what Alan Watts called the "wiggly world." If we were billions of times smaller, we could theoretically navigate through the atoms of our home, but we wouldn't perceive the difference between air, flesh, or wood. If we were billions of times larger, we wouldn't be able to see our microscopic planet. U.S. beekeepers have recently been troubled by mites in the tracheas of their honeybees. These mites are themselves teeming with bacteria, which, in turn, may be infected by viruses. Could there be subatomic universes within each virus? In the other direction, this gigantic universe in which we live could be only a particle in the left front paw of some otherworldly dachshund.

We were made aware of the reality of other visual worlds by the inventions of the microscope, telescope, and X-ray. Our world changes when we wear infrared goggles at night or when we look at a drop of pond water through a microscope. My radiology world changed with the advent of ultrasound and magnetic resonance imaging. In one way, radiologists were therefore able to see the body in cross-section instead of in front-on and side views.

Our reality depends on the ability of our senses to perceive. While jogging one evening, I saw a small, dark animal scurrying toward my ankles. Lurching away from the impending bite, I watched the "thing" (a harmless piece of dark paper) blow into the gutter. A dog's world differs from ours because of its superior olfactory capabilities and ability to hear high-pitched sounds. Elephants hear very low-frequency sound waves (infrasound), which we can't hear, and these pachyderms communicate over long distances using it.

Bees are able to see ultraviolet light, and bats can catch insects by perceiving the ultrasound waves generated by the insects' wing movements.

Accuracy of memory determines reality to a variable extent. Our memories are more fallible than we realize. We forget, distort, and embellish events, and also "remember" incidents that never occurred.

In a flotation tank, we may choose to be deprived of the senses of sight, hearing, touch, or smell, so that in many ways an external world no longer exists for us. This absence of normal stimuli can lead to an abnormal mental state.

There is no simple, uniform reality, and without it, there is no simple you. However, we do share many perceptions that enable us to interact and communicate effectively.

Virtual Reality

Put on goggles and earphones and stick your hands in a lycra glove attached to lots of wires. Your humdrum work-a-day world is instantly transformed into something quite bizarre, because your reality is suddenly made up of equations residing in some computer's memory. You are able to see in three dimensions because each eye receives an image from a slightly different angle. As you turn your head, the visual field changes because the sensors on each side of your head are activated accordingly. A NASA pilot trainee may find himself flying over London, first over St. Paul's Cathedral and then over Tower Bridge. While flying up the Thames, he turns his head to the right and can see the Tower of London. He then decides to dive into the water and is surrounded by fish.

In the future, sophisticated virtual-reality activities such as scuba diving and mountain climbing may be possible. You could be linked by electronic communications to play tennis with your buddy, or you might be able to see and "shake hands" with someone in another country. All of your senses could be stimulated. Besides sight, sound, and smell, you could experience vibration and all varieties of touch sensation along with proprioception (motion and position detection). Temperature variations could be applied and background music added, and your experience could be enhanced by drugs or other brain stimulation.

A susceptible person could become addicted to this computer-generated environment, because, for some, real life would be boring by comparison. After an afternoon of walking through the great cities of the world, would a wheelchair-bound invalid wish to take off the goggles and return to the *real world*? For those who are mentally unstable and/or drug abusers, such an encouragement to disembody into an altered state of reality could result in catastrophe.

Some virtual reality arcades now serve vitamin cocktails and amino acids that are supposed to enhance the experience. A race is on by entrepreneurs to develop an in-home virtual reality system. Imagine dancing, playing tennis, or having sex with a partner chosen from a large catalog. Philosophically, how can you completely separate the reality experienced with these machines from the reality of everyday life—which is also virtual, since it is dependent on the individual peculiarities of your sense organs and your particular ability to perceive?

In the science fiction movie *Total Recall*, the characters can take a vacation by having their brain stimulated by chemicals and an electronic implant. They are guaranteed that they won't know the difference between the mind event and actually taking the trip. Participants have the option of alternative identities and can "take a vacation from themselves" by choosing the trip and the person they want to be, such as a star athlete or a secret agent. In this movie, while the hero is fighting the bad guys on Mars, he uses a holographic double to act as a decoy, thus creating many plays on what constitutes the real self.

Companies now sell a variety of mind-expanding devices controlled by high-technology electronics. Some are advertised as being able to alter the states of consciousness, such as increasing alpha brain waves to provide relaxation and feelings of enhanced creativity. Some are hyped as being able to increase your IQ, and others advertise subliminal tapes to alter your desire for smoking or eating.

Certain high-technology treatments of reality are, to me, actually better than reality. Many sporting events are better seen on television than in cold stadium bleachers far up in a corner behind a post. On television, you can see slow-motion replays, have a cushioned, free, optimal seat, and hear all of the background commentary. Similar ideas are becoming true with travel. You can check out a number of books from the library on a particular country and several videotapes that have stirring background music and first-rate photography . At your convenience, you can view these in your own living room without worrying about jet lag, inclement weather, gastrointestinal upset, or how many guilders to tip the Dutch cab driver. Not surprisingly, soldiers who served on the front line during the Gulf War complained that their families at home, continuously watching the war coverage by CNN, had a much better understanding of the events. Sophisticated computer technology is improving monthly and provides more access to the information superhighway.

Truth

The pure and simple truth is rarely pure and never simple.

Oscar Wilde

We live day-to-day assuming that there is an objective truth, partly because science has constantly reinforced this idea. However, the truth of science, and even mathematics, is shaky. All institutions that declared "truth" are now in disarray. Religion provided the truth for most of Western civilization. Then science held sway. Now everything is questioned, with quantum mechanics, Heisenberg's uncertainty principle, and Gödel's theorem depriving us of absolutes. Exact predictions are replaced by possible happenings and relative probabilities. Truth is only relative and subject to the fickle perspective of each individual. What experts consider the truth depends upon their many unconscious motives and self-interest, including their own prestige and fear of reprisal by the figures of authority in their particular field.

Science moves through different paradigms (models for thinking) that establish accepted thought patterns. A paradigm shift can be exemplified by the familiar optical illusion of the image of a vase shifting to two faces in profile looking at one another. We are continuously undergoing shifts in our concept of truth. In my lifetime, I have seen a meaningful change in the attitude toward minorities and women. Copernicus and Newton changed the idea of truth about the celestial bodies and caused a revolution in scientific thought, and Darwin's theories caused another paradigm shift in science, as did Freud's thoughts. Scientists never find a final truth and can never say what the world is, but only what it is not. If we define truth as a positive correlation between conscious awareness and reality, it follows that truth must change constantly because reality, ever since the Big Bang, certainly does.

If science is no longer the gold standard of reality, then what about mathematics, its unimpeachable support? In 1931, Kurt Gödel, a Czech mathematical logician, determined that any system of axioms and rules must contain statements that are neither provable nor disprovable by the means allowed within the system. Mathematical truth cannot be contained in any formal system, because there is no way to decide which rules or procedures to use in setting up such a system. Mathematical truth is then also a manmade art.

Gödel also showed that mathematics is not completely reducible to logic. An assertion about a system, including logic, arithmetic, and geometry, cannot be shown to be absolutely true from within the system. The very activity of proving the model correct is itself part of an artificial system. Utilizing any environment outside the system for proof requires further proof of the validity of these external activities. This is reminiscent of the uncertainty principle of Heisenberg, which underlies quantum physics. The act of observation of a system by humans changes the system. The human ability to create new paradigms, rules, and interpretations is as indeterminate as the language in which these new ideas are expressed. How do we prove Gödel's or Heisenberg's ideas are true? We can't. Ultimately, everything boils down to a paradox. If someone says, "I am lying," if he is, he isn't, and if he isn't he is.

Each great philosopher through the ages has tried to define truth; all have failed. One of the problems resides in language and definitions. Ludwig Wittgenstein said that philosophy is a battle against the bewitchment of our intelligence by language. We tend to provide criteria as proof for something, but we then find it impossible to prove that these criteria are true. Nietzsche, in his discussion of truth, mentions that it is constructed rather than found. One cannot use facts to determine whether something is true, because facts come to us via our whimsical culture and the nets of our imperfect senses and final conscious interpretation. Truth, therefore, has dubious origins, making it only a yet-unrecognized falsehood—but only if one is expecting some lasting, final type of truth.

Our very doubts about truth can also be doubted, because these doubts are social constructions, subject to the vagaries of ulterior motives and variably interpreted language. Any criticism of scientific, legal, or theological truths is influenced by the same etiological and cultural factors.

There is no final, absolute truth—including this statement. Truth is only temporary and relative and is soon replaced by another form of truth. When theories and paradigms change, the universe changes.

William James (1842–1910), the American physician and pragmatist, had a pluralistic concept of truth, maintaining that there is more than one truth, depending upon the perspective involved. He declared that truth is a complementary word that we use about sentences (he would have called them propositions) that work, and he taught that even though truth is not absolute, it is helpful and should be viewed in a positive way, like viewing the cup as half full instead of half empty. It is true that Chaucer was a medieval writer, but to the modern student who must memorize Chaucer's archaic language, it is also true that he was a jerk. Viewed from the ground, Mount Fuji is an aesthetic delight, but from a plane flying directly above, it is also true that it is unremarkable.

We are constantly modifying old beliefs and arriving at new truths. This is the evolutionary theory of truth. We alter or drop previous ideas based on evidence that contradicts the truth we held. We then incorporate the old and the new ideas to form a more desirable belief. What is true survives and proves itself to be, at least for the moment, free of countervailing evidence.

The philosopher John Dewey (1859–1952) also espoused pragmatic thinking, stating that there is no absolute truth, only what is true for the time being. This is what he called *warranted assertability*. We create our truth and recreate it, based on contrary evidence. Everything in the world, including our bodies, changes; therefore it is logical to assume that the truth changes.

Contemporary philosophers such as Richard Rorty feel that the old philosophical goals of searching for absolute truth and reality should be altered. The terms should be taken off their pedestal, because they are contingent upon time, space, culture, and history. Truth is nothing but a property of language that is useful; we agree that language serves important human purposes.

We always experience truth under some individual, conceptual paradigm. Rorty proposes that we keep the search going, however, and realize that there are no final answers. Just to realize this is a beneficial end in itself.

We are left with the necessity of coping with truth in the pragmatic, short-term situation as it confronts us.

Free Will

> There once was a man that said, "Damn
> For it certainly seems that I am
> A creature that moves in determinate grooves
> I'm not even a bus, I'm a tram!"

Alan Watts

The free will quandary is the old battlehorse of philosophers throughout Western and Eastern history. Reading philosophers' opinions about free will is like listening to stock market predictions from a group of economists. Opinions are constantly shifting. Those who tend to deny free will—they are often called determinists, reductionists, or scientific materialists—are exemplified by David Hume, George Berkeley, John Locke, Albert Einstein, and B. F. Skinner. The camp that believes that humans do have free will includes such luminaries as Thomas Aquinas, Immanuel Kant, Jean Paul Sartre, Ayn Rand, and Pierre Teilhard de Chardin.

The Determinists

Some determinists who deny free will are also known as *fatalists* and *positivists*. They have a tough-minded, materialistic, mechanistic view of the world. They claim knowledge can be acquired only by scientific experiment, tend not to be religious, and believe that human action is determined by physical, biological, and cultural forces. Like Aristotle and John Locke, they believe that scientific analysis should be based purely on observation, an idea also favored by French philosopher and mathematician Auguste Comte (1798–1857). This group also tends to be reductionistic; that is, they break down complicated problems into their smallest components of biology and physics. They believe that a seemingly free action is simply one that is not constrained by external forces; therefore, the existence of such freedom need not presuppose that determinism is false. Apparent free behavior, including speech, does not exist because all such behavior can be reduced to specific prior actions that determine the action finally taken. Before one can speak freely restrictions must be imposed on others to allow this free speech.

Scientific reductionism was exemplified in the thoughts of Rudolph Virchow (1821–1902), who saw human anatomy and disease in terms of cells and has been called the father of pathology. Psychologists tried to reduce human action to the least common denominator in behaviorism, which brought behavior down to the laws of Pavlovian conditioning. (Pavlov's dogs were conditioned to salivate at the sound of a bell when they associated this sound stimulus with a reward of food.) Of course, in physics and chemistry, substances have been chased down into smaller and smaller particles.

The determinists were also represented by the clockwork universe of Newton. Even with Einstein's concepts, everything could be predicted, such as eclipses, and events could be retrodicted, such as the exact time of an eclipse five thousand years ago. The Big Bang theory, accepted throughout physics, maintains that everything was totally determined at the instant origin of the universe, and all activity will continue inexorably regardless of what we do, perhaps forever. Even though we appear free to choose, our choosing mechanism, which is basically neurochemical, is predetermined. Our actions are inevitable, and we have no more personal responsibility for them than we do for the future of our galaxy.

Baruch Spinoza maintained that the universe has no purpose. There is no free will unaffected by outside forces. Your mind is activated by a cause, and this cause is activated by other things, likewise, to infinity. Schopenhauer also held such a view. He said, "A man can surely do what he wills to do, but he cannot determine what he wills." Even Freud doubted that there was a functional free will, teaching that our unconscious motivations ingrained in early childhood eliminated any true freedom of decision. Karl Marx also doubted free will and contended that the unconscious causes of our behavior are predominantly economic and social. Marx believed that the real nature of man is the totality of social relations, there being no individual human nature. He taught that the individual mind was hostage to the material, social, and political conditions at the time.

It is obvious that we experience degrees of freedom. Just as the homeless bag lady is limited by circumstance, the corporate workaholic is also. Strict religious conformists abrogate a large amount of their freedom. Political zealots confine their minds to a political platform. The Democrats are sometimes happy to squash economic freedoms, and the Republicans often wish to impede social freedoms. The libertarian philosophy declares that you can be only as free as you will allow others to be, thereby supporting economic and social liberty.

The behaviorist psychologist B. F. Skinner instructed that even though we like to think we are free, our actions are completely determined, and our environment is the major determinant of our actions. Our behavior is learned by trial and error and is based on reward and punishment. Skinner believed that we should abandon the illusions of individual freedom and dignity and try to create a better life by modifying everyone's behavior in proper ways. He felt that most punishments for crime are illogical.

Einstein said, "I do not believe we can have any freedom at all in the philosophical sense, for we act not only under external compulsion but also by inner necessity." Sociobiologist Edward O. Wilson, a reductionist and determinist who also doubts that free will exists, argued that evolution is predominantly responsible for our behavior. Our genes endow us with propensities for our personality and mental capabilities.

Some schools of philosophy that have tried to place philosophy on a more scientific and mathematical basis have espoused what has been termed logical positivism. These approaches to philosophy do not leave much room for free will. Such thinkers as A. J. Ayer and Bertrand Russell exemplify these more mechanical aspects of philosophy, where there is an attempt to quantify language and place it into mathematical perspective.

Edward Fredkin, a physicist and computer scientist who is well described in Robert Wright's *Three Scientists and Their Gods*, actually believes that information is the most fundamental fabric of reality in the universe and that the laws of physics are algorithms, with the universe working like a computer. He discerns that the state of every point in space at any point in time is determined by a single algorithm, which is a mechanical or recursive computational procedure that converts one body of information into another. Fredkin, like Einstein, has never really accepted the concept of quantum mechanics, which maintains that reality is random and could not function like a computer. Fredkin thinks that an information process controls the core of physics, and at a

higher level, the DNA of life is controlled by a digital information process, and at an even higher level, our thinking is
controlled by this same computerlike processing. Fredkin's
theory of computer-digital physics could conceivably qualify
as the answer to the search for the grand unified theory that
has so eluded philosophy and science.

The Free Will Advocates

In the camp of philosophers advocating the existence of free
will, the most outspoken was existentialist Jean Paul Sartre
(1905–1980), proclaiming that man can only be thought of as
free. Even though we try to hide from this freedom, there is
no escape from it. In having to make decisions about our
actions, we are alone. We are responsible for our emotions,
and, if we are sad, it is only because we choose to make ourselves sad. To try to escape this responsibility is itself a free
choice. We cannot treat freedom as if it were an object to be
perceived and proved or disproved. It is only a postulate of
action, a possibility rather than an actual entity.

In Western civilization, the Jews were among the first to
entertain the concept of free will. The biblical Garden of Eden
story illustrated the idea that the future depends on our own
actions, for which we are responsible. Although Christian
doctrine also establishes that we are free to accept God's sal-
vation, there is quite a bit of coercion involved, because those
who choose not to accept are threatened with hell.

Immanuel Kant also questioned the Christian idea of free
will. He felt that humans didn't get any credit for being good
if all they were doing was obeying a commandment or trying
to dodge hell. The deserving good person is moral without

any rules or coercion. We cannot be moral if we are not free. We are, however, free to make our own laws and moral restrictions. But as we all know, all laws are not moral. If we lived in Nazi Germany in 1938, the moral people should have disobeyed the many immoral laws.

Objectivist philosopher Ayn Rand (1905–1982) was also a champion of free will. She believed that thinking was an act of choice, and the only secret you live with, yet dread to name, is the fact that humans have volitional consciousness. Philosopher Karl Popper, an opponent of the determinists, has long maintained that quantum mechanics undermines determinism by replacing certainty with propensities, thereby establishing a fundamentally unpredictable world. With modern concepts in quantum mechanics and chaos theory, we realize that it is impossible to know enough about the present to make a completely accurate prediction about the future. Because of Heisenberg's uncertainty principle, the initial conditions can never be known well enough.

Many thinkers address the problem of free will versus determinism obliquely. Mathematician Roger Penrose believes that the future would not be computable from the present, even though it might be determined by it. Our future behavior would still be determined from the moment of the Big Bang, though we would be unable to calculate it. One of the problems in the debate involves semantics. We tend to think of free will as a thing in itself instead of a linguistic representation of a vastly complex thought. The issue is basically insoluble and paradoxical, similar to the incongruity between quantum mechanics and classical Newtonian physics. On many levels they are incompatible yet applicable, but neither one is wrong.

Existentialism

Existentialism is not currently very fashionable for several reasons. Besides being hard to pronounce, it is associated with Jean Paul Sartre, who became a morose Marxist in his later years, and it has always seemed to portray a bleak, meaningless existence for humankind. If we delve into it, however, we find that it does have a positive side. Existentialist philosophers believe that the fact of our existence means that we can also act. They contend that life is basically meaningless but that each of us has free will to create values that give our lives meaning. We can only speak for ourselves in choosing and creating the meaning of life. We have a personal choice for our actions that can be either an opportunity or an agonizing burden.

The existential movement began about 150 years ago with Søren Kierkegaard (1813–1855) and Friedrich Nietzsche, but it was not until after World War II that Jean Paul Sartre popularized it. At a Paris café in 1945, Sartre's lectures spelled out existentialism as a kind of upbeat humanism, with "man being nothing else but what he makes of himself." Most existentialist philosophers have been atheists who didn't derive any meaning from religion in their personal lives. They have said, however, that it is fine for an individual to choose to make religion the most meaningful thing in his or her life. Theologian Paul Tillich and Kierkegaard were religious existentialists.

Existentialist theory emphasizes the consciousness of the individual self and the uniqueness of the individual who has free will. Sartre believed that we are "condemned to be free." Our very existence thrusts freedom upon us. It is up to us to make the most of that freedom. Existentialists stress striving to fulfill yourself, maintaining your independence, and continuing the quest to find the best way of life to actualize your potential. They criticize the many modern efforts to relinquish individuality and submit to blind conformity or submergence of oneself into a group. Existentialism, however, does emphasize the obligation of each human being to others. It has some of its roots in romanticism, with individuals appearing heroic in facing the void alone, free and brave, deciding for themselves how to make their own reality, and having the courage to "be."

Later in his career, Sartre changed his stance and admitted that freedom largely depends on situational and enabling conditions. He thought that even though our family, language, economic standing, and contemporary institutions control us, there is still some freedom. He said, "A man can always make something out of what is made of him." We are still able to give back more than our social background gives us.

Existentialism prevails in the fabric of our contemporary world, for any time we encourage children to be unique, to create, or to take responsibility for their actions, we are employing existentialist thought. Such existential writers as Dostoyevsky, Kafka, Camus, and Beckett have vastly influenced our thinking. Much of modern art is existentialist, emphasizing the absurdity and alienation in our world. Samuel Beckett's play *Waiting for Godot* symbolizes the nothingness in our lives, the emptiness and ambiguous nature of life.

Logical Positivism and Linguistic Philosophy

Since the 1930s, many philosophers have sought to bring philosophy more into the realm of structured science. This was encouraged by the advances made in symbolic logic by mathematicians such as Bertrand Russell and Alfred North Whitehead, who based logic on mathematics so that all logical thoughts could be proven by formulas. Today, these logically recursive math functions enable us to make advances with computers.

Wittgenstein tried to establish a mathematical precision to logic and hence language, dissecting language into deductive and inductive facts that are either true or false. Although he did contribute a mathematical formality to what we think and say, he admitted in his later works that language had a plurality of rules that could not be fully described by algorithms.

The term "logical positivism" arose to represent the work of thinkers such as A. J. Ayer, who considered classic philosophy nonverifiable nonsense because it uses speculative metaphysical sentences that do not express factual propositions. Ayer made an analysis of language and, along with Wittgenstein contributed valuable insights into our understanding of it. Logical positivists believe that a word such as *spiritual* is a linguistic expression without cognitive content; therefore, the word represents only a nonsensical, comforting sound. Modern philosophy is dominated by logical and linguistic analysis, which examines syntax and semantics. Philosophers are indeed trying to be scientists and perhaps have awarded science more status than it deserves, considering the shifting foundation of scientific paradigms.

The ideas of modern existentialism can be contrasted to the relatively rigid structure of the mathematical concepts of logical positivism. The logical positivists have put precision and reason on a pedestal and decorated it with science, but the existentialists insist that meaning comes from within. It can't be imposed on the world. Logic, like math, is culturally constructed and variably perceived by the human mind. There is no unimpeachable rule that says we should be logical. All we can do is face the uncertainty of our lives, and then perhaps we can be truer human individuals.

Eastern Thought

> When we try to pick out anything by itself,
> We find it's hitched to everything else in the universe.
>
> We all travel the Milky Way together, trees and men.
>
> John Muir

As time changes so does the seat of intellectual authority. Following the shift from religion to science and rationalist humanism during the Enlightenment, we are now in the early stages of the acceptance of postscientific Eastern thought. During this transition, there are needs being filled by cults, New Age as well as evangelical religions, and bizarre forms of health care. Western philosophers, as well as many physicists, are now grasping the idea that has been accepted in the East for centuries: that there is a continuous, connecting wholeness in the universe that invalidates the concept of a universe being composed of independent parts. The physical world, our physical body, our mind, and our cultural activity are interdependent.

More specifically, our actions are not separate from the rest of the world but inextricably part of it. In India, each person is recognized as the center of the universe. Many Hindus believe that the distinction between a separate individual, in here, and the world, out there, is an illusion. In the Western world, we assume human beings are split from, and adversarial to, nature, which explains our language: "conquer space," "tame the wild," and "you'll never get out of this world alive." Orientals do not fight nature but "go with the flow." In the myths of India, there is the story of the Net of Indr, where at the junction of each thread with another, there is a gem reflecting all the other reflective gems, everything arising in mutual relation to everything else. No one thing is responsible for anything by itself.

Our bodies are intermediate, complex masses, as ants are part of a colony. They are parts of the local ecology, which is part of planet earth, which is part of the entire universe. The world is our extended body. We are not unique, independent individuals, but only symbiotic, interactive particles subsumed by all of nature.

John Dewey emphasized that experience is active unity between the subject and the object. He thought it wrong to impose artificial divisions, such as humankind versus the world, inner mind versus outer objects, and self versus others. Each is unified and related to a totality that is incessantly changing and unstable. There is no division between means and ends, only a continuum with one existing because of the other. In fact, the end sought in one situation may well be the means to reach some future end. Light does not exist without darkness. Many students graduate from the half of the class that makes the top half possible. Fast does not exist without slow, and left does not exist without right. All are complementary and relative, like the ancient Chinese yin-yang symbol of a circle divided into two gently interlocking parts.

A unity also exists between holism and reductionism, because one cannot exist without the other. Chaos and order are likewise complementary with each being a prerequisite for the other to exist. There is no pleasure without corresponding pain. It is a philosophical as well as physiological impossibility to have a constant series of pleasurable experiences forever, as naive pleasure-seekers soon learn.

We now have agreement in thought between the ancient philosophers and modern physicists. Chuang-Tzu, living in China at the height of Greek influence before Christ, said, "I and all things in the universe are one." With Einstein's thoughts of a time-space-mass-energy continuum, and Heisenberg's uncertainty principle, it is now agreed that the mental and physical worlds are interdependent. What we think of as a single, isolated, subatomic particle can now be considered part of an infinite wave pattern spreading throughout the universe.

The Buddhist philosophy also espouses monism, which means that each of us lives in the oneness of things. The narcissist who indulgences in self aggrandizement is unaware that his life is only relative to others and that the self separated from others does not exist. Buddhism encourages breaking away from the social constructions of reality by eliminating inhibiting thoughts and words. Buddhists are encouraged to cleanse themselves of inner thoughts and feelings, and to appreciate that reality is universal and far above human interpretations of it.

Philosophies frequently disagree with, or refute, one another. Existentialists advise us to find something to make our lives meaningful and unique. Zen Buddhists teach us to eliminate desire, because desire makes us prisoners of our wants. Philosophy and science are interdependent, since science requires philosophy to give it meaningful goals, and philosophy is changed by scientific advances. Because philosophy and science are constantly changing there are no final or absolute conclusions to the philosophical enterprise.

Many years ago I was given the gift of a rock with the words "Free to Be Me" painted on it. Even though I've enjoyed it on my desk for many years, I now realize I'm not really free, there's no valid me, and I'm not even separate from that rock.

References

Anderson, Walter Truett. *Reality Isn't What It Used to Be*. San Francisco, Calif.: Harper and Row, 1990.

————. *The Truth about the Truth: De-confusing and Re-constructing the Postmodern World*. New York: Jeremy P. Tarcher, Putnam, 1995.

Barrett, William. *Irrational Man: A Study in Existential Philosophy*. Doubleday Anchor, 1962.

Barrow, John D. *Pi in the Sky: Counting, Thinking and Being*. Oxford University Press, 1992.

Beck, Charlotte Joko. *Everyday Zen*. Edited by Steve Smith. New York: Harper and Row, 1989.

Briggs, John, and F. David Peat. *Turbulent Mirror*. New York: Harper and Row, 1989.

Burke, James. *The Day the Universe Changed*. Little, Brown, 1985.

Capaldi, Nicholas, John Lachs, and Michael Hassell. *The Giants of Philosophy: David Hume*, audiotape. Audio Classics Series, narrated by Charlton Heston. Nashville, Tenn.: Knowledge Products.

Cartwright, Glen. "Virtual or Real? The Mind in Cyberspace." *The Futurist* (March-April 1994).

Casti, John L. *Paradigms Lost: Images of Man in the Mirror of Science*. New York: William Morrow, 1989.

Compton, John. *The Giants of Philosophy: Jean-Paul Sartre*, audiotape. Audio Classics Series, narrated by Charlton Heston. Nashville, Tenn.: Knowledge Products.

Davies, Paul. *The Mind of God: The Scientific Basis for a Rational World*. New York: Simon and Schuster, 1992.

Diggins, John Patrick. *The Promise of Pragmatism: Modernism and the Crisis of Knowledge and Authority*. Chicago: The University of Chicago Press, 1994.

Edelman, Gerald M. *Bright Air, Brilliant Fire: On the Matter of the Mind*. New York: Basic Books, 1992.

Fadiman, Clifton, ed. *Living Philosophies: The Reflections of Some Eminent Men and Women of Our Time*. New York: Doubleday, 1990.

Ferris, Timothy. *The Mind's Sky: Human Intelligence in a Cosmic Context*. New York: Bantam, 1992.

Gergen, Kenneth J. *The Saturated Self: Dilemmas of Identity in Contemporary Life*. New York: Basic Books, 1991.

Gregory, Bruce. *Inventing Reality: Physics as Language*. John Wiley and Sons, 1988.

Hackett, Stuart C. *Oriental Philosophy: A Westerner's Guide to Eastern Thought*. University of Wisconsin Press, 1979.

Hagen, Charles. "Virtual Reality: Is It Art Yet?" *New York Times* (July 5, 1992).

Horgan, John. "Trends in Mathematics: The Death of Proof." *Scientific American* (October 1993): 93–103.

Horwich, Paul, ed. *World Changes: Thomas Kuhn and the Nature of Science*. Cambridge, Mass.: MIT Press, 1993.

Hunter, Gary. "Existentialism: Practical Classroom Applications." *The Educational Forum*, 57 (Winter 1993): 191.

Kors, Alan Charles. *The Origin of the Modern Mind*, audiotape. Springfield, Va.: The Teaching Company.

Lang, Berel, John Lachs, and Michael Hassell. *The Giants of Philosophy: Plato*, audiotape. Audio Classics Series, narrated by Charlton Heston. Nashville, Tenn.: Knowledge Products.

Lavine, T. Z. *From Socrates to Sartre: The Philosophic Quest*. Bantam, 1984.

Macquarrie, John. *Existentialism*. Penguin, 1972.

Mandt, A. J. *The Giants of Philosophy: Immanuel Kant*, audiotape.

Audio Classics Series, narrated by Charlton Heston. Nashville, Tenn.: Knowledge Products.

Maurois, Andre. *Illusions.* New York: Columbia University Press, 1968.

Penrose, Roger. *The Emperor's New Mind.* Oxford: Oxford University Press, 1989.

Plous, Scott. *The Psychology of Judgment and Decision Making.* Philadelphia: Temple University Press, 1993.

Rand, Ayn. *The Voice of Reason.* New York: Penguin Books, 1988.

Roderick, Rick. *Philosophy and Human Values,* audiotapes. Springfield, Va.: The Teaching Company.

Schacht, Richard. *The Giants of Philosophy: Friedrich Nietzsche,* audiotape. Audio Classics Series, narrated by Charlton Heston. Nashville, Tenn.: Knowledge Products.

Skinner, B. F. *Science and Human Behavior.* New York: Macmillan, 1953.

Staloff, Daren, and Michael Sugrue. *Modernism and the Age of Analysis,* audiotape. Springfield, Va.: The Teaching Company.

Stone, Mark. *The Giants of Philosophy: Arthur Schopenhauer,* audiotape. Audio Classics Series, narrated by Charlton Heston. Nashville, Tenn.: Knowledge Products.

Stuhr, John J., John Lachs, and Michael Hassell. *The Giants of Philosophy: John Dewey,* audiotape. Audio Classics Series, narrated by Charlton Heston. Nashville, Tenn.: Knowledge Products.

Von Altendorf, Alan, and Theresa Von Altendorf. *ISMs: A Compendium of Concepts, Doctrines, Traits and Beliefs from Ableism to Zygoactylism.* Memphis, Tenn.: Mustang Publishing Co, 1991.

Watts, Alan. *The Love of Wisdom. The Tao of Philosophy,* vol. 1. San Anselmo, Calif.: Electronic University.

Wood, Denis. "The Power of Maps." *Scientific American* (May 1993): 88–93.

Wright, Robert. *Three Scientists and Their Gods.* New York: Times Books, 1988.

Zukav, Gary. *The Dancing Wu Li Masters.* Bantam Books, 1979.

17

Conclusions

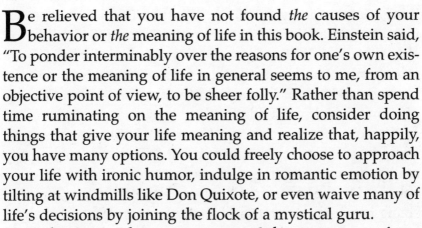

Be relieved that you have not found *the* causes of your behavior or *the* meaning of life in this book. Einstein said, "To ponder interminably over the reasons for one's own existence or the meaning of life in general seems to me, from an objective point of view, to be sheer folly." Rather than spend time ruminating on the meaning of life, consider doing things that give your life meaning and realize that, happily, you have many options. You could freely choose to approach your life with ironic humor, indulge in romantic emotion by tilting at windmills like Don Quixote, or even waive many of life's decisions by joining the flock of a mystical guru.

In this book, I have not promoted the supremacy of one theme in human behavior. So many psychology books today tout the harm of childhood traumas, the importance of your relationship with your father, or the emotional effects of food

additives. Most people have a need to see order in things
rather than chaotic diversity, preferring the idea that there
was a single cause of the fall of Rome or the death of Elvis
Presley. Writers can be very narrow-minded when selling the
predominance of one of the causes of human behavior; they
usually overemphasize one they have picked. When a
teenage tennis star was admitted to a drug rehabilitation program recently, many critics said that, obviously, too much
early tennis caused the drug problem. But they were employing errant *post hoc* thinking. Most avid teenage tennis players
don't have a drug problem, and most drug addicts have
never played competitive tennis. Many other factors, such as
genetics or faulty knowledge, could have been involved in
the player's drug problem.

Trying to blame their clients' criminal behaviors on *one*
thing, defense lawyers exaggerate the effects of temporary
insanity, urban stress syndrome, or previous childhood
abuse, because these play well to sympathetic jurors. We are
more resilient and versatile than we give ourselves credit for,
having survived for thousands of years in an infinite variety
of climates and social relations.

Current pop-psychology "how-to" books espouse one
formula for human "empowerment." They try to simplify
reality by lumping together various concepts of how we
behave. On the contrary, I have gone the other way, emphasizing how many covert and shaky factors affect our behavior. I have tried to dispel simplistic notions explaining our
infinitely complicated actions. Furthermore, I have striven to
discredit pat, unyielding belief systems that support stereotypical thinking such as maintaining that a particular behavior is caused by being Southern, or Catholic, or black, or
Republican.

Not only are we formed and managed by our culture, but our culture itself is volatile and evolving in disparate, chaotic ways. Because our world is changing more rapidly than we can adjust to, we're like a chameleon tumbling around inside a kaleidoscope. Still, our individual, active experience within this culture contributes much to our behavior patterns. A considerable portion of our behavior depends on instantaneous unconscious decisions using time-cost-benefit analysis and weighing mathematical probabilities. We deal with complex cultural problems by employing psychological defense mechanisms that are themselves illogical. Yet genetics governs our actions even more than culture, predominantly establishing our physical appearance, intelligence, and temperament. With genetic engineering, our physiology and our culture have themselves become interdependent, although both are still overruled by forces in our physical environment, from weather to viral infections, to toxic wastes, to mandates from the deterministic Big Bang—and/or blind luck. This mutually dependent web is further convoluted by our alteration of the environment; technology produces pollutants that can affect our actions as well as our genes.

A zillion things influence your actions right now, and a zillion more interface with each of those. As you read this, your mind is being manipulated by everything from hunger to a particle of cosmic radiation zapping a particular neuron in your cerebellum. Many more factors will be discovered in the future.

According to current chaos-complexity theory, we are unable to make accurate predictions. We never have all the data necessary, and tiny inaccuracies in initial data can produce, over time and space, huge differences in final results. For example, in 1961 Edward Lorenz, a meteorologist, used a computer to predict long-term weather forecasts. He incorporated data on wind direction, temperature, and air pressure in his calculations. In his first forecast, he used data with six decimal places; in his second forecast, he used only three decimal places. The two forecasts were completely different. We cannot predict in which slot on the roulette wheel our ball will land because the number of factors required in the calculation is infinite—the exact size of the ball, the force of throwing the ball, air temperature, humidity, and so on. We know from quantum mechanics and Heisenberg's uncertainty principle that we can never accurately measure reality on a subatomic level; we must work only with probabilities. Like it or not, existence is nonlinear and unpredictable.

One minuscule event, over time, can produce enormous effects. Consider that one microsecond when one sperm out of millions penetrated an egg to eventually create Adolf Hitler, thereby influencing the lives of everyone today.

Remember also the science-fiction time travelers who go back millions of years, feed a triceratops a candy bar, then return to the present to find that their act, because of the spreading effect, has completely changed their modern world. Our finger snap today actually affects a particular atom in a star in another galaxy a *very tiny* amount. But a thousand years from now that finger snap might luckily and barely prevent two spaceships from colliding.

Like the renowned butterfly eventually causing a hurricane thousands of miles away, one minor event in early childhood could explain why someone committed murder as an adult. At the opposite pole, like the last snowflake that falls on a huge snowbank and triggers an avalanche, one casual recent event, such as having one too many beers, could also be blamed for the final lethal action. However, we had millions of small events early in childhood, and we have just as many recent influencing events. Chaos theory therefore undermines the defense attorney's argument of simple cause and effect as an excuse for his client's conduct. Chaos theory also discredits any belief system that presumes to possess tidy mathematical precision, such as game theory, logical positivism, and determinism. Reality is not regulated by whole numbers but by the infinite number of fractions between them. The world operates not as a clock but as a lava lamp, swirling chaotically.

Influences on our behavior interact in a meshing wholeness, with each thing existing in mutual relationship to every other thing in the universe. This perfect chaos constitutes a subtle form of order. Chaos and order are thus paradoxically related: each requires the other to exist. Sociologists work to discern orderly patterns in the seemingly chaotic behavior of human populations in the aggregate.

The overwhelming complexity of your behavior is good news. It is so complicated, so impenetrable, that you shouldn't worry about it. It is *impossible* to tell why you did something in a certain way, so any one smug opinion is incomplete, presumptuous, and naive. You are wasting your time guessing about *the* cause of anyone's behavior. Knowing this should actually heighten your sense of humility and make you more tolerant of others and of yourself. Accept the imperfections of all—and relax.

Realize that current philosophic and scientific ideas will be replaced sooner than you think, and those changes will also be superseded by newer paradigms. Recall how Copernicus, Darwin, Freud, and Einstein complicated our concept of reality, and note how scientists and historians today are revising these men's thoughts. Who will transform us next?

In a few decades, today's quarks and black holes may seem as quaint as the four elements (earth, air, fire, and water). Accept that we are people of our times, and our ability to alter that fact is limited. The world is not only weirder than we think, it is weirder than we *are able* to think.

Individualists who are *too* rugged hurt others as well as themselves. Accept the relatedness of your life with your family, humanity, and the entire universe. Spinoza said that you can find real happiness and serenity by viewing things in a loving appreciation of the entire world—not in a self-centered way, but in a rational, impersonal way. Don't frustrate yourself by trying to be a pure, true self with the one, perfect moral, religious, and political belief. Those who must have security by total commitment to a fixed value system will soon find it becoming stifling in our changing world. The mysteries of our awesome universe just cannot be captured in any one, constricted creed. We must be free to reevaluate and adapt.

Understand that our language and our political, scientific, and religious beliefs are all symbols of a socially created reality further filtered through our individual, erring perceptions. There are no tangible, unchanging things out there. Both science and philosophy have deconstructed our premises about reality, truth, and moral values, declaring them contingent, provisional, and based on perspective. Because relativism and situational ethics are here to stay, absolutists who cluck against them will always be distressed because they themselves use these functional ethical standards each day. Since reality does not consist of simple black and white, we have no choice but to learn to become comfortable mucking around in shades of gray. Those who advocate a nostalgic return to the teaching of moral absolutes don't realize that they risk producing moral robots incapable of mature, innovative decisions regarding today's complex problems. Firm beliefs based upon ancient religious scriptures, New Age bunk, or current laws just don't address such issues as gays in the military.

For practical purposes, however, we must live our day as if there is a comprehensible, objective reality. Our psyches have developed over thousands of years assuming a simple reality, untroubled by the uncertainties given to us only a few decades ago by Einstein, Heisenberg, and Sartre. Our minds have not had time to adapt to the postmodern, existentialist world. Even Stephen Hawking and Roger Penrose don't fully understand the relation of thinking and quantum mechanics; Einstein admitted he didn't comprehend much of quantum mechanics. Wittgenstein and Sartre significantly changed their philosophical views during their careers. To remain sane and reasonably happy, we must not dwell too long upon many of the ideas of modern physics and philosophy.

As individuals, we are free to choose our own philosophies. Although many don't realize it, most Americans are pragmatic existentialists, having chosen to accept the ideas of Dewey and James to give their lives meaning. Only *you* can decide the meaning of *your* life. I have become reasonably comfortable with the idea that my beliefs are constantly changing and are conditioned by my social and physical needs. Speaking for myself only, I will continue to maintain a healthy skepticism toward our culture, including the media, politics, and many aspects of organized religion. I will remain skeptical of all "isms," including the now fashionable (and seemingly unassailable) combination of materialism and individualism, which has left us yearning for more romantic purpose and meaning. And I will endure the reality that injustice and deception are the expected background throughout nature, as they are in human relations.

Bolstered by current thinking in quantum mechanics and chaos-complexity theory, I have chosen to assume that free will exists, but I am still concerned that my "chooser" isn't free. Perhaps the freest of thoughts is that free thought might be impossible. Those who deny free will still cannot escape living as if it exists. I also believe people should be held responsible for most of their behavior, but I do not know (nor does anyone) where to draw the line. I accept the necessary change in our decisions of where to draw the line from year to year.

I don't feel guilty about using my psychological defense mechanisms to exaggerate the fortunate things that happen to me and to minimize the unfortunate things. I am aware, however, that I do this. I also use these psychological adaptations to foster a resilient sense of self appropriate to the ambiguity and chaos of our modern world. I have quit trying to *find* my one true self, which does not exist, and now appreciate the good news that I may *create*, and continuously recreate, my self. I have learned to respect the major and more competent aspect of my changing self—my unconscious. I cannot live without a sense of romanticism, such as that of a noble, inspired self. No one can write a book without having exaggerated notions of inspiration. I will continue to voice my present personal opinions and beliefs with measured fervor, but I realize that in a few years most of my thoughts will be considered wrong, even by me.

I believe in an open, real world that is out there beckoning. These conceptions may not be valid nowadays, but they are no more incorrect than anything else, and they are exhilarating and emancipating.

I believe we can actually do things empirically, and I believe the human mind can create order out of the chaos of reality. We can function consciously and effectively despite the unlimited number of variables that determine our behavior. We can go to the moon and back despite innumerable chances for disaster. The best players can win Wimbledon repeatedly, despite numerous possibilities for failure. Doctors, considering an infinite number of confusing symptoms and tests, can make a specific diagnosis and heal a patient. We may have no absolute truth, but what we have is good enough to launch space probes to Venus and to detect tiny tumors in a pituitary gland. The bottom line is that humans do accomplish very specific things.

I will continue to dream the impossible dream and laugh about my broken lances. I will respect and appreciate my warm and loving relationships with family and friends. I will continue to try to be the best doctor I can be, worry about my weak tennis backhand, and occasionally get emotional about college football, recognizing but accepting my illusion that it is important that Tennessee beat Alabama next October.

Life is fabulous! Gleefully join the fray and enjoy it.

Index

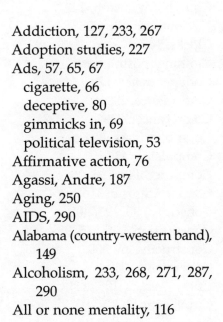